# WORLD MUSICS IN EDUCATION

# WORLD MUSICS IN EDUCATION

Edited by

Malcolm Floyd

SCOLAR PRESS

Published by
SCOLAR PRESS
Gower House
Croft Road
Aldershot
Hants GU11 3HR
England

Ashgate Publishing Company
Old Post Road
Brookfield
Vermont 05036 - 9704
USA


British Library Cataloguing-in Publication data

World musics in education
    1. World music - Study and teaching 2. Music in education
    I. Floyd, Malcolm
    781.6'07

Library of Congress Cataloguing-in-Publication Data

World musics in education / edited by Malcolm Floyd
        p.    cm.
    Includes index
    ISBN 1-85928-144-3 (cloth)
    1. Music--Instruction and study. 2. Ethnomusicology--Instruction and study. I. Floyd, Malcolm.
MT1.W93 1998
780'.7--dc20
                                      96-1790
                                        CIP
                                        MN


ISBN 1 85928 144 3

Typeset by Page One Services, Farnborough, Hants.
and printed in Great Britain by Hartnolls Ltd, Bodmin

# Contents

Contributors                                                    vii

Introduction
  *Malcolm Floyd*                                                 1

A Place for World Musics                                          5
1. Getting in Tune: Education, Diversity and Music               7
  *Ian Massey*
2. Approaching the Musics of the World                          24
  *Malcolm Floyd*
3. A Framework for Intercultural Dialogue in Music              43
  *June Boyce-Tillman*

Practical Applications                                          95
4. World Musics at Key Stage One                                97
  *Judith Deeble*
5. World Musics in Junior Schools                              112
  *Ernest Piper*
6. Music of the Caribbean: The Steel Band                      128
  *Wendy Brett*
7. Perfoming Groups in Schools: A Case Study                   138
  *Malcolm Floyd with Susan Darke and John Tucker*


Directions for Music Education in Africa                       155
8. Music Education in Ghana: The Way Forward                   157
  *James Flolu*
9. Promoting Traditional Music: The Kenyan Decision            186
  *Malcolm Floyd*

Resources                                                                                              207
10. Materials for Schools                                                                      209
  *Rosemary Davis, Malcolm Floyd, Kathryn Howard, Anthony Noble,*
  *Tina Parry-Jones, Ann Tann*

11. World Musics in Higher Education                                              250
      *Malcolm Floyd*

# Contributors:

**June Boyce-Tillman** is Reader and Principal Lecturer in Music at King Alfred's College of Further Education in Winchester, where she leads the World Musics Field. Her work on children's musical composition has found international recognition and led to numerous publications across the world. She is a past Warden of the Music in Education section of the Incorporated Society of Musicians.

**Wendy Brett** is Head of Music at the Connaught School in Aldershot, where the steel bands attract a great deal of interest from a wide area.

**Susan Darke** is Head of Drama at Frogmore Community School in Yateley, and is also very involved in the teaching of Dance. She is currently working for an MA in Related Arts.

**Judith Deeble** is Lecturer in Music at King Alfred's College, Winchester, where she is responsible for much of the Music Education work. Her research is in the early stages of children's musical development in various parts of the world. She is a past Warden of the Music in Education section of the Incorporated Society of Musicians, has been a member of the SEAC Music Committee, and advisor to SCAA.

**James Flolu** has recently completed a D.Phil in Ghanaian music education at York University. After a period as Visiting Lecturer at King Alfred's College, Winchester, he has returned to the University College of Education at Winneba, Ghana, as Senior Lecturer.

**Malcolm Floyd** has taught in primary, secondary and tertiary institutions in Kenya and Britain, and was the winner of the Kenya National Music Festival competition for performance on a traditional instrument in 1984. He is now Senior Lecturer in Music at King Alfred's College, Winchester, where he teaches in the areas of Music Education and World Musics. He is currently doing research on enculturation among the Maasai in Kenya.

**Ian Massey** taught in a range of schools before being appointed as County General Inspector for Intercultural Education in Hampshire. His publications include *More than Skin Deep.*

Ernest Piper has wide experience of teaching in primary and secondary schools, and is a pianist and brass player. He is now Head of Music at King Alfred's College, Winchester, and teaches Special Subject Music courses and on Music and Cultural Studies to Japanese students.

John Tucker is Head of Art at Frogmore Community School, Yateley, where he is also responsible for developing Community Arts Programmes.

# Introduction

*Malcolm Floyd*

There has been an interest in 'World Musics' for quite a long time. Rousseau included samples of Native American, Chinese and European Folk music in his 'Dictionnaire de Musique' of 1768. English ladies in 18th century India composed little piano pieces loosely based on the traditional tunes they heard around them. (Woodfield 1994). However, quite how easy it would have been for the sources of this material to recognise their music is uncertain at best. In the last century 'Comparative Musicology' was the name given to this developing quasi-science which continued into the 20th century, and Helen Roberts defined it as studies that:

> deal with exotic musics as compared with one another and with
> that classical European system under which most of us were
> brought up. (1936: quoted in Myers 1992)

This use of the West as a yardstick has not been unusual, and has certainly not been limited only to music. Even where an individual's intentions are apparently laudable at first sight, the assumptions they may be based upon require serious investigation. Colonel David Stirling had much experience of working in Africa, and disliked much of the racism he saw, but he was not totally immune from it himself. He set up a group called the 'Capricorn Society', and in the 'African News' of March 1954 wrote:

> (Capricorn) rejects both white colonialism and African nationalism
> in favour of the development of a multi-racial society in which,
> however, Western culture and the Christian religion would be
> dominant. (quoted in Gunther 1955:347)

Such principles are still held by many, although not always consciously, or expressed in precisely the same way. What this book seeks to do is to show ways of valuing music on its own terms; of recognizing that diversity is a strength of humanity, and that fear of the unknown may hold us back from experiences that would enrich, develop, and excite us. As the Maasai say:

*Medany olkimojino obo elashei*; One finger doesn't kill a louse.

The phrase 'World Musics' is used to describe the various natures and functions of this music as it occurs around the world. 'World Music' does not perhaps do justice to this variety, and 'Ethnic Music' has implications that only others are 'ethnic', or that the 'classical' or 'art' traditions of the world are to be excluded. One of the functions of this book is to consider not only the new, but how it may relate to what we already know and love.

The implications that 'World Musics' might appear more frequently in schools and colleges has not been entirely welcomed, and how these new demands might be dealt with, if they are at all, is not something that is clearly defined. There is uncertainty, sometimes anger, and something akin to fear felt by many of those who have to deliver the National Curriculum and college courses in the light of this move to include the world in our music education and training. It is towards these fears that this book is directed. It is not a volume 'by experts for experts', and although the contributors have all thought long and hard about these issues, and in many cases have undertaken considerable research, and have much experience, the concern is always to be useful, to support, empower and enthuse those who have to deliver too much, in too little time, with too few resources. The intention is not merely to pass on information, but rather to share the experiences that have affected us, or worked for us, and to provide some pointers and guidelines for the way ahead.

The book is in four parts. The first looks at the nature of the issue; how World Musics may be part of an intercultural policy, what makes them suitable for this function, and goes on to investigate a framework for enabling intercultural dialogue.

The second part looks at practical applications for World Musics in schools, concentrating particularly on discussing experiences, good and bad, and considering the most appropriate ways forward for primary and secondary schools.

The nature of music education in two African countries forms the third part. Ghana is choosing to develop its school music through the dual principles of the importance of traditional music, and the significance of sharing in the creative process. Kenya is emphasising national unity through the sharing of the country's musics, and reducing the previously strong external influences, (although music 'theory' still features strongly). The issues raised are common to many countries around the world, including the use of music to affect society, and the nature of World Musics work going on in universities and colleges, in terms of courses and interests.

It is our hope that this book will be seen as a starting point, with ideas for development and exploration of the 'infinite variety' to be found in the musics of the world.

Bibliography

Gunther, John (1955) Inside Africa  London. Hamish Hamilton

Myers, Helen (1992) Ethnomusicology: An Introduction   London. Macmillan

Woodfield, Ian (1994) 'The Hindostannie Air' in Journal of the Royal Musical Association. vol 119 part 2. London. Oxford University Press

Acknowledgements

The contributors wish to make their first acknowledgement to the schools and colleges in which they have worked, to the pupils and students with whom they have worked, and who have helped them to come to the ideas expressed in this book. The contributors themselves, however, are responsible for any inaccuracies.

We are grateful to King Alfred's College of Higher Education, Winchester, for helping to finance the preparation of this book for publication.

Thanks are also due to James Holmes for the preparation of the musical examples.

# A PLACE FOR WORLD MUSICS

*Baada ya kisa, mkasa; baada ya chanzo, kitendo*
After a reason, a happening; after a beginning, an action
(Swahili proverb)

It is easy to be distracted by the deluge of new material featuring music from a wide range of cultures around the world. It is important, however, to look for some underpinning for our studies into World Musics. These chapters look to see why they might be incorporated into the musical element of intercultural policies, considers starting points for the tasks we may set ourselves, and examines a framework for the systematic investigation of music, which could be tackled in many educational situations.

The proverbs in this book come from
Farsi, S S (1958) *Swahili Sayings* Nairobi Kenya Litrature Bureau
Massek, A ol 'Oloisolo & Sidai, J O (n.d.) *Wisdom of Maasai.* Nairobi.
    Transafrica

# 1 Getting in Tune - Education, Diversity and Music

*Ian Massey*

The pattern of migration into and out of Britain over centuries has inevitably led to a cross fertilisation of cultural components such as language, customs, art and of course music. The trend since the end of the Second World War for European countries to become increasing ethnically diverse has hastened this process.

In Britain the demand for post war labour led to the recruiting of peoples from the colonies and ex-colonies. The details of this are now well documented and focused on the settlement of black/Asian people along with communities of Polish, Irish, Italian, Chinese and Jewish backgrounds.

More recently membership of the European Union and the continuing inequalities between the North and South have contributed to migratory patterns into European countries such as Britain.

In addition to the physical movement of peoples, who bring with them their own cultural identity expressed through religion, language and the arts, has been the development of mass communications and the music industry.

Initially the music traffic was predominantly one way with western classical and especially popular music seeking and gaining access to world markets through records, tapes, TV, videos etc. However, music has often been associated with expressions of resistance and a celebration of cultural roots, events and significant figures. Western music often led to re-discovery of indigenous music or was adapted to modern manifestations of cultural pride. This resistance to cultural colonisation has thrown up a host of old and new artists. Their music, in various recording formats, is now widely available in shops in towns and cities throughout Europe. Western popular and classical and jazz musicians work together on collaborative musical projects for recording and/or touring.

The response of the education system, the curriculum on offer, especially the music curriculum in our schools, to the increasing diversity of England and Wales and the wider intercultural context is the focus of this chapter and the book as a whole.

There are several phases which the education system and schools seemed to have pass through, although the division as Banks (1981) notes 'is blurred rather than sharp'.

## Laissez-faire

The initial response to black and Asian immigration to the UK was, according to Rose et al. (1969), inaction. The assumption was that everyone was equal before the law and, therefore, no special policies were necessary. Immigrants would learn to integrate by working alongside whites. Immigrants were simply strangers who faced temporary difficulties which would be eased by assistance from voluntary agencies. Any tensions caused by their arrival would soon disappear as they were absorbed into an essentially tolerant society. In the early years of post-war immigration, most immigrants were male and saw their stay in Britain as temporary.

Kirp (1979) argues that there was no racially explicit policy at this time and that Government was hoping it would be helping non-whites by not favouring them explicitly.

However, Troyna and Williams (1986) argue that 'inaction or consistent decisions not to act also imply the existence of a policy' (p.2). After all, decisions have to be taken not to act and that will be the consequence of an ideological position. The 'policy' of 'doing good by doing little' did not last long, as some of the assumptions on which it was based began to be questioned by the reactions of white people.

The music curriculum remained largely untouched in terms of content and teaching methods.

## Assimilation via Language and Numbers

In 1958 the first disturbances attributable to racial tension took place in Notting Hill. These led to calls from representatives of white communities at local and national level and for the Government to take more positive action.

There was increasing alarm and political capital to be made out of heightening the concern over numbers. Under the 1918 Nationality Act all peoples of the Commonwealth and colonies had full citizenship rights, including right of entry to Britain. In 1962 the first of several Immigration Acts was passed which restricted the right of entry to drawing a line between those who were born in the United Kingdom and those who were born and resident in the independent countries of the Commonwealth or colonies. The latter would no longer possess automatic right of entry.

The educational response at this time was to offer infant and junior reception centres where children without English as a mother-tongue were given introductory courses. Lynch (1986a) argues that the developing policies towards Commonwealth immigrants contained a conviction of cultural superiority, subliminal prejudice and a secret commitment to racial discrimination through segregation in housing.

This obsession with numbers was reflected in DES Circular 7/65 which gave LEAs permission for the dispersal or 'bussing' of immigrants. This would be done where the quota of immigrants exceeded 33 percent of the school. The justification for such a policy was educational, based on language development and a furtherance of cultural assimilation. However, there were undoubtedly fears of a 'white backlash' as the document notes that:

> It will be helpful if the parents of non-immigrant children can see ....... that the progress of their own children is not being restricted by the undue preoccupation of the teaching staff with the linguistic and other difficulties of the immigrant children.

Although language development was used as the educational rationale for this policy, Milner (1983) has noticed that children were dispersed irrespective of whether they were new arrivals or not, without consultation with parents and 'irrespective of whether they had language difficulties or not' (p.199). There is also no evidence on which to base the notion that white children would be held back by those children who had difficulties with English, or where the proportion of black and Asian children rose above 33 percent (see Little, 1975). As white children were not bussed, the effect was racist and not many authorities implemented or continued to follow the policy. Pronouncements from Government departments and agencies stressed the importance of assimilation and cultural resocialisation. The Commonwealth Immigration Advisory Council report (1964) stated:

> If their parents were brought up in another culture or another tradition, children should be encouraged to respect it, but a national system (of education) cannot be expected to perpetuate the different values of immigrant groups (p. 7).

Assimilation was to be on the terms of the dominant groups in British society but presented in 'deracialised' terms. The policies and practices were legitimised in educational terms.

### Integration through Compensation

The initial policy response of the education system of language tuition was consolidated in 1966 through Section 11 funding by which LEAs could claim back 50 percent (later 75 percent) of the cost of providing English as a second language tuition from the Home Office. It was also about this time that the notion of 'integration' became a popular concept, sometimes presented as a more sensitive development of assimilation. The key to successful integration was, as Barker (1981) wrote, 'linguistic integration as the precondition of social integration' (p.75). Without this, cultural resocialisation was impossible. Accordingly, bilingualism was not considered an option for Commonwealth children. It was considered a disadvantage of learning, impeding social and intellectual development. This was the view of a DES report in 1971 which suggested that black students were at a disadvantage because the language heard at home was their native tongue or pidgin English. So the report went on, 'against a background of this kind the best intentions of school can easily be nullified (p.65).

Consequently a view began to develop of cultural deprivation which, although rooted in language, often reinforced some preconceptions about other cultures' art, music and dance.

Such a view enabled:

i)     The school itself to remain unexamined in its role and method of educating pupils from ethnic minorities. including the nature of the music curriculum.

ii)    Policies and practices to be presented in a deracialised form, with fashionable educational criteria and concepts cited as legitimising agents to a racist posture.

iii)   Any lack or unwillingness to 'integrate' could be blamed on ethnic minorities themselves, as they had been given the opportunities to integrate into British culture.

### Multiculturalism: from Compensation to Cultural Pluralism

The date usually acknowledged as being the beginning of this phase is 1966 when Roy Jenkins, then Home Secretary, introduced the notion of pluralism. This was not to be regarded as a flattening process of assimilation but a recognition of cultural diversity in an atmosphere of mutual tolerance.

However, educational activities based on this approach were a long time in developing. The report of the Select Committee on Race Relations and Immigration (1969) urged teaching about countries from which immigrants had come, including songs, art and costumes to 'help bring immigrant children into the life of the school' (p.42). During the 1970s an approach to multicultural education developed which became known by many as the 3 S version - Saris, Samosas and Steel bands. This was characterised by Rushdie (1982) as 'teaching the kids a few bongo rhythms and how to tie a sari'. Caribbean Studies and Asian History were often additional elements added to non-examination courses, where many West Indian pupils, in particular, were to be found. Most of this kind of work was found only in multi-racial schools.

The music curriculum of these schools was often one of the main areas to incorporate this approach. In practice it took several forms in schools. It appeared as a formal or informal optional extra through GCSE courses or an after-school 'Black Studies Club', or as part of a common core and integrated with work in Moral Education. Finally, it could appear as piecemeal development, where multicultural aspects are featured in some subjects, such as English or Music. The disadvantage, as many teachers and others saw it, was that multiculturalism became compartmentalised, having little impact on the ethnocentric nature of the rest of the curriculum and that it frequently sidestepped the issue of racism.

Bullivant (1981) summarises the key assumption underlying this type of multicultural education as:

i)    By learning about his/her culture and ethnic roots, an ethnic minority child will improve his/her achievement.

ii)   Learning about his/her culture will improve equality of opportunity.

iii)  Learning about other cultures will reduce children's and adults' prejudice discrimination.

What critics of this kind of multiculturalism focused on was the avoidance of confronting racism at school and in society in general, a racism which black and Asian children experienced daily and which had a detrimental effect on their life choices. It was this issue which was to stimulate further development but before detailing those changes in emphasis and ideology it is important to note the changes also taking place in official thinking during this stage.

The late 1970s saw a change in emphasis in official DES documents which now seemed to acknowledge the diversity of cultures as a permanent feature of British society: 'The education system and teachers should take note that our society is a multicultural, multiracial one and the curriculum should reflect a sympathetic, understanding of the different cultures and races that now make up our society.' (DES, 1977, para 10.11)

However, the kind of curriculum developments that awareness of this had led to resulted in the Home Affairs Committee (1981) commenting that a 'black studies' curriculum could become an educational ghetto for black pupils and it urged further consideration of a suitable and relevant curriculum for a multicultural society.

The under-achievement of ethnic minority pupils, especially pupils of West Indian origin became well documented during the 1970s and this led the Government to set up a Committee of Inquiry in 1979 that became known as the Rampton Committee. An interim report was made in 1981 which pointed out that schools needed to take a positive attitude to the richness a culturally diverse society could offer. As Croft (1981b) notes, 1981 can now be seen as a crucial year in that not only were there four major reports on the subject as well as numerous conferences, but also there were major urban disturbances in areas of many cities of Britain with high concentration of ethnic minorities.

Lynch (1996a) notes that it is from this time that 'pluralism becomes acceptable' as part of an ideology that would seek greater social cohesion and in which the education system had a vital role to play.

The Rampton Committee report (1981) came as a disappointment to the growing number of critics of multicultural education because all that emerged on the issue of racism was that schools had a duty to combat the ignorance 'on which much racial prejudice and discrimination is based' (p.34). The Rampton inquiry had internal disputes over the issues which led to resignations and the appointment of a new chairman in Lord Swann who was to complete the inquiry.

Music was a central component which Libson (1976) refers to as "benevolent multiculturalism". i.e. educational programmes which tried to ensure greater compatibility between home and school by the use of culturally relevant material. From this grew the view that such work would have a positive effect on white pupil attitudes and values towards other cultures and people. This multicultural approach became restricted to multi-ethnic schools and a few areas of the schools curriculum.

Despite the lack of evidence that multicultural education could do any of this, LEAs began to base policies on such questionable assumptions, ILEA's document (1984) stressed the need for cultures to be 'respected, differences recognised and individual identities secure' (p. 4). Manchester's document (1980) emphasised the need to combat the ignorance about cultural minorities as a way of improving relations between races. Not only were such policies criticised theoretically, they were also condemned by members of ethnic minority groups, usually for the failure to include the issue of racism.

## Anti-Racism: from Steel Bands to Struggle

The late 1970s and early 1980s saw reports and research confirm the existence of racism in the wider society. The PEP (Political and Economic Planning) research (Smith, 1977 and Brown, 1984) revealed the continuing extent of discrimination in employment and housing. The 1991 Home Office Report on Racial Attacks showed that racial victimisation of Asians was 50 times higher than that of white people and 36 times higher than for West Indians. The report noted that many people of Asian background reported racial abuse and violence as a common but unwelcome feature of British life. Discriminatory practices and overt and covert racism were revealed in other institutions such as the police (see Smith and Gray, 1983). Leaks from the delayed Commission for Racial Equality study into immigration rules show that whereas 1 in 140 visitors from the New Commonwealth was refused entry, 1 in 1,400 from the Old Commonwealth (mainly white) was refused entry. Their conclusion was that the immigration rules were racist in operation.

This period has also seen further controls placed on Commonwealth Immigration through Acts of Parliament in 1968 and 1971. At the same time, race relations legislation was also passed (1965, 1968 and 1976). It was not until the 1976 Act that both direct and indirect discrimination on the basis of colour, race and ethnicity were included as well as coverage of the education system. Lynch (1986b) refers to these responses as examples of Britain's 'Janus-faced' attitude to ethnic minorities. Further tensions and accusations of racism were caused by the passing of the 1981 Nationality Act which created three distinct categories of British citizen: those born in the UK or to UK parents, citizens of dependencies (like the Falklands) and those born in former colonies. Only the first category had automatic right of entry to the UK and these were, of course, mainly white.

The weight of evidence and argument produced a climate in which it was possible for some LEAs to take a positive stance against racism. Policies began to be formulated not on basis of cultural understanding but rather on the need for equality and social justice, involving the combating and dismantling of racism in all its forms, personal and institutional. LEA policy statements called on the schools themselves to submit and publicly declare policy statements opposing racism. They called on schools to review their practices and procedures especially in dealing with racist bullying, abuse and attacks and also to review their curriculum along anti-racist guidelines outlined by the authority and their advisers. Berkshire and ILEA were early examples of this development in 1983, followed by other LEAs, such as Bradford and Birmingham.

These policies marred the first real attempts at a more racialist concept of the nature of schooling and society and the black and Asian experience within that. As a result, anti-racism came to be seen as a radical political movement because of its emphasis on inequality and the need to understand the roots of British racism, which lay in the economic and power structures of Britain. The implication that white teachers were collaborating in the perpetuation of an unequal racist society did not always go down well with educators and politicians who professed a political and ideological neutrality.

Policies reflected the aim that institutions need to change through a close examination of formal and hidden curriculum, assessment, streaming. staffing and how racist incidents were dealt with. To have any effect on the pattern of racial inequality, it was argued the emphasis should be on equality of outcome rather than the equality of access (Hatcher and Shallice, 1983).

Multiculural education had no effect on under-achievement and some critics saw it as part of State policy (see Carby, 1982) to control and contain the resistance of black youth. Anti-racism, as it became known, was seen as the radical alternative to multiculturalism, challenging all types of racism and championing racial equality and justice.

ILEA's (1983) anti-racist statement committed the authority to the elimination of racism, suggesting that all its educational institutions follow a process which included:

i)      Placing the issue on the school/college agenda and making time for discussion and development.

ii)     Coming to grips with what racism is and its historical context.

iii) Considering how racism can and does operate in the school/college.

iv) Analysing both directly conscious racist behaviour and what the Rampton Interim Report termed 'unconscious racism'.

v) Analysing both individual behaviour and the policies and practices of the school/college.

vi) Analysing the behaviour and practices of individuals and services that impinge on the life of the school/college.

vii) Drawing upon the advice and experience of others.

Guidelines were also issued to schools to determine their own policies, which would include:

i) A clear, unambiguous statement of opposition to any form of racism or racist behaviour.

ii) A firm expression of all pupils' or students' rights to the best possible education.

The curriculum should seek to create an understanding of an interest in different environments, societies, systems and cultures, noting the achievements made outside the western world. An historic appreciation is argued for in understanding the entrenched nature of racism due to colonial exploitation, slavery and repression, together with the ways which this may openly and unintentionally influence curriculum content. Materials should be assessed for racism and negative stereotyping (a process which had, of course, been going on for many years).

Such policies enabled music teachers, along with others, to re-examine their professional practice, content of syllabus and cross curricular opportunities. However, this was still largely confined to multi ethnic contexts.

The Swann Report was finally published in 1985 and although disappointing for some anti-racists in its treatment of 'race' did play a significant role in refocusing the issue on the education of all pupils. It is perhaps worth recalling what the main recommendations were:

The essential steps on the argument for our concept of 'Education for All' are as follows:

a)  The fundamental change that is necessary is the recognition that the problem facing the education system is not how to educate children of ethnic-minorities, but how to educate all children.

b)  Britain is a multi-racial and multi-cultural society and all pupils must be enabled to understand what this means.

c)  This challenge cannot be left to the separate and independent initiatives of LEAs and schools; only those with experience of substantial numbers of ethnic minority pupils have attempted to tackle it, though the issue affects all schools and pupils.

d)  Education has to be something more than the reinforcement of the beliefs, values and identity which each child brings to school.

e)  It is necessary to combat racism, to attack inherited myths and stereotypes and the ways in which they are embodied in institutional practices.

f)  Multi-cultural understanding has also to permeate all aspects of a school's work. It is not a separate topic that can be welded onto existing practices.

g)  Only in this way can schools begin to offer anything approaching the equality of opportunity for all pupils which must be the aspiration of the education system to provide.

Verma (1989) comments that for the first time the report made it clear that the issues and needs of ethnic minorities are tied up with the education of white children and that the notion of diversity in unity, which the report was promoting, was a bold challenge to the education system.

The late 1960s saw the beginnings of the backlash against these trends. Academics such as Professors Flew and Scruton began a series of articles and books aimed at discrediting the principles behind both anti-racism and multiculturalism. Headteachers, such as Reg Honeyford, gained high profile coverage with their stance against this product of 'progressive education' which was undermining standards and British culture and values. There were numerous media campaigns against Labour authorities with explicit anti-racist policies and training programmes. Many of these were fictitious and part of a broader campaign against local authorities, some focused solely on the occasional excesses. During this time though, many 'all white' authorities and schools did receive extra funding for a variety of training programmes and developing resource bases, many of these benefited music teachers directly and stimulated curriculum initiatives which enhanced pupils' experience of music in the classroom.

## Contextual Pragmatism

As anti-racism became increasingly difficult to sustain as an operational concept, almost akin to multiculturalism, the search in the 1990s has been for terminology which is not only accessible but is appropriate in the context of the Education Reform Act, LMS, National Curriculum and the Framework for the Inspection of Schools.

Education for Racial Equality, Anti-racist multiculturalism, Equality Assurance and Equality of Opportunity are all terms to be found in the discourse of race, culture and education. The term used often depends on factors such as the location of the school, urban, rural, the political complexion of the education committee, TVEI involvement, the nature of the school and its community. Such factors shape the direction of the policy and the music curriculum, as well as national curriculum requirements.

## Education Diversity and Music

Whatever the terminology chosen it is the restrictions and opportunities of the National Curriculum which often shape what goes on in the classroom.

In the DES Circular 5/89, the Education Reform Act 1988: The School Curriculum and Assessment, which outlined the framework for the development of the National Curriculum the requirements are quite clear.

16. Section 1 of the Act, which came into force on Royal Assent, states the aims of the curriculum as a whole and places them in the context of the needs of pupils and society. It says that the curriculum should be balanced and broadly based, and should:

a) promote the spiritual, moral, cultural, mental and physical development of pupils at the school and of society; and

b) prepare such pupils for the opportunities, responsibilities and experiences of adult life.'

17. This restates and extends the list of central purposes for the curriculum in Section 7 of the 1944 Act; in particular, it emphasises the need for breadth and balance in what pupils study, and that cultural development and the development of society should be promoted. It is intended that the curriculum should reflect the culturally diverse society to which pupils belong and of which they will become adult members. It should benefit them as they grow in maturity and help to prepare them for adult life and experience - home life and parenthood; responsibilities as a citizen towards the community and society nationally and internationally; enterprise, employment and other work. The requirements of Section 1 apply to all pupils - regardless of age - registered at all maintained schools, including grant-maintained schools, except that they do not apply to pupils in nursery schools or nursery classes in primary schools.

In many of the working groups of the core and foundation subjects there were often heated debates on what is 'our cultural heritage'. This was particularly acute in subjects such as History and Music. The draft orders often extended the debate further in professional associations, journals and the popular media. The final orders often contained an attempted compromise between an often politically inspired emphasis or an anglo/eurocentric tradition and a more dynamic view of cultural interdependence. This emphasised developing in pupils a wider understanding and appreciation of other cultures' contributions to human knowledge and their experiences.

National Curriculum documents laying out the Programmes of Study always featured sections dealing with cultural diversity and equal opportunities. In Music the general requirements stated that:

Pupils should perform and listen to music in a variety of genres and styles from different periods and cultures ... with examples from ... a variety of cultures, Western and non-western.

This indicates opportunities for teachers of music to legitimately adopt a 'world musics' approach. However, the above statement has particular problems. As Glynne-Jones (1993) points out "the use of 'other' or 'non' to define a category is in this case divisive and ... leads to a view of different but not equal".

One consequence if not considered carefully could be a return to the kind of tokenism associated with previous phases of education with stereotypical choices being matched to the ethnic composition of the school.

An important and significant aid to avoiding this and ensuring that what is on offer to pupils is appropriate is the guidance to be found in *Equality Assurance* (1993) (The Runnymede Trust and Trentham Books). This fills the gap left by the failure of the NCC to publish guidance to teachers on implementing the multicultural dimension. *Equality Assurance* provides indicators of good practice with Key Stage examples along with whole school principles.

The National Curriculum and Equality Assurance have had considerable implications for teachers of music, raising questions over teaching styles, access, assessment and resources as well as personal and professional knowledge and skills in order to effectively deliver such a curriculum.

There has been a great deal of support from professional associations and LEA inset providers, often with considerable success. The Dearing review noted this and did not recommend any major changes to the Attainment Targets or Programmes of Study and commented that the National Curriculum had "facilitated much positive work in music".

Indeed, this comes through in the advice offered to inspectors using the OFSTED 'Framework for Inspection'. In evaluating the school's provision for pupil's spiritual, moral, social and cultural development it focuses on the contribution music can make to pupils cultural development. It advises that:

> In music pupils should experience and respond to a range of musical styles and senses, including music from a variety of cultural traditions.

In addition the guidance on evaluating the under 5s curriculum states that:

> Schools should ensure that young children learn to be at ease with their own cultural background and respect different cultures and customs. Many aspects of the curriculum such as art, music, play and stories contribute to social and cultural development (p.79).

In order to support the effective development of opportunities in music it is helpful if the music curriculum and its Key Stage Plans reflecting not only the requirements of the music National Curriculum but a wider whole school policy directed towards preparing pupils for life in a culturally and ethnically diverse society. The knowledge, skills, attitudes, and values in music need to be reflected elsewhere in the curriculum and school environment.

**Figure 1.1 School policies on equal opportunities teaching and learning**

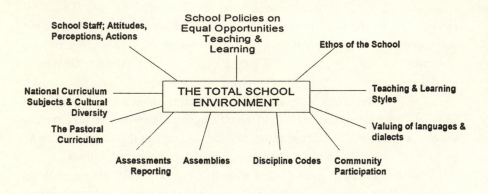

Such whole school approaches take time and in the process of developing staff awareness and an understanding of issues relating to cultural diversity, music can have a key role. It can provide enjoyable experimental examples of how pupils' learning is enriched by an intercultural dimension; the inter-relationship between cultures; the demolition of myths and stereotypes; its contribution to challenging the possible development of pupils racist frames of reference. Within a whole school framework the cross curricular possibilities can more easily be developed. Opportunities have continued to exist and be pursued in Key Stages 1 and 2 due to the nature of teaching and learning styles in primary schools, but this can also be the case at secondary level. For example a joint History/Music and RE module on Black People of the Americas at Key Stage 3 could involve the following:

## Figure 1.2 Black people of the Americas at Key Stage 3

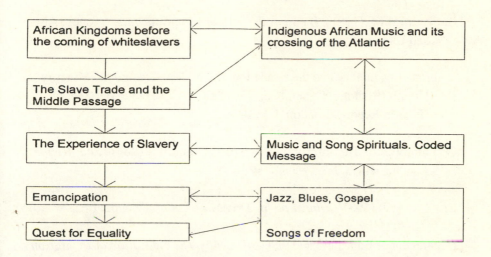

The whole module will meet National Curriculum requirements in Music and History, agreed RE syllabus, provide assessment opportunities, meet the aims and values of a whole school policy on diversity and anti-racism; as well as providing an exciting learning opportunity for pupils.

The education system and schools in Britain have passed through many phases in coming to terms with cultural and ethnic diversity and the challenge of racism. Music has frequently been both used and misused as a means for promoting intercultural awareness and understanding. Sometimes this has resulted in the reinforcement of certain cultural stereotypes and marginalisation. The errors of judgement of the past can be avoided with more accessible understanding of the conceptual issues involved and useful indicators of good practice. Set within an appropriate framework which takes account of conceptual factors, music is well placed to make an even more significant contribution to education for cultural diversity.

## Bibliography

Banks, J.A. (1981) *Multi-ethnic Education: Theory and Practice.* Boston. Alleyn and Bacon

Barker, M. (1981) *The New Racism.* London. Junction Books

Brown, C. (1984) *Black and White Britain: The Third PSI Survey.* London. Heinemann

Bullivant, B.M. (1981) *The Pluralist Dilemma in Education* Sydney. Allen and Unwin

Committee of Inquiry into the Education of Children from Ethnic Minority Groups (Rampton Committee) *West Indian Children in our Schools.* (Interim Report). London. HMSO

Commonwealth Immigration Advisory Council (1964) *2nd Report.* London. HMSO

Croft, M. (ed) (1981) *Education for Diversity.* London. Falmer Press

Department of Education and Science (1965) *The Education of Immigrants 7/65.* London. HMSO

Department of Education and Science (1971) *The Education of Immigrants* (Education Survey no. 13). London. HMSO

Department of Education and Science (1977) *Education in Schools; A Consultative Document.* (Green Paper mnd 6869) London. HMSO

Department of Education and Science (1989) *From Policy into Practice.* London. HMSO

Department of Education and Science (1990) *Music.* London. HMSO

Gibson, M. (1976) Approaches to Multicultural Education in the United States: Some Concepts and Assumptions. In *Anthropology and Education Quarterly.* Vol. 7 no. 4 pp 7 - 18.

Glynne-Jones, M., King, A.S. & Reiss, M.J. (1993) *Music: Respect for Persons, Respect for Cultures in The Multicultural Dimension of the National Curriculum.* London. Filmer

Hatcher and Shallice (1983) The Politics of Anti-Racist Education. In *Multicultural Education.* Vol. 12 no.1 pp 3 - 21

Home Affairs Committee (1981) *Racial Disadvantage 1.* London. HMSO

ILEA (1984) *Race, Sex and Class*. London. County Hall

Kirp (1979) *Doing Good by Doing Little.* London. University of California Press

Little, A. (1975) 'The Educational Achievement of Ethnic Minority Children in London Schools' in Verma, K. and Bagley, C. (Eds) *Race and Education across Cultures.* London. Heinemann

Lynch, J. (1986a) *Multicultural Education - Principles and Practice.* London. Routledge & Keegan Paul

Lynch, J. (1986b) Banks, J.A. and Lynch, J. (eds.) *Multicultural Education: Agenda for Change in Multicultural Education in Western Societies.* London. Holt, Rinehart & Winston

Manchester LEA (1980) *Education for a Multicultural Society.* Manchester

Milner, D. (1983) *Children & Race Ten Years On.* London. Ward Lock

OFSTED *Framework for the Inspection of Schools.* London. HMSO

Rose, E.J.B. et al (1969) *Colour and Citizenship.* Institute of Race Relations. London. Oxford University Press

Runnymede Trust (1993) *Equality Assurance.* Stoke on Trent. Trentham Books

Rushdie, S. (1982) The New English in Britain. *New Society*, 9 December

Smith, D.J. (1977) *Racial Disadvantage in Britain*. Harmondsworth. Penguin

Smith, D.J. & Gray, J. (1983) *Police & People in London*. London. Policy Studies Institute

Troyna, B. & Williams, J. (1986) *Racism, Education & the State.* London. Croom Helm

# 2 Approaching the Musics of the World

*Malcolm Floyd*

I have spent quite a lot of time with the Turkana and Samburu peoples who inhabit the northern part of Kenya. I have listened to many songs as part of my researches but when things have really got going they have been reluctant for me just to sit and listen. I have been included in the singing and dancing, even though my knowledge of the languages is minimal, and my jumping ability, the main element in the dancing, has caused more amusement than admiration. The essence is inclusion; being part of a community which expresses its fears, hopes, humour and aggression through music; which gives individuals a strength and significance through sharing communal aspirations and articulation in an art form which perhaps is the closest to peoples' hearts. I am often intrigued by what the reciprocal arrangement would be: a Music Hall night in a local concert hall? Attendance at the local choral society's performance of the 'Messiah'? Joining in the singing at an international rugby fixture? In a sense, of course, the response to all of these would be yes, as they have all become important and tangible features of our culture in the West, even if participation may occur in a rather different form to that previously experienced by our visitors.

In any case, my Samburu and Turkana acquaintances want me to join in their richest experiences, and are not unduly concerned by my lack of skills, although they are very eager and pleased to see them develop. For me the transformation of my mind happens because of the way the music is expressed physically: song and dance are inextricably intertwined, each lends energy and structure to the other. Also, because one is part of a sizeable group (perhaps 20 to 30), there is little concern about embarrassment or exposure, and even when someone drags you into the middle of the circle to do some 'display jumps' you are always with at least one partner, and can feel that your partners think it is appropriate for you to join in at this more involved and public level. In short, I am placed by them in a peak musical (and cultural) experience, with sufficient support, encouragement and explanation to enable me to feel truly part of it, and the experience itself convinces me of the value of what I am doing. It transmits certain musical and cultural elements, but equally importantly transforms my understanding of them, and facilitates the beginning of assimilation. In this chapter I shall be looking to see if and how this transmission and transformation can be made through experiencing world musics in educational situations, particularly in Great Britain.

There is a clear expectation in National Curriculum Music documents that we will draw on a variety of source materials in our teaching. Consider the following extracts; firstly from the 1991 Proposals:

**The aims of music teaching in school...**
there are of course many different styles of music, appropriate for different purposes and offering different kinds of satisfaction and challenge, excellence may be found in any style of musical expression.

The study of music ... should provide for the progressive development of ... awareness and understanding of traditions, idioms and musical styles from a variety of cultures, times and places. (DES 1991:7)

**Equal opportunities in music**
Music provides exceptional opportunities to experience the cultural heritage of others, from within the United Kingdom, and from other countries and from different religious and ethnic origins. ... Pupils can be introduced to music from other cultures through recognition of their common elements as well as their differences. Different kinds of music should so far as possible retain their cultural and stylistic integrity. (DES 1991:51).

and then from *Music in the National Curriculum* (1992)
**General requirements for programmes of study**
Pupils should perform and listen to music in a variety of genres and styles, from different periods and cultures. The repertoire chosen should be broad ... (and) should include examples of works taken from ... a variety of cultures, Western and non-Western. (DES 1992:3)

The Curriculum Council for Wales reinforces these ideas in its
'Non-Statutory Guidance for Teachers (1992)'
Pupils should be encouraged to develop open-minded, yet sensitive and discriminating attitudes to the music which they encounter. Participation in musical activities and the study of music should ... develop in pupils ... essentially transferable skills

and attributes: (including) awareness and appreciation of a wide
range of cultural traditions (CCW 1992:6)


### Cultural heritage and diversity

It is important that all pupils, wherever they live in Wales and
whatever their ethnic or cultural roots, should experience music
from a variety of cultures. (CCW 1992:7)

This emphasis on a breadth of experience is also made clear in the document
for Northern Ireland, *Curriculum (Programmes of Study and Attainment
Targets in Music) Order* (1992).

Firstly in the **General Requirements for Programmes of Study:**

At all key stages, pupils should perform and listen to music from a
widening range of genres, styles, cultures and historical periods
(DENI: 1992:3)

Later, in the **Detailed Requirements** we find:

Pupils should have opportunities to ... develop some awareness of
the social, historical or cultural content of some of the music they
hear and perform. (DENI 1992 : 9)

And in the Statement of Attainment for Attainment Target 2: **Responding
to Music with Understanding** the following are included:

Level 7 b. identify characteristics of musical periods and styles.
Level 8 b. understand cultural and historical influences on music.
Level 9 b. discriminate within particular forms and styles of music.
Level 10b. display understanding of the expressive  power  and
distinguishing characteristics of music from a variety of styles and
cultures. (DENI 1992, 26 -27)

The implication is also apparent that this will have been prepared for in work
appropriate for previous levels. In May 1994 there appeared the Draft
Proposals for revisions to the National Curriculum published by the School
Curriculum and Assessment Authority, chaired by Sir Ron Dearing. It is
worth including extracts from the Programmes of Study for Key Stages 1, 2
and 3:

The repertoire chosen for performing and listening should extend
pupils' musical experience and knowledge, and develop

appreciation of the richness of our diverse cultural heritage. It
should include music in a variety of styles from different times and
places ... (SCAA 1994:2)
... it should include music taken from the European 'classical'
tradition;   folk and popular music; the countries and regions of the
British Isles; a variety of cultures ... (Ibid:4)

The latest document, *Music in the National Curriculum*, repeats this
statement, then specifies at Key Stage 1 music 'from different times and
cultures', at Key Stages 2 and 3, 'eg. folk and popular music ... cultures
across the world.' (DFE 1995: 2,4,6)

It is clear that variety is considered important by the authors of these
documents. They are not settling simply for just several cultures, or
specifically 'related' cultures with their apparently greater accessibility. The
variety is proposed in culture, time and place, which gives teachers
enormous scope in choosing material. A very interesting study, for example,
would be British compositions based on Indian music in the 18th century,
using material recently described by Ian Woodfield (Woodfield 1994: 189-
211).

We may also note the emphasis given to authenticity and integrity,  so
that recognition of common and different elements can be made from
accurate reality, rather than from misconceptions and imprecise assumptions.
Guidance is further given in terms of the search for 'excellence', in
considering the various purposes of music and in the pedagogic balance of
providing satisfaction and challenge for each child. So teachers are to include
a variety of authentic musics in the pursuit of excellence in its many forms,
which will challenge students and offer forms of satisfaction.  At the very
least there is an obligation, a duty to come close to fulfilling the letter of
these requirements, and in the interests of our own and our students' sanity
and enjoyment we might do well to explore the spirit as well.

However, teachers are expected to find suitable material, have
sufficient expertise, and be able to provide suitable experiences and
opportunities for their students when they may have very limited experience
themselves, and significant reservations about such policies.

It is sometimes the case that teachers in primary schools feel a lack of
confidence in their musical skills, and in their capacity for providing rich
musical learning experiences beyond singing and some instrumental work.
This is not to say that there is not excellent work going on in many places;
rather that such work may depend overmuch on specialist co-ordinators able
to empower and support colleagues. To add musics from other cultures at

this point is to inhibit confidence further. The reasons for this lack of confidence are not difficult to find; unsatisfactory musical experiences at school, the perception of Music as a specialist and therefore elitist pursuit, limited training in class music possibilities at College and in other teacher training, and unrealistically low expectations of children's music in some situations.

In secondary schools the situation is rather different. Almost all the music teaching is done by specialists, who may well have had a very thorough and rigorous training in performing and analytical skills. It will almost certainly be the case that this training will have concentrated, perhaps exclusively, on the Art Music of Western Europe, although some courses are more varied now, (see Chapter 11). It may be felt that to deal adequately with this will take all the time a music teacher has with her students; to add other musics will simply make an already complex task unmanageable. I suspect that there are now few secondary schools where this is entirely the case, however, as many incorporate work on popular idioms, and have performing groups which specialise in non-European music, (You may wish to read about some specific examples in other chapters in this book). Many secondary school music teachers consider themselves well equipped to transmit skills and concepts from other world musics, or to locate and employ others with suitable skills to make sure there is some cultural diversity within the music curriculum. It is, of course, sensible and practical to employ an expert who has a thorough knowledge of another music, and good results may be expected where the teachers themselves support such work through active involvement in its delivery. Where this is not the case, the music teachers are seen to be apart from the activity, and not sufficiently cognisant of its intentions and so the student cannot be expected to have any greater involvement.

We seem to have, then, a cohort of teachers in all sectors who wish to implement curriculum requirements as fully as possible, but may not feel sufficiently secure or experienced to fulfil them, or may not be convinced by the value of the related activities. Ian Massey, Intercultural Inspector for Hampshire, writes in the previous chapter about the significance of an intercultural strand in education, and the place of music as a thread in that strand. It is necessary, however, to consider some reasons for including music in the general intercultural schemes that exist or are being developed in schools.

Peter Fletcher includes among his objectives for music education:

to impart knowledge and understanding of musics of various
ethnic and social groupings within contemporary culture.
(Fletcher 1987:182)

and Kwami is eager to use elements from other musics as sources for
composing, performing and listening and refers to a 'universality of musical
practice'. (Kwami 1989:132). F. Musgrove, however, condemns much
attempted sharing of cultures. In his opinion:

> Cultural relativism (encourages) teachers to transmit cultures rather
> than to transform them. Transmission is the handing on of
> whatever exists and it is likely to produce people armed against
> cross-cultural sympathy tolerance. (Musgrove 1982:130)

and where the culture being 'taught' is included among students;

> Teaching about their culture may be a profound embarrassment to
> Indian and West Indian children. A form of 'exposure' which
> actually increases racial tension. (Ibid:114)

The real situation, of course, is that very few cultures are completely 'pure'
anyway. The radio has certainly seen to that in many parts of the world,
including much of Africa. It would be very wrong, similarly, to neglect the
influence of Black music on contemporary popular music particularly in
Britain and North America. Hungary, by way of contrast, has a very strong
cultural identity, fostered by all official agencies and channels including
education. The desire to maintain 'purity' is perhaps rather simpler for
Hungarians, however, as the population is 91 per cent Magyar (census of
1.1.1970), although the 5 per cent Gypsy are important and Gypsy music
has made a significant contribution to Hungarian music in general.
Furthermore, the Hungarian language is unique and considered difficult,
making international communication problematic at times. Kenya on the
other hand has an official language, English, which facilitates international
links, and a national language, KiSwahili, which serves internal
communication, and at least 42 other languages of the various etho-linguistic
groups within Kenya's borders. Kenya's education policy makes a feature
of sharing its cultures. In 1984 the Presidential National Music Commission
included in its proposals:

>     That music syllabi should emphasise the theory and practice of
>     traditional African music which is relevant to the child's
>     environment. This, however, should be done with the full
>     awareness that there is a great deal of cross-cultural interaction in
>     the present age. (Omondi 1984 :147)

This 'cross-cultural interaction' is not only a purely internal phenomenon.
Many Kenyans have studied abroad; in the UK, USA, India, Canada and so
on; they have decided to move to cities, to adopt Western fashions and eating
habits, and enjoy listening to Western popular music and learning to play
Western instruments  (as much as any instrument can be placed in such a
category).  This shows acculturation at the personal as well as at the national
level.

Consider the cultural context of a child in Britain in 1994. She will see
people with a wide variety of skin pigments, her birthday party food may be
hamburgers or pizza, and might later include items from Chinese, Japanese,
Thai, Greek, Indian, Indonesian, French, Mexican, Spanish and a multitude
of other outlets.  Music will come from radio, television and video-games,
with their pre-programmed background music and the sound combinations
created by the players' actions. Holidays will take her to the USA, Spain,
Greece, France and potentially anywhere else in the world.  And although
there are many attempts to make foreign holidays as much like home (with
sun) as possible, the sharing of holidays with travellers from other countries
makes that an increasingly difficult task. A Mombasa hotel must cater for its
American, British, French, German and Italian guests, and not forget
Kenyans either.

So what should we, as educators, look to find in searching for
authentic music to challenge and satisfy our students?

We should be aware of; have experience of; know music from other
cultures in the first instance because this will enrich, widen and transfer our
own individual cultural make-up.  It needs to affect us first: anything that
does not may lead to disinterest at best, and create or reinforce negative
attitudes which could spill out into the community beyond school at worst.

The second reason for including serious study of world musics, after
personal individual enrichment, is to share the learning and perceptions that
can be found in the immense variety of the musics of the world. This
becomes a two way process as we became aware of shared techniques, such
as the layered ostinato *pes* accompanying the melody in 'Sumer is icumen
in':

SUMMER IS ICUMEN IN

Sing cuc- cu nu sing cuc- cu

Sing cuc- nu Sing cuc- cu nu

(BL Ms. Harley 978)

and the layered patterns in the accompaniment of the boasting songs of Samburu *ilmuran*, (warriors), such as 'Entoremama':

ENTOREMAMA

(transcr. M Floyd)

We will also become more fully aware of differences, as in the realisation of ornaments in the *Ordres* of Couperin, and the ornamentation in the improvised praise songs of Luo *nyatiti* (lyre) players from Kenya. This assists in the process of contextualisation; it makes it more possible to see the constraints and freedoms of our own culture, and thus enhance and strengthen enculturation in what we like to consider "our own" from a point outside it. Seeing Samburu grandparents singing traditional songs with their grandchildren, reminded me vividly of my maternal grandfather teaching me Scottish songs. He approved of them most when I got close to performing them with a Highland accent. The purpose of this was to provide a balance to the very English culture and traditions I have inherited from my father.

Understanding the music of a people is a step towards understanding the heart of a community and the core of its culture; it gives insight into the things societies think are important. This cannot, and perhaps should not, be an easy process, but it seems to be a significant and worthy one to follow.

The musician and anthropologist, John Blacking, said;

> The ultimate goal is personal and social transformation: music making must be used to enhance personal consciousness and experience in community.
> (Blacking 1987:131)

It may be useful to see how two Nigerian societies approach this integration of individual and community through their musical ideas and practices.

M Anagah talks of the Izhiangbo people of north eastern Nigeria. The stories of the origin of music are not of elite composers or performers, but rather linked to the environment, and daily activities. One story talks of man learning to make songs by listening to birds, imitating them by whistling, then becoming creative. Another says that men imitated the sound of the hoe, which went 'fu fu' in soft ground, and 'geng geng' in hard ground. Each man brings his own hoe to work, so each makes different notes. (Anagah 1987:277) The community, as audience, are very much part of Iziangbo performances, and in competition they will judge and correct competitors. When new songs are brought from other areas they are subjected to the community for approval before they are adopted. (Ibid:147)

From south east Nigeria, Joshua Uzoigwe describes the composition process for *Ukom* music, performed at specific rituals. He starts by emphasising that a composer needs social and musical creativity:

social:   thinking and creating as a person living in a social environment

musical:   thinking and creating as a musician and. composer, having to restrict activities in certain formal ways.
(Uzoigwe 1981:131)

He then goes on to define the creative principle:

> *nkwa na agba abuo abuo, oke na.* Music operates in the division of twos, male and female. (Ibid:137)

In this the male is classified as active, virile and forward, the female as passive and receptive. This leads to a creative pattern, the essence of which is layered integration:

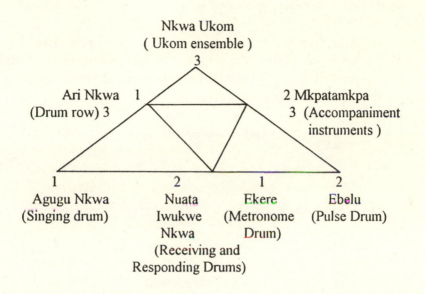

In this we see a solo, lead drum being answered by other drums creating the element called by Uzoigwe the 'Drum Row'. The accompaniment to this is made up of drums playing the pulse of the music, and a metronomic beat. These parts combined, the Drum Row and the accompaniment, create the complete *Ukom* ensemble.

1:      male
2:      female
3:      performance combination
                    ( Ibid : 141)

Such processes may not be universal, but they are effective and functional, and our minds may begin to posit connections with our own work in schools.  It is quite possible to develop every day sounds into structures allowing musical performances. We may already include an audience of some sort in appraisal processes. There are many ways of linking motifs and concepts to produce layers that can be built upon to create a musical whole. If, as Keith Swanwick suggests:

The first and unique aim of music education is to make musical processes explicit (Swanwick 1988:118)

then the *Izhiangbo* and *U k o m* ways of working through communal involvement in standard processes go a long way towards achieving that aim.

Is the task we are setting ourselves achievable? Are there sufficient links between musics for us to progress through our processes? Let us consider some of the things involved in music around the world. Here is a list, which is by no means exhaustive:

## Functions and Uses of Music

motor development

| | |
|---|---|
| intellectual development | games |
| inform | drinking |
| educate | entertain |
| mnemonic | warning |
| aid work | satire |
| encourage | call to arms |
| display | evoke  loyalties |
| description | mourning |
| ritual | catharsis |
| praise | soothe |
| express feelings | love |

It may be worth pointing out the distinction between *function* and *use* here. The *function* tends to be the intended purpose of the music, as decided upon by individual composers and communities. It is the reason for the existence of the music. The *use* is what actually happens to the music in practice. In many cases the two will coincide, but it is certainly not inevitable. Enculturation is also a major function and use of music, but it is not used separately here as it is, in essence, a synthesis of all these purposes of music.

At this point I want to suggest some actual examples for several of these categories to indicate the nature that links might take. For each particular function/use I shall give a named piece of music from European 'Art Music', another World Music, and from a popular idiom.

## 1. Develop Motor and Intellectual Skills

Bach:           Fugues

Kenya (Luo):  *Nyatiti* praise songs

(the lyre player improvises songs to praise important people, in addition jingling leg bells and striking the lyre arm with a metal toe ring)

AC/DC:      *Thunderstruck*

(this makes use of several sophisticated techniques for the guitar, including bariolage, and 'Alberti Bass' figures)

(AC/DC 1990)

## 2. Description

Vaughan-Williams: *Sinfonia Antarctica* (Symphony no.7)

China: P'ip'a (pear shaped short lute) battle pieces (full of accurate sound effects)

Japan ( group) : *Ghosts* (Japan 1984)

## 3. Praise

Vivaldi:        *Gloria*

Benin (Bariba): Court ritual

O Bangana, your name is like a great house. Everyone can find shelter in it. The cow elephant will always give birth to an elephant. You will always belong to a great family. (Bariba 1974)

Ladysmith Black Mambazo:

*Ithaya Lamaghawe* (Home of the Heroes) (Ladysmith Black Mambazo 1987).

**4. Express Feelings**

Tchaikovsky:     Symphony No. 6 (Pathetique)

Papua New Guinea (Kaluli): Bird songs
                (the mournful calls of certain birds are imitated in
                song, with the explicit intention of evoking sadness in
                the audience ) (Feld: 1990)

Sonny Boy Williams: *Born Blind* (Blues).    (The Ultimate Blues
                Collection 1989).

**5. Love**

Puccini :        O Mio Babbino Caro
                ( from *Gianni Schicchi*)

Hungary:         Rab vagyok erted        You hold me captive
                Alom esett a szememre  Sleep closed my eyes
                Hajnal vesse ki belole  Dawn should wake me
                Ha a hajnal ki nem veti  If dawn doesn't wake me
                Kisangyalom ki oleli    Who will  embrace my
                                        sweetheart (Teka 1989)

van Trees:       *Achy Breaky Heart*

**6. Call to Arms**

Anon (11th century): Chevalier mult estes guariz
Ethiopia:        Zira! Zira!        (Floyd 1990)
Schonberg & Boublil: *Do You Hear the People Sing?*

**7. Entertain**

Walton:          *Façade*
Slovakia: (Gypsy)

                Elment Otilka          Otilka went
                Megfesulkodni          To comb her hair
                Nem is fesulkodott     She did not even
                meg jol...             comb her hair well...
                En vagyok Hella,       I am Hella,
                Az oreg Tuta lanya     the old Tuta's daughter
                Ribiza lanya           Ribiza's daughter
                Szombatrol             from Szombat
                                       (Kovaksik 1985: no 38 )

Ellington & Mills: *It Don't Mean a Thing*

These suggestions are, obviously, from just one person's perspective, but they do at least show that similarities exist among the musics of the world; that links can be made. Exactly what those links consist of, and how close the similarities really are requires rather fuller investigation, and it may be that June Boyce-Tillman's work (see Chapter 3), will be of considerable help in structuring such investigations. Below is a much expanded list of musical functions, given by Kaemner in *Music in Human Life* (1973)

## Functions of music

| | |
|---|---|
| Aesthetic: | enjoyment, value, affect, humour, skill |
| Play: | expression, ritual, order and complexity, socialisation, physical control |
| Self expression: | catharsis, love, sexual expression, to gain prestige |
| Communication: | in a lullaby; to express love, to entertain the child, and to put it to sleep, courtship, link with the supernatural, internalise roles (including gender), legitimise other activities, distinguish types of behaviour, make criticism and complaint acceptable, disseminate information, build and maintain group identity, symbolise identity of generations, emphasize ethnic identity |
| Politics: | symbolise conflict, mobilise sentiment, instil courage and enthusiasm, perpetuate differences, control conflict, mark status of superiors, distract attention from political matters, indoctrinate populations, develop nationalist sentiments |
| Pragmatic: | courtship, lullabies, aid work processes, disguise gaps in social events, to create breaks in social events, drown cries of initiates, assure necessities of life for musicians, encourage future employment, teach other things, transmit ideologies, mnemonic aid |
| Ritual: | against sickness, against ghosts, assure general well being, cause rain, change of pace, release of emotions, express sadness, bring about trance, sponsor musicians and performances. (Kaemmer 1993: 151-168) |

It would prove an interesting if exhausting process to find music for all of these!

One of the principal difficulties, of course, is that music is perhaps the least tangible of all cultural expressions. It is relatively easy to describe and analyse techniques of composition and performance, methods of delivery, and the social contexts of much music, and it may be that these methods of approaching music can bring us closest to an eventual true understanding of it. It is probably true that music designed to entertain and inform us will be readily accessible; that would seem to be a principle requirement and may explain the strength and ubiquitous presence of "popular" musics around the world. It may also be the case that music intent on the expression of our most intimate feelings will be very difficult for others to comprehend fully.

There is no requirement, however, that we approach the most difficult first. As with many educational processes it is necessary to start with the possible and progress towards completion and perfection. We may start by looking to see which functions are common, then go on to decide which are useful or important for us and our intentions, and which functions we might choose to avoid. We might wish to consider particularly the overarching function of enculturation, enabling the observation and assimilation of culture, through immersion in music, especially at a time when the cry is often that people in the West have lost their own cultural identities.

Without a well structured philosophy and method for approaching world musics there are difficulties for music teachers which have the potential to become dangers. Firstly, music is not a universal language. The problems we sometimes have when encountering unknown music are evidence enough of that. It could be argued that it is a sort of universal alphabet, in that it has common elements; pitches, rhythm, etc., but differences of emphasis, pronunciation, syntax and presentation make that argument of little real or practical value. Each music has to be regarded on its own terms, and teachers must be wary of making assumptions.

The second danger is an over-concentration on the trappings and epiphenomena of musical performance. Costumes, body decoration and ornaments are interesting and important in providing an insight into authentic modes of performance, but they are by no means always essential. Knowing the social context of a performance gives an understanding of the significance of a piece of music, and its place in a community, but there is a temptation for our interest to be engaged only by the more unusual and arcane rites and rituals, particularly where they pose a contrast to the attitudes and actions we may consider appropriate and proper. Our central aim is to enrich our understanding, not to evoke disapproval and confusion.

The third danger is that a limited inexpert exposure which has no remit to transform our minds can lead to false impressions that knowledge has been acquired, and this insufficient 'knowledge' may be used in the justification of racist attitudes and tensions. This is not to say that no attempt should be made to approach other world musics if they cannot be performed with complete accuracy and authenticity. This will never be achievable in the classroom anyway simply because it is a classroom, but we can ensure authentic aspects of particular musics, so that what is shared is based on original realities. Also, culture is dynamic and composers respond to the times, so we will often get a glimpse of music as it was at particular points.

So what should teachers be providing for their students? Students from Frogmore Community School in Hampshire made the following comments after a three day workshop with the London-based Ghanaian music-dance group, Dagarti Arts, in 1992:

> They were very good at what they do and they are very good at teaching other people ...
> It was very enjoyable to work with real experts ...
> I thought they were very educational and I would like to learn about another culture ...
> active ... brilliant ... good dancers ... fit ... intelligent ... persistent ... creative ...
>
> It was good and I had a great time and I would do it again ...
> It was easy to dance to the music and the beat stays in your head ... and how the instruments are like our ours ... They were very good singers dancers and teachers, they helped you even if you weren't participating ...

What is noticeable here is the fact that the students are impressed with the *command of skills* shown by the workshop leaders; appreciation of the *challenges* made upon the students, within the framework of *understanding*, and the *development* of *selected appropriate abilities*, and approval of recognisably *authentic* modes of expression. (More can be read about Dagarti Arts at Frogmore Community School in Chapter 7).

This seems to come down to finding challenge and satisfaction in the excellence of an authentic culture as required of us in National Curriculum documents cited earlier.

Can this be achieved by teachers in schools as well as by visiting experts? Catherine Ellis suggests that pedagogical skills may be suitably transferable:

> Good diagnostic teachers have comparable skills across cultures.
> (Ellis 1985:87)

It may well be that specialisation in one or two areas may be helpful, and such expertise could then be shared between schools. East Sussex, for example, has decided to concentrate on four cultures (see Ernest Piper's chapter later in this book).

How can we select suitable music for our schools? Our answers to these questions may guide us in appropriate directions:

1) What music have we heard?
2) What music have we performed?
3) What music do we enjoy?
4) What music affects us?
5) What music intrigues us?

If we have no answers to any of these, then the first stage is to increase and widen our own musical experiences and background. It is probable, however, that everyone has heard a vast range of music, consciously or unconsciously: from disc, casette, radio, television, video game, or in live performance. Then the job is to provide positive peak experiences, which should aim to lead to understanding, in the form of respectful awareness. These experiences will arise from carefully laid plans, within a coherent framework, with the intention of providing opportunities for the transformation of musical thought, and hopefully:

'increasing the child's power of thought by inventing for him modes of access to the empowering techniques of the culture' (Bruner 1972 : 19)

## Bibliography

AC/DC (1990) *The Razor's Edge.* Atco Records

Anagah, M.I.N. (1987) *North Eastern Igbo Music.* Unpublished PhD Belfast. Queen's University

Bariba Court Ritual (1974) Unesco Collection - *Ritual and Ceremonial Music from Northern Dahomey.* Musical Sources: Ceremonial, Ritual and Magic Music 11-5. Philips

Blacking, John (1987) *A Commonsense view of All Music.* Cambridge. Cambridge University Press

Bruner, Jerome. S. (1972) *The Relevance of Education.* London. Allen & Unwin

Curriculum Council for Wales (1992) *Music in thc National Curriculum: Non-Statutory Guidance for Teachers Cardiff.* CCW

Department of Education (1992) *Curriculum (Programmes of Study and Attainment)* DENI (Circular 1992/19) 1992

Northern Ireland (1992) *Targets in Music Order (Northern Ireland)* Bangor

Department of Education and Science (1991) *Music for Ages 5-14* DES/WO

Department of Education and Science (1992) *Music in the National Curriculum.* London. HMSO

Department for Education (1995) *Music in the National Curriculum.* London. HMSO

Ellis, Catherine J. (1985) *Aboriginal Music:Education for Living.* St Lucia. University of Queensland Press

Feld, Steven (1990) *Sound and Sentiment.* Philadelphia. University of Pennsylvania Press.

Floyd, Malcolm (1990) *Folksongs from Africa.* London. Faber

Gritton, Peter (1991) *Folksongs from the Far East.* London. Faber

Japan *Exorcising Ghosts.* Virgin Records (1984)

Kaemmer, John E. (1993) *Music in Human Life.* Austin. University of Texas Press

Kovalcsik, Katalin (1985) *Vlach Gypsy Folk Songs in Slovakia.* Institute for Musicology of the Hungarian Academy for Sciences

Kwami, Robert M. (1989 ) *African Music, Education and the School Curriculum.* Unpublished PhD. London University

Ladysmith Black Mambazo (1987) *Shaka Zulu.* WEA Records

Musgrove, F. (1982) *Education and Anthropology.* London. Wiley

Omondi, W.A. (Chair) (1984 ) *Report of the Presidential National Music Commission.* Nairobi

Swanwick, K (1988) *Music Mind and Education.* London. Routledge

Teka (1989) *Teka: Hungarian Folk Music Group*    Hungaroton SLDX 18147

*Ultimate Blues Collection* (1989) MCR Productions

Woodfield, Ian. (1994)   'The Hindustannie Air' in *Journal of the Royal Musical Association* vol. 119.pt 2. London. Oxford University Press.

# 3 A Framework for Intercultural Dialogue in Music

*June Boyce-Tillman*

## Introduction

There is a story of an official from Africa who was taken to a Mozart concert at the Festival Hall by his British host. At the end he said: 'That was very pleasant but I understood that your music was more complicated than that.'

It is a story that not only turns on its head the traditional Eurocentric view of European music and its relationship to that of the rest of the world, but also gives us some pointers to the problems involved in the establishment of any framework that will enable us to value music from a variety of cultures. If we look at the many traditions of the African subcontinent, particularly those involving drums, we see immense complexity in the area of rhythm, and limited, if any, development in the area of melody and particularly tonality, and its associated area, modulation. If we think of the Mozartian idiom we find a very simple use of rhythm, with clear-cut phrases and little use of rhythmic counterpoint of any kind. Its complexity lies in the area of tonality and especially, modulation. Mozart's music is complex but the complexity was not in an area in which the African could immediately perceive it. So it is with Europeans faced with African musics; untrained to perceive such rhythmic complexity, they perceive it as simple. And so the absence of cross-cultural understanding is perpetuated, and the excellence and sophistication of some cultures when compared with others, is supported by ill-conceived or wrongly constructed notions of excellence. Any culture, to have survived at all, has, by definition been valued by a certain group of people in a certain geographical location for a period of time and therefore, (the human mind being what it is) has developed a degree of complexity in some areas. To establish a contextual set of values that will allow a certain degree of musical interchange between cultures is the substance of this chapter.

The history of intercultural dialogue in music is peppered with a variety of anecdotes. Most of those familiar to me, because of my own cultural background, work to reverse the assumptions of the opening story and uphold the glories of Western European classical traditions as 'better', 'more advanced' or 'more sophisticated' than other cultures. Academic papers are proliferating, some claiming that it is possible and detailing the caveats, others that it is totally impossible. Books on the subject range from commentaries originating in the traditions of classical analysis on such works as David Fanshawe's 'African Sanctus', to accounts of ethnomusicological journeyings. Musicians from the Western European Classical tradition cite examples of the use of material from other cultures in their own tradition, including the use of Turkish percussion in the Classical period and Debussy's encounter with the Javanese gamelan. Various conclusions are drawn from these. One is that Western European Classical music is a world culture, this being helped by the ubiquity of such phenomena as Associated Board Examinations and the world wide touring of many groups from that tradition. The other is that the Western European tradition is already multicultural in its philosophy and practice, thus rendering current debate unnecessary.

However, such borrowings, to other eyes, may have the feel of cultural highjacking and imperialism. To look at other world musics from this perspective is to treat it like we now treat the Third World economically, by valuing it only in terms of what we can take from it, rather than for itself.

In the world of school music making, policy documents embracing or eschewing multiculturalism within the classroom setting abound and nestle sometimes uneasily next door to classroom texts and schemes of music education that have embraced a variety of cultures, in various ways, long before it entered the thinking of educational policy makers.

For it has long been said by some that music is a universal language, and denied equally vehemently by others. Levi-Strauss puts the dilemma clearly:

> ......music is a language with some meaning for the immense majority of mankind although only a tiny minority of people are capable of formulating a meaning in it...it is the only language with the contradictory attributes of being at once intelligible and untranslatable. (Levi-Strauss 1969: 18)

And so on the one hand music would appear to define culture less hermetically than speech; and yet the acrimony that ensues in the local church when electric guitars are introduced into a particular religious setting, indicates that different cultural groups within a single society are defined by their music, perhaps more clearly than by their language. But as 'less developed' (whatever that may mean), countries open themselves up to the world, one of the first things that they 'export', is often a performing group of some kind. This, presumably is because they believe that people of different cultures are more likely to be able to relate to their culture through music and dance, than through other forms of expression, particularly language. (It may also be that these express more fully the totality of the culture than language.)

In the light of this, it is difficult to retain in its rigid form the argument set out by many and made manifest by Walker:

> One can go further... to claim that discovering the 'inherited riches' of a musical culture cannot be done except through direct experience. For example, only one's presence at a Pacific Northwest Indian potlatch ceremony can convey the true nature of a potlatch song. (Walker 1992)

Such a philosophy not only spells death to any attempts at multiculturalism in education but also gives the lie to people's obvious enjoyment of a performing group from Africa and South America. It is arguable whether my presence at a potlatch ceremony with a background in the Western European tradition, actually enables me to enter into the same experience as the North American Indians, who have been reared in that culture. We all view other cultures, wherever we meet them - 'home or away' - through culturally-tinted glasses. Nothing can change that. We can only be aware of the likely tints and shades that make up the lenses. It is indeed unlikely that we perceive Mozart as he was perceived in the eighteenth century, and yet we would claim that his music has some degree of meaning for us, partly because some of its features are rooted in our culture and partly because of our common humanity. In my research into the work of the medieval composer, Hildegard of Bingen (1089-1179), I am always acutely aware how different were the belief and cultural patterns that governed the world of her day and especially the monastic traditions, from my own belief systems. And yet are we incapable of appreciating Mozart, because we cannot enter an eighteenth century palace and dine there?

Indeed, it can never be clear that the ways in which individuals experience music within a community or culture are all exactly the same. Indeed it is most likely not to be; for each of us has our own personal music autobiography which is unique. Within this, there is the linking of pieces with certain personal events - tragedies and successes - that give certain pieces personal emotional significance that transcends their role within the culture. There is a story of Cecil Sharp, the collector of British folksongs, in search of a particular fiddle tune. He found a fiddle player, perhaps the only player who knew it; however, the last time he had played it, was at the death of a friend, and he had vowed that he would never play it again. Sharp could not persuade him, despite a considerable degree of persistence, to break that vow. The fiddle tune was lost for ever.

It may well be that certain cultures are easier for us to 'know' (whatever that word may mean musically), than others, that musical cultural divisions operate in a similar way to language divisions. It is easier for English speaking British people to make the jump into other languages with a Latin Anglo-Saxon base than it is to go further afield to the pitched tone languages of the Far East, where there are fewer similarities and the very concepts of grammar and syntax appear different. In the same way, it is easier for us to approach Mozart, than the Javanese gamelan. However, the roots of contemporary pop music in the rhythmic traditions of the African continent, may mean that certain traditions of the music from that continent are more easily approached by contemporary adolescents, than the music of Mozart - phenomena clearly seen in our secondary school classrooms.

The thrust towards multiculturalism in the music curriculum has not always been generated from the desire for purely musical outcomes. Its history in Britain and the US shows several strands co-existing; these need to be unpacked to examine the sort of models already in place (even if undeclared) for intercultural exchange in music.

From the beginning of the century there has been literature (that has increased throughout the century) rooting music education in sound exploration. In 1916 the classes in creative music of Satis Coleman (a piano teacher at Lincoln School of Teachers College, Columbia University) started with the sound of instruments. Children were encouraged to collect and construct a variety of instruments. It was a short step, that also coincided with the exhibition at which Debussy heard the sound of the Javanese gamelan and Orff's basing his construction of easily approachable classroom instruments on Eastern and medieval European models, to the examination of the construction of various instruments from various cultures. So Coleman's *Creative music in the Home* (1927) contained information about and instructions for the construction of musical instruments from India, Polynesia, Africa and China. From then on the search for new tone colours in the Western European classical tradition saw other cultures as a rich source for new tone colours, which were often hijacked without much concern for cultural context.

In the US and Britain concern about the status of minority groups socially led to the advocacy of a multicultural music policy as a route to solving social problems. Such bodies as the Music Educators National

Conference (MENC) from 1939 in the States looked at exchanges between the US and Latin America, and 1949 UNESCO founded the International Music Council. In the 1960's courses in ethnomusicology burgeoned in the US and formed part of large conferences at Yale in 1963 and Tanglewood in 1967. Ethnomusicology developed as a separate discipline with its own methodology, grounded more in the sociological sciences than practices of the musicologists rooted in the Western European classical traditions. School textbook publishers consulted ethnomusicologists, in order to introduce elements from other musical cultures into the classroom; but at academic level there was no framework to link this with more traditional classical courses in 'music'. The academic world was, in general, happy to see a separation between itself and these other aspiring methodologies. The result of this was a mish-mash of opportunistic approaches to the study, which often reflected pragmatically what was possible, rather than any conceptual underpinning.

The racial conflict that characterised both the US and Britain in the 1960's led to an upsurge of attempts to find anything that might solve, or at least ameliorate, racial tensions. Moore writes in 1977 of this movement in the States in the 1960s and 70s:

> The concerns of minority students for the inclusion of studies that reflected their culture (Black, Chicano and Native American studies), and accurately represented their ancestors as well as themselves filtered downward to the elementary and secondary levels to become the ground for multicultural education in its beginning stages of implementation throughout the United States. (Moore 1977: 74)

This coincided with a movement to develop the musical potential of every child, and the opening of what was once regarded as the domain of an elite, to all children. Within the context of "music education for all", it was felt that an exposure to a variety of musics of the world would instil pride in the various cultures that made up British and American society.

The ways in which this policy was worked out in practice were various; it was based on a set of social and psychological goals, rather than a unifying underlying philosophy. Two philosophies or perhaps methodologies did, however, emerge. One saw the best route into unifying nations as the creation of a sort of world culture based on the 'universal language' view of music. So the goal was the creating of a sort of 'world style' from an amalgam of various traditions. It could be said that both the classical route of integrating various stylistic elements within its own tradition and the increasing trend in pop music to do the same, are even now working towards this end. And yet the roots of both these styles, and the fact that at present they are still in the hands of First World entrepreneurs, makes the whole movement look remarkably like a cultural form of the geographical imperialism that characterised the last century.

The other line was that of pluralism, supported by John Dewey. He identified a number of dualisms that plagued education:

1. Academic versus artistic study
2. Process versus product
3. Specialised music versus comprehensive musicianship
4. Music for the talented versus music for every child
5. Fine arts versus practical arts
6. Cognitive versus the affective domain.
(Drawn from Steinecker 1976)

The problem and the solution are identifiable in a quotation found in Steinecker:

> Our sense of crisis stems largely from the pluralism of our society; but this unease is related to the expectation that society should, in fact, be linear and non pluralistic. Pluralism does not produce conflict unless the expectation is for unity. Once one recognises pluralism as the dominant fact of our society, the ability to live with and understand and appreciate the divergent ideologies is not necessarily a source of unease. (Steinecker 1976: 7)

The model set out in this chapter is an attempt to understand pluralism and must not be seen as a prerequisite for musical practice within a culture. Palmer (1975) identified four categories of philosophical ideation:

1. The 'global village' concept that saw a world decreasing in size by the development of transportation systems and thus becoming aware of the values of other cultures.

2. The awareness of other value systems than that of the Western aesthetic (I shall return to this later). The presence of functional, ritualistic or religious ends in other cultures led to a questioning of the notion of musical

significance  This became intertwined with an emerging sociological view of music (in the hands of ethnomusicologists).

3. The endangering of other musical traditions by western colonialism, missionary ventures and more recently, urbanisation and scientific technology. Acculturation dominated where change was rapid. Organisations fostering global exchanges were set up, notably the International Society for Music Education and the International Institute for Comparative Music Studies and Documentation. The problems of ethnic minorities within other cultures reinforced the drive towards this.

4. Academic scholarship and increased ethnomusicological field work resulted in an identification of differences in the products but similarities in the processes. Grounds for a universality of music as a language were rooted in psychology rather than in musical outcomes.

The academic world has not so far grappled with the problem to the same extent as the schools. An article examining the state of current research in the US (Jordan 1992) can identify few places where the problem has been addressed in higher education curricula. She lists the following:

1. Butcher (1970) who developed a course in African music as part of a project at Harvard University.

2. Schmid (1971) who developed a curriculum for undergraduate education which contains a rationale and methodology for the study of music of tribal cultures, the music of oriental cultures, European folk music and the folk music of the Americas.

3. Levine and Standifer's (1981) *From Jumpstreet: Television and the Humanities* - a series of 13 half hour television programmes for pre-service and in-service training focusing on America's black musical heritage.

4. Rodriguez and Sherman's (1983) manual designed for teacher training, in which the music of black Americans, American Indians and Hispanic Americans is explored.

5. Gartin's (1981) survey of intercultural perspectives in music appreciation textbooks.

6. Mumford's (1984) research revealing that direct contact is a better method of facilitating attitudinal change in relation to black popular music than lectures and reading.

7. Stephens' (1984) building on Mumford's work, showing that acceptance of Afro-American popular music was greatly affected by the integration of Afro-American popular music into the undergraduate curriculum, by means of a programme of lectures, films, listening, readings and discussion.

The pattern in higher education in Britain is similarly patchy, and few courses have sought to do much more than have a module of ethnomusicology or a particular culture within a traditional framework rooted in Western European classical traditions. Teacher training courses have had to address it in more depth but in the absence of attempts to integrate at the highest levels of academia, few tools for the relating of musical cultures have been developed. Most school educators have adopted a pragmatic approach.

In Britain the move towards a multicultural approach to all education in the late 60s, 70s and early 80s has recently been overshadowed by the debates around the National Curriculum. But multiculturalism has played an important part in this debate and it was the retraction of developments in this area, that was one of the characteristics of the revised consultation document (1992) produced by Pascall and the government appointed working group.

It is important, then, in this context to see *What Schools Have Actually Done* in this area. Originally the approach was one that can be likened to a 'Cook's Tour': it consisted of playing recordings of music from a different culture, learning something about it sociologically and geographically. and then returning home to our own culture, (here defined as Western European classical traditions). with a sense of relief, feeling that the 'foreign' culture is strange, exotic and little able to be grasped.

With the advent of the more integrated approach to the curriculum, favoured in primary schools in particular in the 60s, 70s and early 80s, a change of approach emerged. The curriculum was clustered around themes like 'Water' 'Myself' or 'Change'. Curriculum material in all subject areas was chosen mostly on the grounds of the relevance it had to the topic in question, rather than on the basis of its 'goodness', its cultural origins or, sometimes, its appropriateness for the stage the pupils had reached in their own development.

Because many (often all) areas of the curriculum were integrated in this approach, there was more likelihood that the context for the music would be examined, and that this would be related to contextual considerations within the majority culture.

Another approach has been pressed upon schools by the structure of the National Curriculum. It can be called the 'musical concepts' approach, which says that all musics share such concepts as timbre, pitch. melody. form and structure, rhythm and so on. So examples from musics of the world are now clustered, not around an extra-musical idea, or topic, but around a so-called 'musical concept'.

Although this can result in a 'we're all the same really' approach, - in more skilled hands it can lead to an examination of ways in which we differ, and ways in which we are the same. It is tempting to see it as an 'advance' on the Cook's tour and the Topic work approach. But for reasons that will appear later it is also a minefield interculturally.

Elliott's (1989) analysis of six different *Curriculum Models* that have emerged in North America (drawing on Pratte's book *Pluralism in Education* (1979)) will be useful here, as a way of identifying curriculum models which have, in general, rather like Topsy 'just growed':

1. One focuses on the major musical styles of Western art music, the goal being the establishment of 'good taste', which is defined as the breaking down of students' affiliation with popular and/or subculture musics, especially those of cultural minorities. There are echoes here of the National Curriculum debate in England. Based on the absolute supremacy of Western art music, world unity is to be achieved by establishing the ubiquity of Western classical traditions

2. The second curricular model includes some ethnic and subculture musics (e.g. gospel, rock, Mexican, African,), but views their relevance to the curriculum as related to the way in which they have acted as inspiration and source material for new music within accepted styles and forms. Values of the minority cultures are regarded as a source for potential contributions to the stronger hybrid society. Projects such as 'Debussy and the Javanese gamelan' would fall into this category.

3. In the third model any cultural heritage is regarded as an impediment to progress. Only the contemporary is of value. Musical values are dependent on current fashion and taste, both social and political. Self expression in the here and now validates such fusions as commercial pop and avant garde classical traditions choose to make.

4. This aims to preserve cultural diversity by selecting some of the core repertoire from the largest minority group in the local community. Although apparently more 'multicultural' than models 1-3 this, in fact, provides a very limited choice and is likely to trap students in the culture of their upbringing, rather than allowing them to be more mobile socially. In Britain we see this in such schemes as the introduction of sitar teaching in schools with a high Asian intake. A sad anecdote highlights the dangers implicit in this. A pupil of Caribbean background wanted to be an opera singer. A well-intentioned teacher had asked her whether she might not prefer the steel pans. This is an extreme version of the idea that an ethnocentric curriculum raises the self esteem and academic achievement of children from ethnic minority backgrounds. But in these parameters it can prove limiting and may narrow the path ahead of children, isolating them from an enriched cultural life. This is also a 'backs-to-the-wall' approach to the curriculum, which is now driven by the requirements of a local situation rather than from any philosophical model for curriculum content and teaching strategy. If the sitar is worth teaching, it is worth teaching to whichever pupils will choose it.

5. This model selects musics on the basis of regional and/or national boundaries of culture, ethnicity, religion, function or race. It aims at introducing musics in the same way as they are introduced in their original cultures, in so far as this is possible in a school context. It organises the curriculum according to the musical elements, processes, roles and behaviours accepted by the majority values. And before dealing with Elliott's sixth model I wish to reflect on this approach a little further.

This is the so-called 'musical concept' approach popular in Britain and America currently. It governs course books like the Oxford School Music Course and the Silver Burdett music course. It is, however, important to identify the cultural roots of such an approach. More than the 'topic' approach, it claims to be intrinsically 'musical', and to look at what is actually there in the music. As such, it is firmly rooted in Western aesthetics and schools of analysis. These are proud of their ability to make musical judgements about musical superiority; and these can easily be extended to relate not only to individual works within a culture but also to whole cultures. The grounds for such judgements lie in a view that music can be totally divorced from the culture in which it was created. It is a product of the so-called absolutist school, proud of its so-called 'objective' musical judgements. Cook in his book 'A Guide to Musical Analysis' gives clear insight into the origins of such thinking and schools of analysis. Here he describes the origin of the Western analytical traditions in the teaching of Western classical composition techniques to groups of people. He identifies the 'formal' approach as one centred in the identification of 'themes':

> Certain parts of the music are picked out and identified as themes (and accordingly labelled A, B, B1 and so forth) whereas the rest of the music is regarded as non-thematic - or to use the old-fashioned and rather unsatisfactory term, 'transitional'. (Cook 1987:9)

He goes on to ask on what grounds certain passages are regarded as only transitional even when they may play a significant fact in later musical discourse in the piece.

He then turns his attention to content:

> At the beginning of the century, as indeed nowadays, it was harmony that was regarded as the crucial aspect of musical content - at least in the musical content of the eighteenth and nineteenth centuries. And as the traditional way of analysing harmony was to rewrite it in terms of some simplified notation. It is sensible to begin by briefly considering what a notation is and how it works.

> Essentially there are two analytical acts: the act of *Omission* and the act of *Relation*; conventional musical notation is analytical in both of these respects. It omits things like the complex overtone structure of musical sounds, representing sounds by their fundamentals alone. Even in the way it represents these fundamentals it is schematic, because it reduces to a few symbols and finite number of chromatic pitches the enormous variety of articulations and intonations that string players and singers, for instance adopt. Similarly, conventional notation does not show the fine detail of rhythmic performance; indeed, it makes heavy weather of showing any rhythmic values which are not in the simplest arithmetical relationships. In all these respects, as in others, the ordinary performance score constitutes an informal and rather unsystematic analysis of musical sound, sacrificing detailed representations in the interests of clarity, simplicity and intelligibility. (Ibid:16)

He goes on to deal with the centrality of harmony to the Western analytical systems. He identifies different schools of analytical thought and the relative weight that the world of musicology has given to them. High in the ratings lie the approach of Schenker and the like, who have constructed mathematical systems to define the notion of musical excellence. Firmly rooted in the German harmonic traditions of the late Classical, Romantic and Modern Periods, these set great store by harmonic and tonal frameworks and define structure in these terms. Fortuitously(!) on this scale German works of the last two centuries come high in the list of ratings. Of lesser worth are rated what Cook calls the more psychological approaches to analysis, in the hand of such practitioners as Reti, Meyer and Deryck Cooke. These see a piece in the context of its creator, more in terms of a reflection of his psychology and personal history. This edging towards a more referential approach, or at least one that relates musical meaning to a context, is often regarded as less objective than more 'mathematical, scientific approaches'. The sociological approach in the hands of practitioners more related to the ethnomusicologic field therefore becomes even more suspect; for it embraces referentialism to an even greater extent than the psychological approach. Here music becomes a series of culturally meaningful patterns of sound. The danger inherent in this approach is seen in further quotation from Walker:

> The special sounds of a culture are special symbols which owe their epistemological and ontological nature to an inextricable link between culture and acoustic qualities. I am not happy to see children take the sounds of a koto, a pipa, or a gamelan, and denude them of their special cultural significance in order to make new sonic structures which have only the 'child's curiosity', openness to feelings, and respect for other people's ideas and work as their raison d'être. Using sound as a personal expression is one thing, but using someone else's sound and stripping it of its significance in order to be curious is something else. For me, the worst educational scenario would be to hear a child's rendering of "their tune" played by a sampled koto sound, knowing that the child has no clue about the special cultural codes contained in the koto sounds. (Walker 1992 : 172)

This is a view that I have disputed earlier; but there is a degree of truth in it, as there is in the so-called absolutist position.

It is from the absolutist position that the 'musical concept' approach to the curriculum is drawn. The Western classical tradition is chopped up into its component parts, to which are attributed greater and lesser degrees of value, with rhythm rating well below melody and especially harmony and tonality. The component parts are then parcelled up and channelled down the educational system in a 'top down' methodology, that gives the youngest children 'high and low' while the older students get 'harmony': And yet even the system used for dividing the culture up is to a certain extent culturally conditioned. When, for example, do the multi-timbral drums of Africa become pitched instruments. Are they lesser instruments when they are not? Where does timbre end and pitch begin? Is the absence of harmony within a tradition an indication of lesser value?

To unravel this muddle we need to place the analytical systems used to dissect music in this way and then used as the basis for value judgements based on a hierarchy of 'musical elements', firmly into the context that produced them; this was an aspiring scientific society anxious to conquer the world in the guise of reason and rationalisation. They are European in philosophy and methodology. Viewed in this light, they can rightly take their place in the culture that they serve; their limited validity beyond and outside of that tradition can then be honestly acknowledged.

All traditions have ways of evaluating musical excellence. These are thrown up within a culture, and perhaps above everything else, these have limited cross-cultural use. All cultures have musical leaders (some more open to admitting wider society to their ranks than others), but the methods of selection and the role of these in the society vary from culture to culture. The problem arises when the values from one culture are taken as 'objective', devoid of cultural context and therefore, transcultural. They are indicators only within a cultural frame; they cannot be used as value judgements transculturally.

The way forward lies in the putting together of methodologies taken from both musicology and ethnomusicology. And this brings me to Elliott's final curriculum model.

6. This he entitles dynamic multiculturalism. It opens up the possibility of the generation of unfamiliar values, procedures and behaviours in the interest of understanding or 'knowing' musics of a variety of cultures. It attempts ' to preserve the integrity of musical traditions from the past, but allows students to develop ideas about music that will counterbalance unconscious prejudice either academic or social'. He writes:

The combination of the widest range of world musics and a world view of musical concepts separates the dynamic curriculum model from all the rest. Thus, in addition to developing students' abilities to discriminate and appreciate the differences and similarities among musical cultures, a dynamic curriculum has the potential to achieve two fundamental 'expressive objectives or ways of being musical: 'bimusicality' at least, and 'multimusicality' at most (Elliot 1989 :18)

Although he still leans to the 'musical concept' approach, he does mention the possibility of generating unfamiliar values, procedures and behaviours. It is in this spirit that the framework in the ensuing pages is set out. We need a framework that will enable us to value and relate cultures without necessarily fusing them at all.

And yet we are all products of a culture, and rebellion is as much culturally conditioned as conservatism; to construct transcultural tools presupposes existence of a cross-cultural person who, by definition, cannot exist. None of us can totally rid ourselves of our cultural spectacles, and I cannot claim this for myself. Any individual is a separate being in the context of a particular culture, as, indeed, is any individual work of art within a particular tradition. To analyse in this way is not to deny individual uniqueness. The model also attempts to weld together into some sort of united model the contextual approaches to music and the more absolutist view.

The model is based on the premise that all music can be viewed in a number of dimensions simultaneously. Three of these are Materials, Expression and Form (Swanwick and Tillman 1986, Tillman 1987). So, if we listen to a Mozart Symphony, at one level it is a certain group of instruments playing together and that is at the level of Materials. However, it makes us feel in certain ways at certain times and the flow of the feeling is ever changing within it - the level of Expression. It is also divided into sections, called movements, in the pattern: fast-slow-dance-fast; and, furthermore, each of these has its own internal pattern of some elements that recur and contrasted material; the repetition and contrast is handled differently in each movement. The symphony can be viewed critically in each of these dimensions, although they all exist simultaneously in the music and interact with one another. It is possible to see a calypso played on steel pans in the same way. At the level of Materials, it is a collection of instruments of the ideophonic kind, made from oil drums, playing together; at the level of Expression it has a certain feelingful character, often quite distinctive in that tradition and rooted in the rhythm patterns used. The formal structure often involves a harmonised AABA melody which returns in a variety of variations.

This educational research (Swanwick and Tillman 1986) enabled these parameters to be seen more clearly, by examining the work of children; with them the process of musical knowing and understanding is not yet fully developed. By observing the musical utterances of some 40 South London primary school children over the course of some seven years, a helical form of musical development emerged, showing the children entering progressively into these dimensions of musical understanding. The reason for the choice of the helical form is that once entered upon the level of understanding is not left behind, but added to the musical knowing.

## Figure 3.1 Musical Development

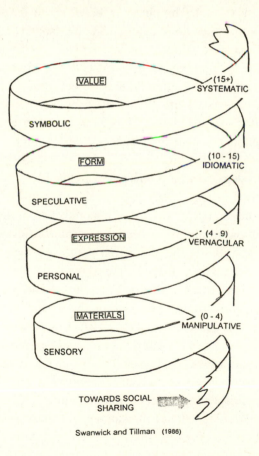

Swanwick and Tillman (1986)

The youngest children are taken up with the quality of the sound itself; the question that they ask of an instrument or their own voice, is what sort of sounds it can make. So they shake a shaker in a number of ways, they rattle a beater around a triangle, and they explore all the possible sounds from a gato drum in a random way. Pitched instruments are treated similarly as producers of different timbres and sonorities: beaters are run up and down the bars, and all parts of the instruments are struck. The world is their oyster; they are embarking on a love affair with the quality of the sound itself. That is a love affair which will last for the rest of their lives; for it is a love of a particular timbre that holds and keeps us in relationship with music all our life. We choose our instruments, whether as composers, performers or listeners, fundamentally on whether we like that particular tone-colour. In the youngest children, this is part of their exploration of the world in general. If you want to find out about an object, you look at it, touch it, lick it, smell it and listen to it. This phrase is therefore called *Sensory*.

The children then seem to organise their sound in some way. This phase depends on their ability to move one part of their body in a controlled manner, the music often being a by-product of the movement. This is often the hand or arm but the Soundscape project shows clearly how other movements can be used with physically disadvantaged children to enable them to pass through this phase. The children often beat out the rhythm of their pulse, explore repeated notes or sequences on pitched instruments, and discover the note that they find easiest to sing with their voices. Because it is linked with physical movement, this phase is called *Manipulative*.

As Rhoda Kellogg (1969) made clear, in her analysis of children's art, children need manipulative control of materials before they explore artistic meaning. In drawing, the child needs to be able to draw a square and a triangle, before drawing the archetypal house. As they enter this phase, children are taken up with the expressive quantities in music. Their improvised songs are delightfully characterful and are part of a total improvised dance or drama. Because of the total concern with personal expressiveness, this phase is called *Personal*. A child sings a song about the sun shining and becomes the sun with a radiantly smiling face; as she sings about a bass drum, she makes herself look fat, and marches slowly about. In instrumental pieces, this concern with expressive character becomes manifest in a delight in crescendi and accelerandi combined, to produce a sense of excitement, and diminuendi and ritardandi to produce a sense of repose. The children invent stories for their pieces. I heard a child in a student teacher's lesson designed to teach the 'concept', high and low in pitch go by steps up a xylophone. 'That goes up' said the student. 'It is somebody climbing the stairs,' said the child. She had entered a different level of musical knowing beyond that being explored by the student teacher.

The advent of the next mode has often been lamented by advocates of the 'creative' school of thought, but it is crucial in our understanding of the enculturation process as it operates in music. After these spontaneous, vivid and novel (to adult eyes) songs, the child wants to sing 'London's burning' or other popular songs; the instrumental pieces become repetitions of ostinati that teachers have heard a thousand times before. The pieces become more organised. There is a definable attempt at phrase structure, clearer rhythms and metre, and a grasp of melodic gesture in song creation; so that they are no longer able to create text and tune together, and prefer to hum a tune separately. All through their lives they have been surrounded by the sounds of their particular culture and now they are endeavouring to join it, by using expressive gestures taken from it. That is why this phase is called the *Vernacular* (a term taken from a paper by Robert Bunting (1977)). Now pupils are more likely to be able to repeat exactly what they have played or sung. They are more able to organise a group piece by combining ostinati. (Before this, organising a group piece meant simply giving out the instruments.)

The beginning of the next mode is often signalled by a desire to surprise. In the Vernacular mode, improvisations often consist of four repetitions of the same ostinato pattern. Now the pupil varies the pattern on the final repetition, and sometimes even says: 'You thought I was going to do the same again, but I didn't, did I?' This use of surprise signals the beginning of the entrance into the world of form. All musical form is based on repetition and contrast. Surprise is musical contrast. The pupils now are taken up with how to create longer musical structures by repeating ideas, creating beginnings and endings and introducing musical surprises. This phase is called *Speculative*. At first these are less well integrated into the structures but as they edge towards the next move they move towards the way in which various idioms have managed contrast. The move to the next mode as with the Vernacular, is marked by a desire to conform to conventions; as it often coincides with adolescence, it often includes the embracing somewhat slavishly of a particular set of beliefs, way of life, friendship group and style of dress. Indeed, the choice of musical idiom may be dependent on the friendship group of the young person concerned. For, in this mode, they choose a musical idiom and immerse themselves fully in it - hence the title *Idiomatic*. Musically, they learn how formal structures within the chosen idiom work - how the balance between repetition and contrast is handled, to give the correct balance for a particular group of people. For any style to become established as an idiom it must have got that balance right for a particular group of people at some point historically and geographically. So, if the person is into the style of the European Classical period s/he will want to learn the conventions of the old harmony teaching regime, which was based on the handing on of the conventions of European high art music between 1750 and 1830 with such progressions as cadential second inversions and the favouring of modulations to keys a fifth away. But if s/he is into a current pop style, different and more repetitive harmonic progressions will be favoured with moves to keys a tone or semitone away, and fades at the end of pieces, rather than clear-cut cadences. The dress worn for performances will differ markedly - evening dress for one, casual gear for the other. The venues will differ; the style of audience involvement will be markedly different. In a religious group this stage will be marked by the adopting of a certain belief system as well. It is important in this mode that the young person does belong to, or is linked up with, a group practising in the style of the chosen group, for most work in this mode requires a group of people to perform it. Within these traditions certain groupings of instruments will have been put together as being typical of that idiom. So, we will not expect to find electric guitars in a classical orchestra or a tuba in a religious group of the folk type. From the infinite variety of tone colours available in the *Sensory* bank, certain have been selected by a particular group of people as 'correct' within that idiom. This includes vocal tone colours; for it is the singing style that sets an operatic idiom most clearly apart from a choir singing plainchant, or North American Indian chanting traditions.

I shall break off from the model here to look more closely at the formation of a musical idiom. This appears to come about, as implied in the description above, by the selection and clustering of elements, taken from the infinite variety of sounds available at the base of the helix. This model of Western music drawn up by Jenny Scharf shows clearly how this might be set to work:

**Figure 3.2**

| | SOUND | | | |
|---|---|---|---|---|
| PITCH | DURATION | VOLUME | | |
| TEMPO | MELODY | DYNAMICS | TIMBRE | SILENCE |
| PACE | HARMONY COUNTER POINT | TEXTURES | | |
| COMPOSITIONAL STYLE | STRUCTURES | | | |

## MUSICAL ELEMENTS

Scharf (1993)

The National Curriculum debate in Britain has identified the problems of defining 'musical concepts' and this model shows how they are gradually created by a coming together of various elements. It begins to make sense of such questions as:

When does sound become pitched?
What is the relationship of harmony to texture?
Is melody a function primarily of pitch or rhythm?
How is a musical phrase created?
Is the concept of what constitutes a melody and its sense of being finished or unfinished, different in cultures that have developed a harmonic tradition, from those that have remained monophonic or developed other textural patterns?
Is accent a function of dynamics or metre?

Such questions bedevil the glossary of musical terms at the back of the National Curriculum document (1992) that sets out to be a guide to musical terminology for the uninitiated generalist teacher. It shows the nature of the minefield; and we have, as yet, few maps for crossing it. I can remember the dilemma of trying to analyse a so-called plagal cadence at the end of an Andrew Lloyd Webber piece, and realising that the very concept of cadential progressions and the common patterns that formed the basis of the traditional harmony syllabus, cannot be transplanted effectively from the European Classical tradition from which these concepts were drawn.

However, if we see the creation of a musical idiom as a clustering of phenomena from the infinite bank of sound that exists at the base of the helix the reasons for certain identified phenomena become clear.

For example, May and Hood (1962) experimented with teaching Javanese songs to a first and a fifth grade class of elementary-age children. The younger group grasped the non-equal-tempered system of the pelog and slendro Javanese tuning systems more quickly than the older ones. This is not surprising in the light of the model. As children get older, they are increasingly learning clusterings. When they are younger, these clusterings are less tightly fixed and formulated. As they are fixed by the process of enculturation (including education), it becomes more difficult to embrace other systems. Palmer makes the point that:

> restraints on musicality of peoples are culture bound rather than intrinsic limitations of the human intellect and musical capacity. (Palmer 1975:142)

Arthur Koestler (1964), in his book *The Act of Creation* describes how it is relatively more difficult to create a sense of surprise as the set pattern of habit becomes more firmly established. The contemporary composer, Paul Patterson told a story of how a choral work of his required three women to make what we would regard as unusual vocal sounds into an open grand piano where they would set the strings vibrating in sympathy, and the problems he had in getting them to do it. He would have had little difficulty at the age of five, when the process of enculturation had not set up a notion of which sounds are appropriate for a classical choral work. In order to do this, the women had to return to the infinite bank of sounds that were open to them their childhood, and make a different selection.

It is, after all, like this with language. Most people learning English as a second language, have to return to that bank, and find again the 'th' sound, that few other cultures appear to have chosen in their sound base. So the model of musical culture is beginning to look like a tree, rooted in an infinite variety of sounds; from these selections are made; these form the larger limbs of a musical culture; from these issue the smaller branches of various idioms within these; from these come the smaller twigs and the individual leaves of individual musical products (see Fig. 3.3).

**Figure 3.3 Cultural Formation**

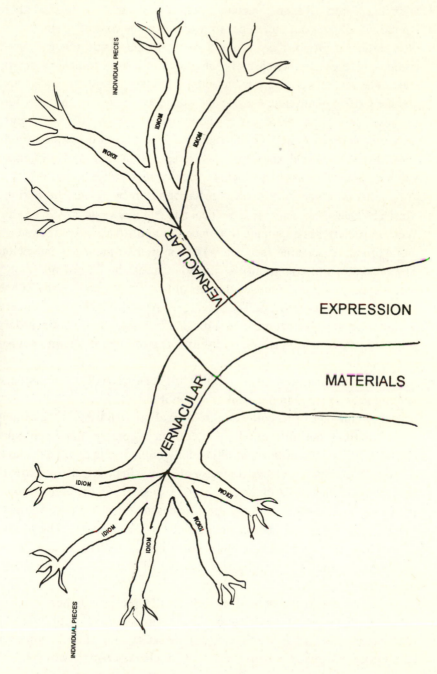

To return to the modes of the helix, the next - the *Symbolic* - sees a widening of musical taste to include works from a variety of musical idioms. An individual personal preference prevails over one controlled by the taste of a particular group; there arises a desire to get inside other styles. In composing, these are increasingly integrated into the composer's personal style. S/he becomes more articulate about expressive intentions and aware of the likely effect of different choices upon different audiences and in different venues. There is an awareness of the expressive power of music and an increasing capacity to be articulate about it. The student becomes articulate about his/her musical knowing, and aware of his/her own systems of valuing - how s/he uses music, what it can express and so on.

This entrance into musical metacognition brings us the notion of Musical Value - how and why individual and cultures value artistic products. Western society has attempted to reduce the multi-faceted value system of more 'primitive' societies (see below) to a system of monetary interchange. The breakdown of community in the 80s caused the loss of many of the sociological functions of music; this has unfortunately reduced the richness of a variety of value systems. The valuing of music for its healing properties is expressed in payments made to a music therapist, while relatively larger sums are paid to those passing on information through music in television advertising.

I was made acutely aware of the conflict between different systems of valuing in an Australian museum of art. In it hung a wooden fish, with an account of the date of its collection from an aboriginal tribe; then came the statement that the aboriginal people from whom it had been taken, considered that this was the controlling deity of the fish in their lake, and that when fish stocks were low, they would pass their hand over the fish sculpture and then put it in the pond; the fish stocks in the pond would be increased. There was no apology for the devastation of the removal of this image, which was not just an image but the divine itself. The Western system of valuing by hanging on museum walls and monetary payment, had no comprehension of the religious valuing of the tribe in which it had originated.

To return to the helical model, finally the established composer reaches the phase of creating her/his own personal style, which is recognisably Mozart's or Hildegard's. Because this often involves the creation of recognisable individual musical characteristics, which become acceptable to a certain group of people, this mode is entitled the *Systematic*. As such, it includes such phenomena as Schoenberg and the twelve-note System and individual jazz performers' treatment of the twelve bar blues.

Although drawn from an observational approach to children composing the model has value as a tool for understanding and relating world cultures. It would seem likely that young children the world over explore the sound-making materials that are to hand in various geographical locations. Two pieces of wood are knocked together all over the world: in the Australian desert they are two pieces of mulga wood; in South America they are two pieces of rosewood. The ways in which they develop control are also similar - pulse patterns, patterns linked with rhythmic movement of some kind, where the sound is a product of the rhythmic movement, and the finding of one's own individual note in singing.

The cruder expressive gestures also seem to be common; so that if music is fast and loud we feel empowered and strengthened, and if it is slow and quiet we feel more at peace. If it is very rhythmic, we think of rhythmic movements such as marching and dancing; if the metre is unclear we think of freer images such as meditating and birds circling. If there is one instrument alone, we imagine one person or animal alone; if more instruments are added we think of a greater number gathering. If it is high in pitch, we think of sky and mountains and so on. I have asked people in various countries to allow a free play of images in their minds while listening to a piece of Chinese folk music, and it is amazing how similar the images created by it in the minds of the listeners are.

All of these modes seem to be common to all cultures; but the point at which they diverge, as the name could suggest, is at the onset of the Vernacular; at this point the children make the gestures of the surrounding culture their own. They have, of course, been receiving these since and even before birth (Woodward 1992). But the deliberate attempt to enter the surrounding culture appears around the age 7. It is not by accident that many 'schemes' of music education start at this age, many instrumental tutoring books and, indeed, the programmes of individual instrumental teachers themselves. Most 'schemes' are designed to initiate children into a culture. Kodaly's aims are very clear, in that he wanted to pass on the Hungarian musical heritage to the children. Here is the root of the dilemma when it is transplanted into other cultures. There is a sense in which each culture requires its own Kodaly, who analyses the structure of his/her own tradition and decides the best way to hand it on. This cannot be done by someone from outside it. From the Vernacular onwards the traditions diverge; nevertheless in the Systematic mode, composers often widen their cultural base and attempt to make new syntheses like David Fanshawe in *African Sanctus* and Hildegard in her use of some melodic systems from the East in her plainchant. (But this is only possible if the culture allows a degree of innovation).

Because it is rooted deeply in the nature of music itself and the way in which human beings 'know' musically, it is possible to use this model as an analytical system for individual pieces of music, and from there to move to comparing cultures by means of it. Of any individual piece a series of questions related to the modes of the spiral can be addressed:

What is making the sound and how is it produced?
What patterns therefore become easier to play and characterise music for that
    instrument?
What does it make you feel? Are any images conjured up in your mind?
What culture does the piece arise from? How is that manifest in the music -
    the choice of scales, metres, length of phrase, melodic shape?
How is contrast achieved in the music? Do any aspects of the music recur?
For what particular purpose was the music written e.g. for religious ritual,
    for ceremonial occasion, to accompany eating and drinking, for
    commercial profit?
How does this manifest itself in the choice of instruments, tone quality for
    the voices, texture of the music, the degree of repetition and contrast
    and the way it is handled?
Are there any influences from other cultures?
What is it that makes this particular piece unique?

From these questions it becomes possible to structure the approach to any individual piece or to any culture.

In the area of Materials, the ethnomusicological classification of instruments into idiophones (with its subdivisions into concussion, striking, stamping or tapping, shaking, scraping, friction and plucking), membranophones or skin drums, chordophones or string instruments (with one or more strings attached at both ends to a sound box and including the violin, harp and zither and lute families), aerophones or wind instruments (Myers 1992) becomes appropriate. Viewed in this way, it is possible to compare the banjo from the United States, the electric guitar which is becoming ubiquitous now, the Russian balalaika, the Japanese samisen. the Indian tambura and the West African kora and examine both the similarities and difference in the methods of sound production and the tune quality produced. These can be examined in detail, in the context both of the geographical situation that produced the raw materials, and also of the surrounding culture in the visual arts, that produce styles of shaping and decoration. Studies in musical instrument technology and construction characterise the Sensory mode when used in the context of Critical Studies in Music.

From this develops the examination of patterns that are easy to play on any particular instrument. Some of these will be common to many instruments within a certain classification, such as chords on the fretted plucked string instruments and patterns produced by certain patterns of footwork on shaken idiophones that are tied to the dancers' legs (like the bells of the Morris dancers and the shakers of some African traditions). This linking of the structure of the  instrument with certain physical movements (as in instrumental studies in European classical traditions) characterises critical exploration in the Manipulative mode.

The exploration of Expression begins with a personal and individual response to a particular piece, and can include imaging of various kinds. There is scope here for cross cultural research. I have already hinted at certain common factors in my own experience above. It is possible to relate songs connected with certain tasks found in various cultures by means of expressive character. Lullabies are a clear example, as are baby bouncing songs, marches and counting songs. It cannot, however, be said with certainty yet that such gestures and feelings transcend all cultural boundaries. There is work to be done here about the relation of music to feeling, looking in more detail at the work of Suzanne Langer (1953). The flow of human feeling is more often than not made up of an admix of a number of emotional strands. Music, more than words, is capable of encompassing a number of differing emotions simultaneously; this is not only shown clearly in operatic ensemble (like the famous quartet from Verdi's *Rigoletto*) but in different instrumental gestures within a complex orchestral texture. And so there is a complexity in the area of feeling in music that cannot be encompassed in any verbal description of the experience. This can lead to different cultures appearing different in their use of what appear to be general musical gestures. It is at this level that an examination of the therapeutic uses of music in various cultures is appropriate. The use of music by certain shamanic traditions for excitement and emotional catharsis is attracting interest in British and North American society.

In this mode also is the examination of simple attempts to represent sounds from the everyday world by means of musical sound gestures. This would include aboriginal imitations of various bird and animal sounds on the didgeridoo and some explorations in programme music in Europe, including such phenomena as Beethoven's imitation of bird song in the 'Pastoral' Symphony. These can be taken beyond this as they are woven into a musical texture; but cultures and individuals demonstrate this strand in their musical 'knowing'.

In the Vernacular mode we find a selection from the infinite variety of tone colours, manipulative patterns and personal expressive gestures clustering together in certain cultures to produce a distinctive vernacular musical style and producing musical stereotypes; so that pentatonic scales on plucked string instruments conjure up China, the short phrases of the call and response tradition with certain vocal tone colours transport us to Africa and the combination of a free metre, the use of church modes and certain singing styles recalls the European plainchant traditions.

This is like the structure of language, in which, from the infinite variety of sounds produced by the human infant, certain are selected by the surrounding culture and put together in blocks called words; these are then clustered into certain syntactical combinations that are meaningful within a particular culture, but less comprehensible outside of it. The child learns the appropriate selection, by having it reinforced by those around him/her, sometimes deliberately, as in the case of carers teaching a child to talk, and sometimes unconsciously, by the presence of a particular pattern of spoken words around the child all the time.

So it is with music. In some cultures music is deliberately passed on by teaching of one kind or another, from the gurus of the Indian subcontinent to the instrumental teachers of Europe and America; but also, in every culture, the child is surrounded by music making; and our 'wall-paper music' culture is no exception. The problem of the growth of a world-wide pop culture (or, indeed, any world-wide culture) is the creation of a 'world musical vernacular' that threatens to iron out the richness of the current diversity of world traditions.

In this mode, it is appropriate to examine the variety of divisions possible within the infinite range of frequencies available that produce ragas, diatonic scales, pentatonic traditions and so on, the ways in which various traditions handle metre, such as the syncopated treatment of the 4/4 metre that characterises traditional jazz, the 3/4 metre that characterises Maori songs (although this was possibly imported from Europe on the ships of Captain Cook) and the length of the units of musical meaning (phrases), varying from the short units of the call and response traditions of Africa to the long sweeps of nineteenth century Romantic melodies in Europe.

With the Speculative mode comes the examination of how contrast can be created in the various parameters of music - the uses of the changes of metre and syncopation, changes in scoring and thickening and thinning of the musical texture, the changes of timbre and scoring, modulation in the tonal traditions, the use of contrasted rhythms simultaneously in contrapuntal compositions, the use of a programme to define musical structure and so on. One aspect of this is the way in which closure is achieved in various traditions - the gradual fade out in some traditions and the clear definition of endings within others. In conventions about the start of piece, there are traditions in which tuning is incorporated in the piece (the origin of the lute prelude) and where the gradual arrival of people shows a gradual build up of resources, as in various Pentecostal worshipping traditions. There is an examination of the way variety is created in various cultures, such as the use of contrasts of tonality in European classical traditions and the continuous melodic variations of the sitar traditions, and the part the audience plays in the defining of musical contrast.

The role of the audience becomes much more significant in the Idiomatic mode. Most idioms are created in response to certain social requirements; so that there are musics for dance, for religious or other rituals, to summon people to war, for ceremonial occasions and so. The purpose of a musical product in a culture may be similar, although the product itself may sound quite different. To create an idiom the selection of elements from the infinite base that we call sound, has greater definition and the clustering is tightened up to produce more clearly defined patterns than in the Vernacular (see Fig. 3.3). So in a Mozart symphony, for example, out of the infinite variety of sound colours available at the level of Materials, certain have been selected and clustered to form a classical orchestra. This makes certain melodic gestures possible and certain impossible, as seen in the unavailability of certain notes on the brass instruments at that time. Certain feelings and moods are selected, partly by the composer and partly by the established pattern of moods involved in the tempi that characterise the symphonic structure. The music is created from an arrangement of notes that we call tonal. The phrases are often four or eight bars long, with clearly defined beginnings and endings, often having a strong-weak rhythmic pattern at the close. Metres in two and three time prevail and there is little use of syncopation. All these make up the vernacular of that time and the place. Contrasts are introduced by means of changes in the tonal centre and changes of tempo and metre from movement to movement. Tunes are sometimes contrasted in expressive character. The purpose would probably have been for the arrival of a visitor to the court. The idiom would be characterised by certain distinctive harmonic progressions and modulatory patterns. These would be central to the make-up the idiom of the piece. So it can be seen how the musical elements are clustered; and yet each individual Mozart symphony, within these parameters, is a unique work of art.

If it were a piece of calypso music for steel pans, a different clustering would have been made, including the selection of a very different tone colour (from the percussive metallic sounds) which make certain manipulative patterns likely (including the distinctive tremolo used to sustain the notes), and a different general mood; diatonic scales would be used but with much less modulation, different rhythmic formulae, a formal structure more dependent on melodic repetition and variation and so on.

The formation of a musical idiom is about the getting of a balance between repetition and contrast that is right for a certain group of people at a certain time in a certain place for a particular purpose. If there is too much repetition an audience calls it boring, and if there is too much contrast, they cannot understand it. This is why an audience that likes pop music finds it difficult to understand classical avant garde music, while the audience familiar with avant garde traditions of Europe finds the pop traditions boring. Similarly, it needs to be right for the purpose. It is often said that the music for a film is good if it is not noticed; the degree of contrast here needs to be less than music designed to be listened to in a concert hall. That is why the playing of pieces in a concert hall out of the context for which they were written, sometimes leads to unjustified pejorative judgements less possible were they heard in context. All music is not intended to be listened to for itself. The concept of great music requiring our full attention is an invention of twentieth century academics within the European classic tradition. Through the centuries people have used music to accompany a variety of tasks, from the most humdrum to the most transcendental. Wall-paper music is not a twentieth century phenomenon. What was the purpose of Mozart's cassations, divertimenti and, indeed, many operas right through the Romantic period in Europe? What is the intention of the creators of wedding and funeral music the world over and the carnival traditions of the Caribbean and South America? Fitness for purpose is as valid a musical intention as the creation of masterpieces for concert hall listening. An examination of traditions in the Idiomatic shows this clearly.

Catherine Ellis (1985) in her book on 'Aboriginal Music', (pp17-18), and drawing on the work of Strehlow (1971) and Berndt and Berndt (1964), identify clearly the purposes for which music is used in aboriginal culture. I have identified them in other world cultures:

1. The history of a people is preserved (such as African narratives of great heroes and also our 'museum-type' concerts, made up of masterpieces from the past).

2. The laws of the people are maintained (such as the socialising function of music in political systems such as Communism).

3. The entire physical and spiritual development of the individual is nurtured (such as the contemporary use of the personal stereo and the cathartic effect of music theatre).

4. The well-being of the group is protected (such as the association of music with religious ritual in many traditions).

5. Supplies of food and water are ensured through musical communication with the spiritual powers (which is retained in such traditions as harvest festival in Western society).

6. Love of the homeland is poured out for all to share (as in patriotic songs).

7. Illnesses are cured. Under this heading she examines in some detail the relationship between developments in Western music therapy and aboriginal understanding of it, concluding:

> What we have learned through observations of both Aboriginal and white response to music in a therapeutic situation is that the same techniques in the music of several traditions (e.g. the unbroken, metronomic pulse of Indian tabla playing, the unbroken pulse of the beating accompaniment in Aboriginal singing and the unbroken pulse of Ravel's 'Bolero', produce similar stabilising responses. From this it seems that there are some physiological responses to certain musical techniques which do not depend at all on association for their effectiveness. (Ellis 1985:30)

8. News is passed from one group to another and here she cites the example of the observation of an Adelaide housewife who lit a cigarette every time the tune from the advertising jingle was played, as an example of how television advertising communicates information.(p25)

I should like to add one more to Ellis's list, one also drawn from the aboriginal traditions, and developed by Bruce Chatwin (1987) in his book *The Songlines.*

9. Geographical and emotional maps are set out. Chatwin writes:

> It was during his time as a school-teacher that Arkady (Chatwin's companion) learned of the labyrinth of invisible pathways which meander all over Australia and are known to Europeans as 'Dreaming-

tracks' or 'Songlines'; to the Aboriginals as the 'Footprints of the Ancestors' or the 'Way of the Law'. (Chatwin 1987:2)

These are the geographical maps of the Aboriginals. You sing your song about the journeys of the Kangaroo Man in the Dreamtime and follow in his steps and you will know where to find water and food. It is likely that the Aeneid and the Odyssey are the last remains of the European songlines. Although we no longer use music as geographical maps, we do use it as a feeling map and Beethoven and the like, through their symphonies, show us a map of feeling that might guide us on our journeys.

As soon as we look into the uses of music in other cultures we come back to our own culture with new eyes and must question the declared ways of aesthetic valuing that characterise education based on the Western European classical traditions in the context of a society that has elements of other value systems present within it.

In the Symbolic mode we look more closely at the process of symbolising in musical form and becoming articulate about it. We look at ways in which we value music, drawing on the explorations of the Idiomatic mode. The role of personal and cultural contexts in the attribution of musical value is examined alongside ways in which value is given and expressed. We look at how, as individuals, we give a personal value to an individual piece or style, and how societies express their own values, including payment for musicians, use and frequency of performances, popularity and prestige given to the musical elite, and the role of the media in this respect in the West, the role of social factors in the determining of musical worth (including gender and race in this), and the way in which music is retained e.g. which pieces were chosen to be notated by the medieval musical scribes of the middle ages, which traditions developed notation systems at all, and at other forms of recording and retaining.

In the Systematic mode, there is an examination of outstanding individual pieces and performers/composers from different cultures. How are musical elites created and how do they function? How do individuals within these transcend them? What is the level of objectivity possible in musical judgements? How is the notion of excellence within a culture constructed?

Figure 3.4 illustrates the use of the helical model as the basis for a Critical Studies course in World Musics:

# Figure 3.4 A Framework for World Musics

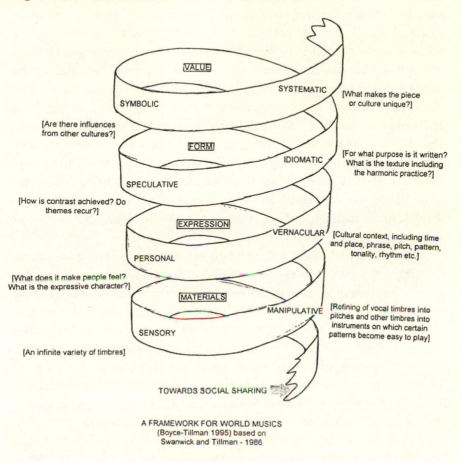

A FRAMEWORK FOR WORLD MUSICS
(Boyce-Tillman 1995) based on
Swanwick and Tillman - 1986

By examining a culture and cultures by the critical use of the helical model, we are able to reappraise our own musical autobiographies. In Britain today, this will almost certainly reveal, not a single culture but a multi-cultural society. In my own past I can locate experiences of a variety of different idioms. My paternal Grandfather brought me up on the popular dance tunes of the Victorian/Edwardian period and my other grandfather on the parlour songs of the same era. In terms of fitness for purpose, these score high; for they were about the building of a community, one at a village level and the other at a family level. They do not rate high on Schenkerian methods of aesthetic musical analysis. Victorian hymn tunes were my first songs and only at seven did I encounter much of the classical tradition of Western Europe through private piano lessons. (My grandfather had one classical record - of Jose Iturbi playing Chopin's Fantasie-Impromptu). At school we sang Cecil Sharp's watered down versions of the English folk tradition. We were taken to hear a concert performance of Smetana's opera *The Bartered Bride*, which I did not understand. It was a pathway that was rooted primarily in the popular traditions of Britain, and I had to learn the classical tradition, a great deal of it from books, because it had not been the culture with which I had been surrounded as a child. I had not been saturated in it in the way that characterised the experience of those of my male contemporaries at Oxford who had been cathedral choristers. It took a long time for me to absorb it as my musical vernacular. I was taught to devalue my own tradition, in pursuance of a high art tradition, that was no more mine, than the music of the Caribbean that I first encountered in Notting Hill in the 60's. Value was expressed in the so-called objective standards of the absolute music tradition, and not in the more contextual terms that this model makes possible.

So the model offers a chart to guide journeyings into more distant cultures, one's own musical background and experience and the current multicultural musical scene in the West. It provides a way of making sense of whatever tradition is encountered. It combines more absolutist ways of viewing music with more contextual ways; and so provides a broader base than the methods developed within the context of any high art tradition.

Any system has cultural roots. But the use of this model for a field in World Musics in the context of a modular degree and its use to help teachers and students in teacher training programmes in the use of music from a variety of traditions in the classroom has proved very successful.

In terms of analytical work it offers the possibility of comparing music from a variety of cultures on a level playing field. Our students in the World Musics field have to use it to compare two pieces for their first assignment.

In terms of assessment the helical model offers the possibility of comparison of performances and compositions in a variety of styles. The following criteria based on the model that we have been using for the past three years enables us to compare a bass guitar performance with one on an African drum; and another on a violin.

# Figure 3.5 Grade Linked Criteria For Performance Assessment

*Third*

There is a degree of technical competence with little or no expressive characterisation. There is no perceivable grasp of structural relationships in either performance or associated notes.

*Lower Second*

The technical grasp is sufficient to make a certain degree of expressive character possible. There is clearly identifiable mood. The general principles of the conventions of the style are grasped and identifiable e.g. clearly defined phrases, if appropriate. There is in associated notes or performance evidence of a grasp of structural features.

*Upper Second*

The technical grasp is secure. Expressive and structural elements are organised coherently within a style appropriate to the idiom of the piece. Contrasts are well managed and there is evidence in associated notes of a grasp of both the form of the piece and the general principles of that particular idiom.

*First*

Technical mastery serves musical communication. The listener's attention is focused on formal relationships and expressive character which are fused together in an impressive, coherent and original musical statement made with commitment.

*Note:*

Within the classes the fine tuning is made by interrelating intention and achievement which can be done by means of the associated notes. For example, a performance that has a clear intention towards expressive character but with poor tone production or tuning (which is in the area of technical grasp) would be placed in the lower part of the lower second class.

Composing assignments use the following criteria. The students develop their own personal style, as well as being taught a variety of techniques from differing traditions e.g. Bach chorales and Nigerian highlife:

## Figure 3.6 Criteria for Assessment of Composition

1.  How far the writing is suitable for the instrument/s chosen (not how easy or how difficult is it, but how much does it exploit the instruments' potential?).

2.  How far the composer has succeeded in creating the expressive character intended.

3.  How far the musical form hangs together.

4.  How far the style is coherent (whether the composer has worked within the context of a particular historical or geographical style)

5.  How far there is evidence of the composer's own individuality.

6.  How far the composer is able to reflect on and be articulate about own processes of composition.

In terms of classroom practice within schools, it gives us various ways of unpacking a culture. Students can be guided in their entrance into another culture. Given a live performance or recording from another culture, the listening can be focused by the following questions, which can be linked by repeated playings of the piece:

1.  What is the instrument made of? How is the sound made on the instrument or with the voice? How is the sound changed?

2.  How does the music make you feel? What images are conjured up in your mind? What title would you give the music? Which part of the world do you think it comes from? How do you know this (e.g. through the instruments used, the scales chosen, the rhythmic patterns etc.)?

3.  How is contrast achieved in the piece? Do certain parts of the music recur? Can you perceive any pattern in this? Why do you think this piece was composed/performed? Has this affected the musical structure in any way?

4.     Did the composer have a specific audience in mind for the piece? Have
       the audience a role in the piece at all (e.g. clapping, joining in the
       singing, shouting out or screaming)? How will the piece affect the
       audience - both the one for which it was written and other ones? How
       are these social/psychological effects achieved in the music? Why will
       that audience come to hear the piece? How do they express their valuing
       of it and their commitment to it? Would you regard this as an
       outstanding piece of music? How have you made that judgement? How
       far is it coloured by your own cultural experience? How is it viewed by
       the culture from which it comes? By other cultures? (It is interesting to
       discuss works that are regarded as the 'classics' of their culture, like the
       Beatles' *Sergeant Pepper*, in this way.)

Such questions focus audience listening activities and provide a route into
otherwise strange and exotic sounds, by viewing a culture by means of its
different levels of meaning. Once unpacked in this way, bridges can be
formed to the culture of the students and the possibility of links of various
kinds is opened up.

It helps us generate a curriculum with appropriate activities for various
ages and stages of development. With the youngest children it is appropriate
to get together simpler instruments from various cultures, and allow pupils
to explore them freely and develop certain patterns on them (the Materials of
sound). In the area of Expression, older children can look at how music
makes us feel through imaging, writing, moving, writing poetry and
combined arts work of various kinds. Pieces from various cultures can be
compared and responded to (the Personal mode). Then we can look at the
scales and metre and phrase lengths (which is well taught through dance)
that characterise certain cultures (the Vernacular). As the students' interest
shifts to musical Form, older children can explore how surprise can be
introduced, looking at the various parameters of sound (the Speculative
mode). Certain idioms then are chosen and examined in some detail
(preferably with the help of experts from within them (the Idiomatic mode).
Students can then be helped to widen their personal taste and be articulate
and aware of their own value systems and those of the surrounding culture
and then of other cultures. Finally through awareness each person can
achieve their own musical potential.

It is also a tool for examining the systems of thought and values of a
particular society. Gooch, in his book *Total Man: Towards an Evolutionary
Theory of Personality* (1972) postulates that within each person there lies a
polarity and at any given time we will favour one of the two sides. This will

affect the form of communication that we find most satisfying. He also draws attention to this polarity within literature, legend. religion and language. He defines two systems of thought and labels them A and B. These paired words give some indication of the distinctions between them:

| SYSTEM A | SYSTEM B |
|---|---|
| doing | being |
| objective | subjective |
| impersonal | personal |
| thought | emotion |
| thinking | feeling |
| logic | magic |
| detachment | involvement |
| discrete | associative |
| proof | belief |
| scientific knowledge | non-causal knowledge |

He claims that these lie within human beings and that we have a choice which we use and societies decide which they prefer. The Western world has clearly chosen System A; other societies favour System B. Clearly the balance lies somewhere between them; so Gooch sets up a third, reconciling the polarities:

| System A | System B | System C |
|---|---|---|
| male | female | whole |
| doing | being | alive |
| thinking | feeling | reasoning |
| reductionist | associative | creative |

There are echoes and parallels here to the helical model with its swings from left and right in which the left pole represents more individual experimental work, whereas the right represents a greater desire for social sharing. It was clear from the children studied, that at certain times children wanted to experiment and at others they wanted to learn and be encultured into the patterns of their culture. There was also some indication that personality factors influenced this as well, individuals preferring one or other polarity. It is clear too that the established composer needs to keep a balance between the two poles. Too great a swing to the more experimental and innovative lefthand side will lead him/her to the position of the misunderstood genius starving in a garret, whereas too great a lean to the right hand pole will produce a 'hack' composer producing the music that the public wants, but failing to express his/her own individuality.

Towards the back of her book, Catherine Ellis (1985) attempts to synthesise Gooch's thinking with that of Gregory Bateson (1972) in his book *Steps to an Ecology of Mind*. In this he defines 'learning as a process which denotes change', and suggests that it is often used incorrectly to describe situations of habituation which imply no change or minimal change of response. This he classifies as 'zero learning'. He postulates three levels of learning beyond zero learning:

Learning I:  The extinction of habituation.

Learning II:  This covers most of what we consider learning. It involves changes in sets of alternatives from which choice is made, a process of leaning to learn.

Learning III:  This he regards as difficult and rare for it is concerned with spiritual issues and requires a profound reorganisation of character.

From these and other writings by Assagioli (1965), Le Shan (1975) and Reimer (1970), Ellis draws up the following diagram (Fig. 3.7).

**Figure 3.7**

| Theoretical outlines of levels of Learning I, II and III | |
|---|---|
| SPIRITUAL VISIONARY (level III) | Perceiving Alternate Realities (Le Shan) which go beyond formal, self-centred learning and reach toward the higher self (Assagioli) and universals. This may be experienced through the act of aesthetic creation (Reimer) |
| COGNITIVE TECHNICAL FORMAL (level II) | Formal training; learning to learn (Bateson); centred on the conscious self (Assagioli) |
| INFORMAL (Level I) | Informal learning; extinction of habituation (Bateson) |

Catherine Ellis (1985 : 192)

There are clear echoes of the helix here, particularly if we extend it further by using the writings and experience of outstanding musicians within a culture. There often appears in their writing, and it often becomes more pronounced as they get older, an increasing sense of the numinous, of music as having meaning of a cosmic or transcendent kind.

Richard Wagner (1813-83) is reported in a conversation with Humperdinck of 1880 towards the end of his life to have said:

> I am convinced that there are universal currents of Divine Thought vibrating in the air everywhere and that anyone who can feel those vibrations is inspired, provided he is conscious of the process....I believe, first of all that it is this universal vibrating energy that binds the soul of man to the Almighty Central Power from which emanates the life principle to which we all owe our existence. This energy links us to the Supreme Force of the universe of which we are all a part... in that trance-like condition, which is the pre-requisite of all true creative effort, I feel that I am one with this vibrating Force, that it is omniscient, and that I can draw upon it to an extent that is limited only by my own capacity to do so. Why did Beethoven appropriate it to a far greater degree than Dittersdorf, to name only one of the many minor composers of that period? Because Beethoven was much more aware of his oneness with Divinity than was Dittersdorf. (quoted in Abell 1954:137-9)

And here Ravi Shankar writes of what happens in a good performance:

> When, with control and concentration, I have cut myself off from the outside world, I step on to the threshold of the raga with feelings of humility, reverence and awe. To me, a raga is like a living person, and to establish that intimate oneness between music and musician, one must proceed slowly. And when that oneness is achieved, it is the most ecstatic and exhilarating moment, like the supreme heights of the act of love or worship. In these miraculous moments, when I am so much aware of the great powers surging within me and all around me, sympathetic and sensitive listeners are feeling the same vibrations. It is a strange mixture of all the intense emotions - pathos, joy, peace, spirituality, eroticism, all flowing together. It is like feeling

God....the miracle of the music is in the beautiful rapport that
occurs when a deeply spiritual performer performs for a receptive
group of listeners. (Shankar 1969:57ff)

Similar themes were found by Catherine Ellis (1985) amongst the musical
elders of the Aboriginals. She also draws attention to other ventures like
Rabindranath Tagore's university in Calcutta, entitled 'Santiniketan' (Abode
of Peace).

I am therefore extending the helical model to include a further turn that
I have labelled 'Transcendence'. The left hand pole I have entitled Spiritual
for it represents an acute awareness of the Divine, the Other, often a
searching through systems that link music with this Ultimate Reality. The
right hand pole I have entitled Mystical; it represents a new integration of
these elements into a personal belief system that influences all the person's
musical activity (see Figure 3.8).

Before proceeding further it is important to remember how the helical
model was intended to be viewed. It was not a stage-by-stage model but was
a three dimensional helix which lies coiled up in each person. The swings
indicate the main thrust of interest of a musician at any given time and the
experienced musician freely revisits the lower levels in all musical activity.
Technical control (the Materials level) is necessary for any performing
activity; a composer has always to bear in mind the capabilities of the
group/voices/instruments for which she/he is writing. And similarly there
will be indications of the upper levels, even in the work of the youngest
children. On the wall of my study, I have a picture of two children in a
nursery exploring a drum. The camera has caught the look of wonder in their
eyes at the magic of its sound. I saw that same wonder in the eyes of
Messiaen when, towards the end of his life, he talked of his choice of the
gongs that were part of one of his symphonies. The difference is that
Messiaen was able to be articulate about his experience and had systemised
his musical belief system over the course of his lifetime as a composer.

This expanded model can now be compared with the one in which
Catherine Ellis (1985) synthesises the work of Gooch (1972) and Bateson
(1972) and her own thinking. It can be seen in Fig. 3.9 on page 83.

## Figure 3.8 Musical Development

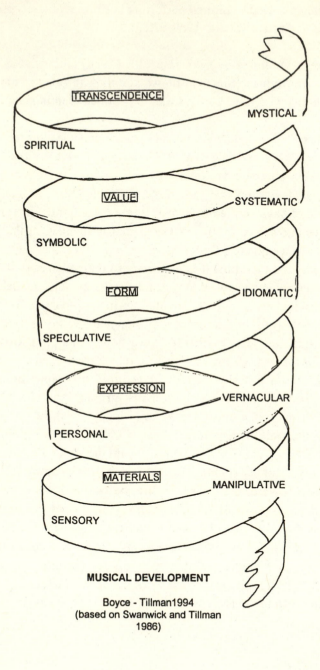

TRANSCENDENCE

MYSTICAL

SPIRITUAL

VALUE

SYSTEMATIC

SYMBOLIC

FORM

IDIOMATIC

SPECULATIVE

EXPRESSION

VERNACULAR

PERSONAL

MATERIALS

MANIPULATIVE

SENSORY

**MUSICAL DEVELOPMENT**

Boyce - Tillman1994
(based on Swanwick and Tillman
1986)

**Figure 3.9**

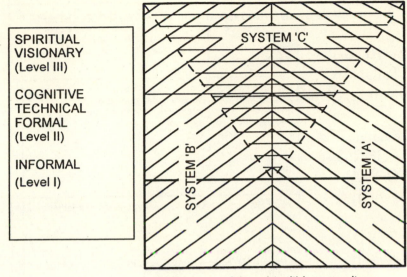

SPIRITUAL
VISIONARY
(Level III)

COGNITIVE
TECHNICAL
FORMAL
(Level II)

INFORMAL
(Level I)

Systems of thought within any culture

Catherine Ellis 1985:194

Here the relationship to the helix is clearer, with the swings from left to right and also echoes in level one of the Materials level; in level 2 of the Vernacular but especially the level of Form. Level 3 then represents something similar to the levels of Value and Transcendence.

She goes on to develop further in another interesting model, in which she represents side by side the process of 'ethnocentric' and 'acculturated' education.

**Figure 3.10**

| Three levels of Learning occurring in two distinct contexts | | |
|---|---|---|
| SPIRITUAL VISIONARY (level III) | Heights of spiritual experience | Maintaining supreme levels of quality experience in more than one culture |
| COGNITIVE TECHNICAL FORMAL (level II) | Formal education which enables questioning ('How?'"Why?') and application of techniques to answer the questions | Considering the experiences gained in other cultures and accepting, integrating, discarding and re-experiencing |
| INFORMAL (Level I) | Informal and unreflective learning about one's own culture | Unreflective experience of another culture |
| | ETHNOCENTRIC (Stage I) | ACCULTURATED (Stage II) |

Catherine Ellis (1985 : 196)

This is helpful in distinguishing the strands of musical education which have often become confused. It is possible that, as has happened for a long time in Britain, the task of ethnocentric education is taken on by the teachers of individual instrumental and vocal traditions, while the task of the musical classroom and the university lecture room, which contains a variety of experiences and backgrounds, is that of the 'acculturated' strand.

Her final diagram goes further by postulating a third stage that she calls 'Transcendent'. (She uses this somewhat differently from the way I have used it in the helix: see Fig. 3.11)

This is a visionary model that few educational institutions have aspired to. As such it remains to be proven and worked out in practice. It also highlights the difficulties implicit in the making of models for musical knowing. Music is such a multidimensional art form that it is impossible to represent its totality even in a three dimensional model. People have taken the helical model and tried adding all sorts of shapes to it (Woodward 1989).

**Figure 3.11**

| Progressions of learning within and across cultures | | | |
|---|---|---|---|
| **SPIRITUAL VISIONARY LEARNING (Level III)** | Heights of experience and communication of these within one culture through aesthetic or religious processes | Heights of experience in aesthetic or religious forms which derive from sources in different cultures | Being universal |
| **COGNITIVE FORMAL LEARNING (Level II)** | Intellectual activity whithin and about one's own culture, and one's own position in it, as well as intellectual activity based in one's own culture, but *about* another culture (e.g., anthropological study) | Intellectualizing and experiencing across cultures | Researching and discovering and experiencing universals. Intellectualizing and feeling about the nature of culture as a prop for daily behaviour |
| **UNREFLEC-TIVE, INFORMAL LEARNING (Level I)** | Unreflective informal learning about one's own culture | Experimental learning about another culture or sharing experience of own with another | Awareness of unimportance of cultural difference (We are all children of the universe) |
| | ETHNOCENTRIC (Stage I) | ACCULTURATIVE (Stage II) | TRANSCENDENT (Stage III) |

Catherine Ellis (1985:198)

There is, indeed, a danger in models of any kind - that they limit and restrict experimentation and encourage a blinkered approach that supports a rigid view of reality that the theologian Mary Daly (1973) calls 'methodolatry'. It has the same dangers as 'idolatry', that no reality can be fully contained in a single form

The helix is a wider model than we have had before. But there is a danger in the bottom to top layout. This might be seen to deny the fact that in a piece of music of the highest quality within a culture all the levels are handled equally well and resonate with one another. The materials of sound are well handled, with attention paid to the capabilities of the chosen instruments and voices, the expressive character enables people to form an emotional bond with the music and enable the feeling structure to resonate within themselves; the formal structure allows for the right amount of repetition and contrast to satisfy the particular audience; the work is set within a commonly accepted value system.

The danger is that one of these levels will be valued above the others. In the Western classical tradition form has tended to be regarded as more significant than expressive character. People familiar with this model have attempted to turn it on its side so that Materials, Expression, Form and Value run upwards in strands of equality and the importance of social sharing is marked on a vertical axis, reflecting the fact that at certain stages in our development we need to be innovative and at others more concerned with belonging. It could look something like this:

## Figure 3.12 The Formation of a Vernacular

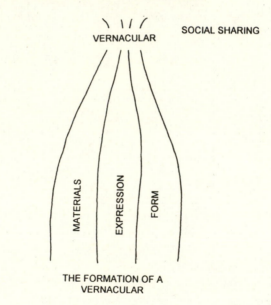

THE FORMATION OF A
VERNACULAR

This makes it somewhat similar to one set out by Eleanor Stubley (1994) identifying the narrowing down process of enculturation. Earlier in the chapter (Fig. 3.3) I suggested another form for this. This needs to be extended further to include the potential phenomenon of Transcendence. This is approached through a particular culture; by experience within a tradition and through the pursuit of novelty, uniqueness, individuality we can again enter the infinite world that was our heritage as children. This is, of course, with the eyes and experience of the adult, and an ability to reflect and be articulate (to some degree) about the experience. In this we can share in depth with people from other musical cultures, as shown in Figure 3.13.

**Figure 3.13 Enculturation and Transcendence**

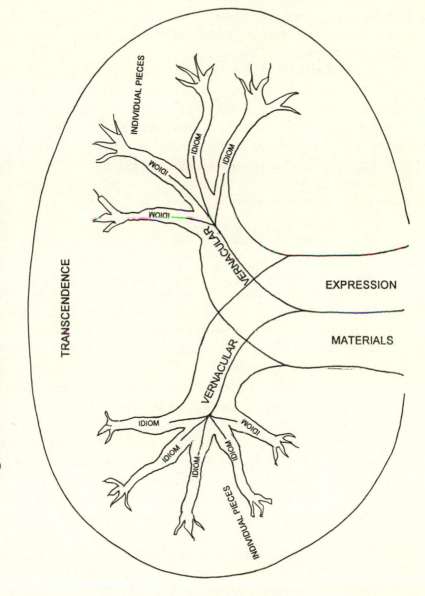

Such discussion and model-making serves to illustrate the complexity of the subject in hand and the transitional nature of thinking about it at this time.

It is the helical form (Fig. 3.4) that has generated most of the work in this paper. I have examined here its strengths and weaknesses and the echoes it contains of people working within other cultures. It attempts to merge a variety of ideas from musicology and ethnomusicology. It has already proved useful as the foundation for a field of study in World Musics at undergraduate level, in curriculum planning in schools at every level, in bringing together a variety of schools of thought, as a useful tool in cross-cultural assessment. It represents an attempt to meet some of the challenges set out in the literature on multimusicality in education at every level. Research would need to be done with people who had passed through a system based on such a model which attempts to address the fundamental issues as set out by Schwadron:

> Put simply, we are not agreed on matters of values or directions of study. In the US there is still some confusion between liberal outcomes and socio-ethnic goals which identify more readily with such movements as affirmative action, equality of opportunity, and other concerns for minority rights. The idealistic hope is that by searching out value systems in music cultures throughout the world, music education will assume an inclusively valuable humanistic role - one that is alert to cultural differences and commonalties while nurturing aesthetic self-realisation from a rich field of musical potential. (Schwadron 1984:94)

The 1970s in Britain and the States was the heyday of examining such notions. The nationalisation of the British educational system has not aided the exploration of models that might guide this process. Dolce (1973) outlined several characteristics of multicultural education that would still seem to have validity and are relatively unexplored musically:

1.    Multiculturalism is a reflection of a value system which emphasises the acceptance of behaviour differences deriving from differing cultural systems and an active support of the right of such differences to exist....Advocates often wrongly assume that all share basic cultural values.

2.  The concept of multiculturalism transcends matters of race. A one-to-one correlation between race and culture is simply not supported by the evidence.

3.  Multiculturalism is not simply a new methodology which can be grafted onto an educational program. The concept of multiculturalism in education is based upon a different view of society than that which appears to exist.....a single course on multicultural education in such a setting is an attempt to capture the appearance without the substance.

4.  A multicultural state of affairs is not one which is devoid of tensions. All differing cultures are not complementary. The interaction of such cultures will tend to create new tensions and possibly increase existing tensions.

5.  Based upon mutual respect among different cultures, multiculturalism is not a euphemism for disadvantaged. Cultures are neither inherently superior nor inferior to each other.
    (pp282-3)

I have hovered in my thinking uneasily between the terms multicultural and intercultural. People have defined both terms in many different ways. In the end, I guess, it is a question of perspective, like whether you look at music as sounds set in silence or silence broken up by sounds. As I feel that it is possible for transcultural relationships to be set up, I shall settle for the relationships implied in the term interculturalism, with all the weaknesses that some feel are implied by it in terms of imperialism and takeovers. In the end it is about differing value systems and the regarding of difference as a richness rather than a drawback, so that tensions are seen as potentially fruitful, as well as potentially damaging. Within music we have the potential for wholeness by valuing divergent systems. Rabindranath Tagore writes of his own educational experience:

> In the usual course I was sent to school, but possibly my suffering was unusual, greater than that of most other children. The non-civilised in me was sensitive: it had a great thirst for colour, for music, for the movement of life. Our city-built education had no need of that living fact. It had its luggage-van waiting for branded bales of marketable result. (Tagore and Elmhirst, 1961:53)

There is a saying 'To know all, is to forgive all'. Musical knowing which includes both experience and understanding can enable existing tension to be lived with. 'If your neighbours appear to be dancing rather strangely, they may be dancing to different drums' (adapted from Thoreau). In the end we all dance to our drums tuned to our own rhythms and the rhythms of the culture that we find ourselves in at any given time. I hope that the model set out here may guide the steps of those who are prepared to try new steps and new formations based on older traditions. Only time and practice will tell.

## Bibliography

Abell, Arthur M.(1954) *Talks With The Great Composers*. New York. Philosophical Library

Assagioli, Roberto (1965) *Psychosynthesis: A Manual of Principles and Techniques*. Harmondsworth. Penguin

Bateson, Gregory (1972) *Steps to an Ecology of Mind*. New York. Ballantine

Berndt, R.M. and C.H. (1954) *The World of the First Australians*. Sydney. Ure Smith

Bunting, R. (1977) *The Common Language of Music, Music in the Secondary School Curriculum*. Working Paper 6, Schools Council, York University

Butcher, V. (1970) *Development of materials for a one-year course in African music for the general undergraduate student*. (Research project No. 6 -1179, Final Report) Washington: U.S. Department of Health, Education and Welfare. Bureau of Research

Chatwin, Bruce (1987) *The Songlines*. London. Picador

Cook, Nicholas (1987) *A Guide to Musical Analysis*. London. Dent.

Daly, Mary (1973) *Beyond God the Father*. Beacon Press. Boston.

Department and Education and Science (1992) *Draft Order for Music*. 27th January
Department of Education and Science (1992) *Music in the National Curriculum*. (England) London. HMSO

Dolce, C.J. (1973) Multi-cultural Education - some issues, *Journal of Teacher Education*. 24, pp282-285

Elliott, D.J. (1989). Key Concepts in multicultural music education, in *International Journal of Music Education*. 13, pp11-13

Ellis, Catherine J. (1985) *Aboriginal Music Education for Living*. Queensland. University of Queensland Press

Gartin, B.A.B. (1981) *Intercultural Perspectives in Music Appreciation*: *A Survey of five college textbooks*. Unpublished doctoral dissertation. University of Massachusetts. Amherst

Gooch, Stan (1972) *Total Man: Notes Towards an Evolutionary Theory of Personality*. London. Allen Lane, Penguin Press

Jordan, Joyce (1992) Multicultural Music Education in a Pluralist Society, in Colwell, Richard (ed.,) (1992) *Handbook of Research on Music Teaching and Learning*. New York. Music Educators National Conference, pp735-748

Kellogg, R. (1969) *AnalyzingChildren's Art*. California. Mayfield Publishing Co

Koestler, Arthur (1964) *The Act of Creation*. London. Hutchinson

Langer, Suzanne (1953) *Feeling and Form*. New York. Charles Scribners Sons

Le Shan, Lawrence (1975) *The Medium, The Mystic and The Physicist*: *Toward a General Theory of the Paranormal*. New York. Ballantine

Levine, T. and Standifer, J. (1961) *From Jumpstreet: Television and the Humanities*. A Workshop on multi-cultural Education in secondary schools. Washington. WETA-TV. (ERIC document Reproduction Service No. ED 220 388)

May, E. and Hood, W. (1962 April-May) Javanese Music for American Children, *Music Educators' Journal*. 48, pp38-41

Moore, M.C. (1977) *Multicultural Music Education: An analysis of Afro-American and native American folk songs in selected elementary school textsbooks of the periods 1928-1955 and 1955-1975*. Unpublished doctoral dissertation, University of Michigan. Ann Arbor

Mumford, J.E. (1984), *The effect on the attitudes of music education majors of direct experience with Afro-American popular music ensembles - A Case Study*. Unpublished doctoral dissertation, Indiana University. Bloomington

Myers, Helen (1992) *Ethnomusicology: An Introduction*. London. Macmillan

National Curriculum Council, (1992) *Consultation Report: Music in the National Curriculum*. York. N.C.C.

Palmer, A.J. (1975) *World Musics in Education: A critical analysis*. Unpublished doctoral dissertation, University of California. Los Angeles

Pratte, R. (1979) *Pluralism in education: Conflict, clarity and commitment*. Springfield. Charles C. Thomas

Reimer, Bennett (1970) *A Philosophy of Music Education*. New Jersey. Prentice-Hall

Rodriguez, F. and Sherman, A. (1983) *Cultural Pluralism and the Arts. A Multicultural Perspective for Teacher Trainers in Art and Music*. Lawrence: Kansas University School of Education (ERIC Document Reproduction Service No. ED 832795)

Scharf, Jenny (1993) *Progression in Music*.Unpublished fellowship paper. The University of Ulster.

Schmid, W.R. (1971) *Introduction to tribal, oriental and folk music: A rationale for undergraduate music education curricula*. Unpublished doctoral dissertation. University of Rochester. Eastman School of Music, Rochester

Schwadron, A.A. (1984) *World Musics in Education*. International Society for Music Education. 11, pp92-8

Shankar, Ravi (1969) *My Music, My Life*. London. Jonathan Cape

Steinecker, J.L. (1976) *John Dewey's empirical pluralism: Implications for musical education*. Unpublished doctoral dissertation, Temple University. Philadelphia

Stephens R.Y. (1984) *The effects of a course of study on Afro-American popular music in the undergraduate curriculum*. Unpublished doctoral dissertation, Indiana University. Bloomington

Strehlow, T.G.H. (1971) *Songs of Central Australia*. Sydney. Angus and Robertson

Stubley, Eleanor (1994) Play and the Field of Musical Performance: Implications for Practice in Music Education, Paper read at the *Philosophy of Music Education International Symposium*. Toronto. June

Swanwick, Keith (1983) *The Arts in Education: Dreaming or Wide awake?* Special Professorial Lecture, London University Institute of Education

Swanwick, K. and Tillman, J.B. (1986) The Sequence of Musical Development: A Study of Children's Composition, *British Journal of Music Education 3*. (3) November, pp305-39

Tagore, Rabindranath and Elmhirst, L.K. (1961) *Rabindranath Tagore. Pioneer in Education: Essays and Exchanges between Rabindranath Tagore and L.K. Elmhirst*. London. John Murray

Tillman J.B. (1987) *Towards a model for children's development in music: A Study of children's compositions*. Unpublished doctoral dissertation, University of London Institute of Education

Walker, R.(1992), in Commentary on Swanwick. K., Open Peer Commentary: Musical Knowledge: the Saga of Music in the National Curriculum, in *Psychology of Music* Vol. 20, No.2, pp 162 -179

Woodward, Elisabeth D.(1987) *Children's Compositions*. Unpublished MA Dissertation, Reading University

Woodward, S. (1992) *The transmission of music into the human uterus and the response of music to the human fetus and neonate.* Unpublished Doctoral dissertation, Johannesburg

## Practical Applications

*Mwanzo wa ngoma ni 'lele'*
The beginning of a musical celebration is one person singing 'lala'
(Swahili proverb)

For most of us, after we have read about World Musics, studied them, considered how we might integrate them into our curriculum, we have to take a step forward and do something; create an activity. Each of us may think of ourselves being the 'one person singing "lala" '. The chapters in this part look at what various people and schools have done, and assesses what has been most successful and why. There are suggestions for work from Key Stage One through to Key Stage Four, the implication being that children can usefully learn from and through World Musics at all stages of their school careers.

Hopefully, we will discover that the 'ngoma' will be worth launching into our first 'lala' for.

# 4 World Musics at Key Stage One

*Judith Deeble*

> The knowledge of the world is only to be acquired in the world,
> and not in the closet. (Lord Chesterfield)

Everything we do with Key Stage One children is of immense value. They
are keen and interested in the world around them. They are unprejudiced in
their thinking and willing to hear new sounds. At Key Stage One we are
encouraging concepts and skills which will become the habits of the future,
and all following key stages will build on the work done at this key stage.

## Why World Musics?

The music curriculum orders have stressed that children should be given
opportunities to be aware of the music of other times and lands. We are
asking them to experience musics other than those of their home cultures (the
sounds with which they were brought up). It is the intention of this chapter
to show how an introduction to World Musics can contribute to the musical
development of children at infant level.

## What are Key Stage One children learning?

Children come into school with varied preschool musical experiences. They
may have sung nursery songs with their relatives and friends. These are
more likely to be Western than non-Western, but depend on the background
of each family. They will probably have heard music on the radio and
television. There may have been music attached to films or videos. They
may have experienced music in places of worship. They may have attended
ceremonies such as a wedding or a funeral and heard the related music.
Children may be learning to play an instrument or respond to music through
dancing. The range of possibilities is wide and encouraging. However, in
practice, most children will only have shared a few of these forms of music
and some will come into school having heard or experienced none of these.
    Children come into school with great aural and imitative skills. They
have mastered the basics of one language and may be equally proficient in a
second. The range of musical skills these children possess is also wide.
Some may be used to singing by themselves or with an adult. Some will

sing regularly. Some will only have sung along with recorded music. Some will have had encouragement to respond to music by movement in songs, gymnastics and dancing. Some will have listened actively to music, encouraged to listen for specific melodies or elements within the music. Some will have had their music making shared by their principal carers and we know how much this adult interest can encourage children. Some will have been told to 'Be quiet!' Again each child will have a different set of experiences.

This means that the role of the Key Stage One teacher at year R and beyond is to consolidate previous experience and to open up the whole of the sound world to children. A Key Stage One curriculum may be said to stimulate the children and develop their imagination. By improving their coordination, skills are developed and improved, which enable children to work cooperatively. Conversation stimulated during this cooperation and successful activities lead to a sense of satisfaction in work and in personal worth. Music provides strong opportunities to further these aims.

According to the Swanwick and Tillman model of musical development, (1986) children develop musically by increasing their experience of materials and using them in conjunction with increasing intellectual skills. So they are constantly revisiting areas of musical activity in their music making, throughout their music making and a structured curriculum gives them suitable and relevant experiences. Their increase in skills and understanding allows them to function at an increasingly higher level up the spiral of music development. Most Key Stage One children are functioning at the sensory and manipulative levels of musical development. They are discovering the vast assortment of available sounds, which music at school can give them. For many this is their first opportunity to make noise legitimately and they need to explore what they are able and permitted to do. Once they have control over sounds they are able to produce a desired sound by a particular way of playing the instrument. Then they are in a position to produce, for instance, a pattern of quiet and loud sounds intentionally. It may be necessary to revisit one area of experience in more depth for one child than another. World Musics can provide an opportunity to look again at concepts and skills with completely new and exciting material.

It is the role of the teacher to extend the children's experience and to open up the whole range of sounds available to the child. It is one of the aims of this chapter to show how this may be done, but first:

# What do we see in school?

At the moment the position of world musics in school is tenuous. The amount varies according to the interest and experience of the teachers concerned. Music may be introduced in several ways:

## Assembly

Music is often played in the hall as the children go in to assembly. The choice may be left to an individual teacher or it may follow a more structured plan, developed by the consultant or agreed by the whole staff. If there is an interest in non-Western sounds this piece of music may be a piece from a different culture. Perhaps it will be introduced by name and some details of the players and the composer will be given. It may be set into a cultural context. Generally the children are told to sit and listen. Very often there is one class moving in or out at the same time. Such movement is rather distracting and removes concentration from listening to the new music.

## Listening

Sometimes a piece of world music is chosen as a listening exercise in the classroom. There is a range of strategies for asking the child to use her/his ears. The child is talked through the music and then listens to the whole piece. Extracts are listened to and these are then set into context within the whole piece of music. Sometimes the children write a story or paint a picture whilst the music is going on.

## The topic approach

By far the greatest use of music from other cultures comes during cross-curricular topic work. The teacher may select a piece of music by its title to fit in with a topic on animals. Alternatively a topic such as 'India' is supported by the playing of music from India. Songs maybe sung and sometimes a parent or visitor is available to teach the works in the home language. The music for assembly or to accompany or stimulate movement is associated with the country. Sometimes it may be a foreign pastiche such as most of us would recognise in the Spanish music of Bizet's *Carmen*.

However, all these approaches tackle the music of the rest of the world as something rather exotic and strange and therefore in need of special attention. This may be true for the teacher, but for children so much of the world is new and exciting, and a piece of music from around the world is no more different than a piece of mediaeval dance music or an electronic composition of Stockhausen, for example. My own approach has been to use examples of music from many musical cultures in whatever musical task I am doing with the children.

One of the problems with the introduction of world musics to the infant classroom has been the perception that you must be an expert to deliver it well. It is felt that without a thorough grounding in the musical constructs of other countries and a thorough understanding of the place of each piece of music within its home culture, we cannot deliver an introduction to world musics. We do not have to be system analysts to deliver information technology effectively in the classroom. Thus we do not need to understand everything about each world music tradition to start to use them effectively in the classroom. (Please refer to other chapters within this book to find longer and better justifications.) What we Key Stage One teachers need to realise is that we already organise activities and use materials and instruments which contribute to an understanding of musics from different times and places. We must decide how we can build on this and develop our knowledge and the experience of the children and then have the confidence to go on and do it.

## Exploration of the National Curriculum

The National Curriculum orders list the following musical elements: pitch, duration, dynamics, speed, timbre, texture and structure. Not all cultures classify music and its components in the same way. For instance within our element of timbre, classical Chinese music has eight tones associated with eight different materials found in nature from which the sounds are made:

### *Ba - yin* **or Eight Tones**

| | |
|---|---|
| Metal | (in an instrument such as a bell) |
| Stone | (such as a chime) |
| Silk | (zither, *zheng*) |
| Bamboo | (flute) |
| Reed | (*guan* or *sheng*) |
| Clay | (*xun*) |
| Leather or Skin | (drum) |
| Wood | (woodblock) |

This provides us with a categorisation of sounds which in our classification are of timbre of sound. However they read more like a classification of instrument families such as our strings, brass, woodwind and percussion.

## Practicalities

But first you need to get the instruments to the children. Take a class of twenty five children with a table full of sound sources. How are you going to allot instruments to players? If they all go at once a child or an instrument will be damaged in the melee. There will be chaos as each one pushes a way to the table and inevitably those at the back will not have 'the only one I wanted, Miss'. A more structured approach is preferable.

Before the children come in, arrange the instruments for the session. Lay the instruments in the centre of the room, if the children will need to select from them during the session. If not, you could lay them out on a side table.

A circle is a useful shape to work in. Try sitting with the children in this circle around the instruments. You may only need to introduce one new one. When presented with a new sound source what is the first thing which YOU want to do? Play it, of course! Children are just the same. Therefore the introduction of sounds is structured so that they are all given the chance to play the sound. If they do this all together at the same time then it is very difficult to focus unpractised ears on the difference between sounds. However, if the instruments are introduced one at a time over the course of several sessions many of these problems are alleviated. One suggestion is a little song like:

> What can you play?
> What can you play?
> What does the ................... say today? (inserting the name of the selected instrument in the gap).

The instrument is passed round the circle during the song and at the end of 'today', the child with the instrument is encouraged to play a little. Accept all offerings with encouragement and praise if appropriate and go on to encourage the children to produce a different sound, if they can think of a way of doing so. It is very rare to find a child who does not want to play, but if one refuses, do not force her/him to perform in public then. We all know how exposed it feels to play in front of peers.

Select a variety of classroom instruments from a variety of world music traditions. A common selection might be castanets, xylophone, drum, maracas, African thumb piano or *kalimba*, *shekere*, slit drum, wood block, claves, tulip block and Chinese bell tree. This is probably a selection which you could find in your school. We can use these to explore the National Curriculum elements of music.

## Timbre

You can sort these instruments by sound and sight into sets according to the main material, for instance sort by metal and wood. Then you can listen to these without the children using their eyes and then match sounds heard to instruments from the sound, perhaps selecting from the floor. This can be recorded verbally in class discussion or, by sound on tape or by children's pictures or writing. You may be able to sort by rattle or other natural material.

## Duration

Once familiar with some of the sounds you are able to listen to a sound in more detail. Some of the sounds last for longer. You could give each child an instrument and ask her/him to make one sound (one strike, one shake). Then listen to them and put them into order with longer sounds at one end of the line of children playing and shorter sounds at the other. There is always much discussion as to which sound is actually the shortest amongst the children. A visual record of children playing their instruments in order could be a satisfying corridor display.

## Pitch

By now children will have noticed that you can make more than one sound from some instruments. Select those that do. By same or different questioning careful listening to sound can be encouraged and children may learn to recognise up and down in pitch.

## Dynamics

Children can match sounds using these instruments from different world music traditions to copy how the teacher plays. Each instrument needs to be taught by the child to use its speaking voice, its shouting voice and its whispering voice. Conducting games are a fun way of allowing children to explore the range of dynamics.

Devise signs to cover the changes from loud to quiet and the rate of change in consultation with the children. Generally they will have a lot of good ideas which may well tend towards the Western accepted notations.

## Speed

Have you tried this one? Each pair of children in the movement lesson has an instrument. The child playing guides the speed of a repetitive movement of the other child by his/her playing. Alternatively the player is guided in his/her sound making by the speed of movement of the child moving. You can extend this with sequences of movement.

## Texture

Select one child to play a pattern on one instrument. Listen to the start, the playing and the end. Try combining two patterns from different children and listen to the effect. Children listen effectively with their eyes closed but it is easier to maintain this attention if the sound source is screened from the children, so that they have to listen to the patterns without any visual distractions. Experiment with more than two patterns to hear how they interconnect and allow the children to comment on their effectiveness.

## Structure

The simplest structure is 'play and not play'. Much song uses a chorus, a repeated pattern of words or melody. Some songs are based on a leader calling and the whole group responding. These are all structures. Investigate the structures of the songs which you are singing and use these as a basis for classroom composition.

All of the above ideas are suitable for use with younger children or those with very little formal musical experience. We need to know what to do next.

## Upper Infants

Once children are familiar with these ideas and are able to predict the sounds of instruments, they are able to start thinking about ordering them. This is composition. A very early example of this is when a child is presented with the range of available sounds and chooses which sound to start with, which to follow and how to end. He/she should be able to tell you why this decision has been made. In practice the teacher generally imposes limits on the composition too, by making some of the decisions for the child in advance. The teacher probably limits the number of sounds available. The teacher may give a theme to develop or a structure to work within.

Let us look at some examples of using a piece of music from another culture. We shall look at some ideas from it and then take some of these ideas on to use in the children's compositions.

## A piece of Ameridian music

This is a chant which uses very limited vocal sounds and a simple rhythm:

**Ayo**

The number of different notes used is limited to three. There are plenty of places to get a breath. The overall beat is steady. You can teach this to children as a call and response, a very common structure in folk musics. In British folk music an example of call and response would be a shanty.

How can we add a steady rhythm to this music to add more interest to our performance? Try a steady hand clap at the *.

## Ayo (2)

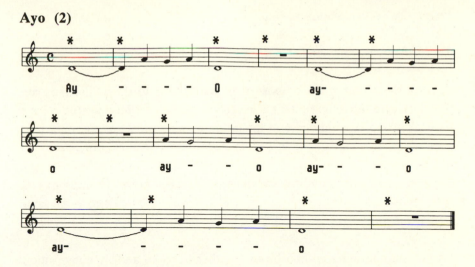

Can we put anything into the gaps between lines of chant? Try this one:

## Ayo (3)

Now make up your own.

Movement can be added quite easily by making use of a steady step which adds rhythmic emphasis to the music. Take your right foot and touch your toe to the floor with the knee bent. Put the heel down firmly to make a noise. Do the same with your left foot (toe heel) so that you end up with the pattern:

toe heel toe heel, toe heel toe heel.

Practise doing this while you sing.

This activity can be extended in many ways. You could:

1.  Ask the children to compose their own chant to do whilst they are moving round the room in the toe heel step. You may find it useful to have half the group moving and half the group making music at any one time, because children may find it difficult to chant and move at the same time.

2.  You can ask the children to develop two (or more, as appropriate) patterns of drum beats which will go together, and to play them at the same time in the group.

3.  Put the children's compositions together to make a class composition. For instance it might go:

*Ayo Chant || Group A || Ayo Chant || Group B || Ayo Chant.*

**Cherry Blossom**

This melody is well known in the West; indeed the children may already be familiar with it through hearing it on the television, where it has been used for scene setting. It uses only a limited number of notes, which are linked together into what we would refer to as the pentatonic scale[1]. You can

([1]Note: Cherry Blossom is, in fact, not entirely pentatonic, since in its whole range it uses 6 notes. To make the instruments truly pentatonic for the children to compose in the Japanese style, the note D should also be removed.)

achieve this on your classroom xylophone by removing the note G. This will make it easier for you to play to the children. It is a slow and stately piece, so there is no need to rush.

What can the children do with you to make the performance more Japanese in feel? We need to ask questions such as all or some of the following to make our own arrangement:

* Shall we add some sounds to the long notes?
* How about using small bells to have a light ripple there?
* Is there an instrument we could add which would play on the first count of each two?
* What could we add to the count of two?
* Do we want to have everyone playing during the melody or do we limit the number of people playing with the melody?
* Do we want to have every instrument playing all the way through? (This is a matter of taste, because each classroom arrangement is special to the group with which you do it. I arrive at a consensus, through discussion with my class.)

You might end up with something like the arrangement on page 108.

How could we extend this work?

1. We could listen to the piece played on authentic Japanese instruments from a live or recorded performance. We could compare this with ours looking for the differences and similarities. We could say which we liked and why. We could listen to similar pieces. We could discover how many instruments are playing and describe the texture of the music.

2. This piece is called 'Cherry Blossom'. Can you write a piece of music with the same title and same mood?

3. Give the children prepared instruments with the same notes only. In groups, let them compose a piece of music which has an aspect of Japanese style.

## Cherry Blossom arrangement

## An example from the Chinese tradition

Chinese music from the high art tradition is based on firm aesthetic and philosophical principles. It is beyond the scope of this chapter to give exhaustive detail of these here. But let us take some of the limits of Chinese music and use them to frame the children's composition.

> Melody is based on a simple set of notes. (This may sometimes be pentatonic).

> Form: this is often based on the aesthetic principle of *Qi - Cheng - Zhuan - He* (Which translates as: Start - Continuation - Change - Synthesis)

This is a structure which we could use with infants. We need to decide on melodic idea, go on and play more of the same (in its simplest form a repetition would work), develop it differently in the next section and finish it with something that sounds like an ending to what has gone before.

## Using the way in which instruments are constructed or played to guide the children's composition

Folk instruments tend to be divided into families, according to how the sound is made. There are:

Striking sounds: Claves, split bamboo, castanets, coconut shell, slap sticks, wood blocks, guiro or rasp, chimes, gongs and bells.

Resonating sounds: drums.

Reeds sounds: comb and paper

String sounds: guitar, string over wooden box, elastic bands.

The problem of making a specific sound has fascinated man since he first had some spare time from survival. There are examples of bird bone whistles dating from prehistoric times in museums and the range of instruments got larger as man had more time and more materials with which to experiment.

Children also enjoy this exploration. Give a group a limited choice of material and see how many different ways they will combine them to make sounds. Perhaps the simplest to do is to give the children a range of containers, with and without lids, a range of possible rattling sounds such as seeds, lentils, pasta, small stones, nuts, shells, and glue to combine them. Pride in the finished product leads children to wish to decorate the sound source of which they are proud and it is exactly this motivation which leads to instrument makers placing inlay on a harpsichord: it serves no musical function. There are plenty of books on the market which give detailed descriptions of how to tackle such instrument making.

Once children have experimented with how to fasten rattles inside a hollow container, they can see how a maraca works and why it is used as it is. Once they have fastened the rattles on the outside of the instrument they are understanding the problems of making and playing a *kabasa*. Natural products will be more fragile than man-made, so they will see why in Africa 'guitars' have been made out of oil cans, which are strong, rather than gourds, which are brittle.

## Conclusion

The range of activities which World Musics present to the busy teacher is vast. It gives access to a whole new and exciting collection of sounds with which to explore how sounds are ordered to make music. It allows the teacher to draw on songs linking the children's activity to faraway places. This in turn introduces them to a respect for the culture of others - through an understanding of their humanity and through having shared similar (in this case musical) problems. There is an opportunity for the teacher to learn and explore with the children, and a shared experience is one which is remembered for a long time. It is not necessary to be an expert on music from another part of the world provided you are prepared to listen with an open ear and let the sounds speak for themselves. There are many selections of materials and recordings on the market which are available for use in school and it is possible to work with the local junior or secondary school to share resources and invite common visitors. This has the added advantage of making the activities less expensive. There are grants available to encourage visitors into school for specific intercultural experiences and these can only enrich the life of the whole school. There are also some very good tunes.

# Bibliography

Swanwick, K. and Tillman, J.B. (1986) The Sequence of Musical Development: A Study of Children's Composition, *British Journal of Music Education 3*. (3), November, pp305-39

# 5 World Musics in Junior Schools

*Ernest Piper*

## Introduction

In many areas of human endeavour the gap between what is conceived of as a realistic goal and what is eventually achieved varies greatly in different situations according to the diverse influencing factors. The same influencing factors will lead to a variation in the concept of what is realistically possible when humans in differing circumstances are faced with an identical challenge. Should the challenge itself be one which allows freedom of interpretation there will be further variation in the definition of attainable targets.

Schools, when presented with a common challenge, have to take into account a number of variable factors including such matters as number of children on roll, proportion and mix of ethnic groups, intake area, geographical location, size and design of buildings, qualifications, competencies and interests of teaching staff, overall curriculum design, class organisation, influence and help of advisory bodies, resources, etc, etc.

Discussion of the educational justification for the inclusion of world musics into the curriculum is outside the scope of this chapter and, regardless of educational reasons, the most significant stimulus for many schools to start working on the world musics challenge is the statement in the National Curriculum Order for Music that:

> Pupils should perform and listen to music in a variety of genres and styles from different periods and cultures. The repertoire chosen .... should include examples of works taken from .... a variety of cultures, Western and non-Western. (General Requirements for Programmes of Study)

Attainment Target 2, Key Stage 2 is defined as:

> The development of the ability to listen to and appraise music including .... a knowledge of our diverse culture and a variety of other musical traditions.

The revised Draft Proposals of May 1994 are not more specific and teachers are left with important decisions to be made on the content and quantity of world musics in the curriculum. This observation is made not to criticise the National Curriculum planning team but to point out a further influence leading to the great diversity of both theory and practice of world musics in schools.

A survey of primary schools carried out for this chapter reveals that some admit to having no specific world musics input during the academic year 1993 - 1994 (although they were planning to organise something in the following year). In contrast one school has already developed and put into operation a policy which attempts to link world musics into all aspects of the music curriculum. Schools with little or no world musics presence in their curriculae, when faced with an approaching Ofsted inspection, will more fully appeciate Dr Johnson's famous dictum that 'when a man knows he is to be hanged in a fortnight, it concentrates his mind wonderfully.'

## Strategies

The strategy adopted by a school will be influenced by the factors mentioned at the beginning of this chapter. The presence on the staff of a teacher with skills, confidence and general interest in music can lead to the early establishment of world musics in the school. It is appropriate at this point to mention that, in the scramble to cope with all the requirements of the National Curriculum, many schools have understandably opted to concentrate their efforts into organising the core subjects, and it is not difficult to find primary schools lacking a written policy or curriculum for music. The strategies listed below are, of course, crystalisations of approaches and emphases and in many cases have become so intermingled as to be inseparable.

## Opportunist

This is not really a strategy but it has served in several schools as a starting point. A teacher whose turn it was to take assembly played to the school a tape of Bolivian pan-pipes. These evocative instruments attracted much attention and in the following days both pupils and staff brought into school similar tapes and discs which were listened to and discussed. The Opportunist will take advantage of any world musics-related activities or events occuring in the locality, in national or international news or the arrival in the school of pupils or visitors who can offer some sort of musical performance. The Opportunist approach militates against forward planning although some teachers have gained enough confidence from such initial ventures to enable them to explore the world musics field in a more organised fashion. It might also be said that there are few teachers who would fail to take advantage of a golden opportunity should one occur. Indeed, one headteacher claimed that he and his music teacher had an 'active Opportunist' policy which enhanced the planned intercultural work of the school.

## Assembly Based

The value of classes preparing and presenting aspects of their work to the rest of the school in assemblies is accepted. Two very positive aspects of this type of activity are:

i)      a clearly defined goal for classwork
ii)     a performance to an audience

A well-tried and successful approach is to base some assemblies through the year on important festivals such as *Hanuka, Divali, Holi* and *Yuan Tan*. These assemblies inform pupils of the significance and meaning of the festivals, introduce related cultural aspects and share the celebration of the festival with any relevant ethnic groups in the school. Festivals generally have music associated with them and present a unique opportunity to investigate and perform different musics. 'Added value' factors are that the class shares its learning with other pupils and teachers in the school and that the yearly return of the festivals and their celebration helps to counteract the disturbing tendency of many children to forget what they learnt last year.

## Topic Based

Topic-centred work is firmly entrenched in British primary schools. Many (but not all) topics allow the logical inclusion of music, particularly those with a historical, geographical or ethnic base. A topic on the Tudor period which ignores music is not only leaving out an important aspect of Tudor social life and cultural achievement but is also denying the pupils the experience of learning and performing some delightful music which is well within their capabilities. The place and function of music in modern Western Europe is different from the experience of music in other cultures, and the topic based approach can be helpful in placing a music in its cultural context.

There could be a place for music in any topic with an intercultural element. Apart from topics on specific countries and cultures, topics on world religions, festivals, rites, dance, storytelling, drama, and so on, can all offer the opportunity for an input of related music. The combination of elements such as story, costume, lifestyle, art, dance and music make a much stronger and more memorable impact on many children than any of these studied in isolation.

## Visit Based

i) Visits out of school

Pupils and staff visit a centre, workshop, exhibition or performance and follow up the visit with class projects. The opportunities for this activity vary according to the location of the school. Schools situated in or near large urban centres are much more likely to arrange visits without formidable expense and long travelling.

ii) Visits into school by specialist groups

Location here is much less important. Many professionals in the area of world musics are very happy to travel considerable distances. Real people delivering live authentic performance and responding to pupils' questions can bring to life a new area of experience and understanding far better than any book, sound or video tape. Artists who specialise in school work nearly all have developed well tried follow-up activities.

The effectiveness of successful visits into and out of school cannot be denied. The problem here is, of course, cost, particularly in economic situations where financial resources are already stretched. A useful strategy for the funding of a visit into school is to find another local school or cluster of schools willing to participate in the event and share the cost. Should a high profile visit be considered there is always the possibility of finding some sponsorship (See below, Case Study 4).

## Music Curriculum Based

In this approach world musics are used primarily to develop and broaden pupils' musical skills and understanding. Indian music may be used to introduce pupils to the instruments, techniques and characteristics of Indian music, and a *raga* could serve as a model stimulating pupils to develop improvisation over a drone accompaniment. Caribbean music may similarly be used to develop pupils' awareness and skill in syncopated rhythms. Music from different cultures and periods may be used in the teaching of basic concepts. To develop pitch awareness the pupils could listen to recordings of a didjeridu, double bass, Tibetan monks chanting and the closing of Tchaikovsky's 'Pathetique' Symphony as examples of low sounds, while high sounds could be illustrated by pan pipes, an ocarina and an excerpt from Vaughan Williams 'The Lark Ascending'. Plucked strings as a sound source could include rock guitar, sitar, balalaika, koto and Pizzicato Polka by Strauss. A musical curriculum based approach requires teachers with good general knowledge in world musics and must be supported by good resources including a collection of relevant recordings. This approach could lead to a situation where musics are studied without reference to their cultural background.

## External Course Based

Many teachers have found published music curriculum schemes or schools music broadcasts to be very useful. Recently published schemes of work are devised around National Curriculum requirements and include a variety of world musics. The world musics content of broadcast programmes varies greatly but many contain at least an intercultural slot. The advantage is that the necessary information and development activities with sound and visual illustration are all given. This is particularly helpful for schools lacking relevant resources or where the teachers feel ill-equiped or unconfident about tackling world musics. The disadvantage is that the teacher has to accept what is in the course and the world musics content may not link with other cross-curricular projects. Reliance on broadcast programmes has a significant effect on forward planning as programme content changes from year to year. Unless the teacher carries out follow-up activities, the pupil may regard the music lesson as just another television programme.

## School Case Studies

Five of the schools visited for the purpose of this study have been chosen as case studies. These schools have established effective but but very different working plans for dealing with world musics. Interestingly one school deliberately set up an intercultural programme (with associated music activities) because the school population was totally white Anglo-Saxon, while another school developed its intercultural work because of the rich cultural/racial mix in its pupils.

## Case Study 1

Rural primary school in small village
No. of classes in Key Stage 2: 3
Ethnic mix: Almost completely white Anglo-Saxon

The school has no music specialist on the teaching staff but the Headteacher has both competence and enthusiasm in music. School policy is that all class teachers operate their own music lessons and each class should have a music lesson once a week.

To help those teachers less competent in music and in the interests of consistency between classes the music curriculum is based upon a selection of appropriate lessons from the Silver Burdett scheme. BBC music workshop have also been used when they fitted in with planned work. In addition all children are taught to play the recorder, starting in Year 3. Teachers try to relate music to other curriculum areas when reasonably possible.

The school's approach to intercultural issues is carefully thought out and well established. Over a two-year period three of the major topics studied are specifically intercultural: Indian celebrations; the Caribbean; Jewish festivals. The head teacher would like to set up a fourth intercultural study related to the Far East. She believes, however, that four is the maximum number of such major topics her staff and pupils can comfortably cope with. The Indian Celebrations topic is centered round a visit to a Sikh temple where pupils are introduced to Indian religious and cultural traditions, including instruments, music and dance. The Silver Burdett scheme offers useful ideas and resources for related music lessons. The Jewish and Caribbean topics are not related to visits but as with the Indian topic, Silver Burdett provides the resources and lesson content which can be operated by non-specialist musicans.

Festivals such as Divali, Chinese New Year and Hanuka are also celebrated with presentations in school assemblies. Tapes of non-Western music played in assembly very often provoke an interested response from the pupils. The Silver Burdett tapes are currently used as the major world musics sound resource in the school but a wider collection is gradually being assembled. Instruments and artefacts are borrowed from the County Intercultural Resource Centre.

The school has a tradition of lively curricular and extra-curricular music. Music is introduced in assemblies with explanatory comments. A yearly drama/dance/music event is produced and there is a weekly Music Club for pupils.

## Case Study 2

Inner city junior school
Number of classes at Key Stage 2: 8
Racial/Ethnic mix: 90% from Indian sub-continent; 10% white Anglo-Saxon.

Many of the notices in the school are written in four languages: Bangla, English, Punjabi and Urdu. Pupils from the sub-continent are actively encouraged to practice and develop their skills in the language of their country of origin. A visiting music specialist takes all classes for music, covering basic National Curriculum work. The world musics input largely takes place in assemblies. The deputy head has musical training in both Indian and Western traditions and encourages music in the school, particularly through assemblies for which groups of pupils prepare and enthusiastically present aspects of their culture to the rest of the school. A group of Indian children, for example, may introduce and perform a dance in costume, accompanied by a tape or by pupils performing: a group of Pakistani pupils might perform and teach a song in Punjabi. The pupils will happily learn songs in any of the languages prevalent in the school.

Assemblies are, of course, sometimes used to celebrate the religious festivals, giving another opportunity for the introduction of a variety of musics. This is not a systematic approach, nor does it promote the appraisal skills (which are developed in music lessons) but it gives pupils a familiarity with diverse musics and helps children to develop a sense of joy and pride in their cultures. Teaching staff are convinced that this confident sharing of cultures has a very beneficial influence in relationships within the school. Sometimes musicians visit the school to demonstrate their music and its instruments. There are also extra-curricular clubs for choir (which sings mainly in English), keyboards, recorders and *dholki*.

# Case Study 3

Primary school in North London
Number of classes in Key Stage 2: 4
Ethnic/racial mix: 50% white Anglo-Saxon; 25% Afro-Caribbean; 15% Asian; 10% mixture from East Europe, the Far East and Oceania.

There are multilingual signs on display but these proclaim a commitment to interculture rather than serve a functional purpose. There are too many first languages spoken in the school to allow them all to feature on notices. One of the class teachers is a specialist music teacher who takes all the classes for music. The school draws on the richness of the cultures represented by the pupils. Music and dance performances from different cultures often feature in 'showcase' assemblies for which groups of children prepare presentations. Class topics include Light and Life (intercultural and interfaith festivals), Explorations and Living in the Community. Some music from different cultures features in each of these topics.

Last year the school joined six other local primary schools for a week-long festival of arts focusing on carnivals. The pupils from this school worked with an African music/dance/drama group. Before this event the school had already participated in a joint Latin-American festival. Classes have visited the local public library to hear stories and taped music from all over the world. The School Association, run by parents, organises a series of 'International Evenings' for adults and children where world musics are often presented along with associated dance, costume, food, literature, customs and so on.

The music teacher has devised her own curriculum programme with a significant world musics input including songs which contribute to class topics. She attended a workshop on Arabian drumming and has taken classes to workshops on African drumming and the gamelan. Projects in these three areas feature in her programme of work. The gamelan workshop, with a follow-up session conducted in school by the gamelan teacher, has proved to be very worthwhile. Pupils, using classroom instruments, have practised gamelan music and have used gamelan techniques to compose and perform their own compositions. They were subsequently able to give a public performance of gamelan music on gamelan instruments and of their own compositions on classroom instruments in a concert at the London South Bank Centre. The music teacher feels that her pupils have gained much from the gamelan project, especially in the areas of general self confidence, composing skills, co-operation and awareness and self-discipline in ensemble work. The school has invested in a classroom set of African drums. The school resource of recorded world musics is still undeveloped, the music teacher having difficulty in finding suitable recordings.

**Case Study 4**

Primary school in rural dormitory area
Number of classes in key stage 2: 5
Ethnic mix: completely white Anglo-Saxon

A welcome notice in several languages at the entrance of the school is indicative of a vigorous policy towards interculture. For the last eight years a working relationship has existed with an East London school having a large percentage of Bangladeshi students on roll. This is an ongoing relationship designed to compensate for the absence of different racial and ethnic groups in the school. Exchange visits for pupils and staff are made between the two schools every term. During these visits there is often musical activity such as the Bangladeshi children teaching a song to the English children and vice versa.

There is a music-specialist consultant who organises the music curriculum, but class teachers take their own classes for music lessons. The music policy is not primarily biased towards world musics but is consistent with the school approach to interculture and attempts to bring different musics into regular music lessons. Music work links into appropriate year topics such as festivals and Judaism.

A great variety of taped music is played in assemblies and some of the intercultural topic work, with its associated music, is presented by pupils. The school acquired a collection of resources when a local intercultural resource centre closed down. Three years ago the school collaborated with another primary school and a local comprehensive school to put on a week's festival of performances and workshops given by Kathakali, an Indian dance and drama group.

Following the great success of this venture a week-long festival was organised last year, led by Dagarti Arts, an African group presenting Ghanaian music, dance, song, story telling and creative arts. Four schools were involved in workshops during the day and in a public performance given one evening for the local community. The cost to each school was greatly reduced by the sponsorship attracted to such a high-profile local event.

## Case Study 5

Large middle school on outskirts of a medium-sized country town
Numer of classes: 17
Ethnic mix: 99% white Anglo-Saxon

This school has a music specialist teacher and an assistant specialist teacher who take all classes once a week. The music teacher has a long-standing interest in intercultural aspects of music and has devised and established a music curriculum which integrates world musics and Western music.

Her music policy states that the curriculum will endeavour to widen the range of pupil's experience so that different musics become a normal and expected part of music lessons. World musics are used alongside Western music in the teaching of musical concepts and in practical work wherever possible. Topics in the Music curriculum include projects on West African drums and rhythms, the gamelan, Chinese pentatonic and an intercultural vocal project.

Cross-curricular links are made where possible and appropriate with the year topics, one of which is Africa. Music also connects with a Religious Studies project on Ceremonies, sometimes resulting in assembly presentations where taped non-Western music is played or pupils give live performance such as a Jewish or African song. A steel band teacher and an African dance/music/drama teacher have given workshops in the school.

The teacher has built, over several years, a good resource of world musics tapes and is continually looking for suitable material to enlarge her collection.

There is a busy schedule of extra-curricular activities including choir (which includes African songs in its repertoire), orchestra, wind band and steel band which has raised the profile of music in the school. The music teacher feels (despite what has been achieved) that she needs more time for personal development in world musics.

## The Gamelan

Among the various musics introduced to primary and secondary schools in recent years gamelan music appears to be increasingly significant. Many schools within reach of gamelan teaching centres take groups of children for workshops. Gamelan courses for adults also attract a number of school teachers. In asking and answering the question, 'Why do the gamelan?' the intention here is not to present gamelan music as 'a better' or 'the best' method of involving children in a non-Western music but to examine the value and potential of a particular path and identify principles of learning and experience that could also inform ventures into other ensenbles such as steel pans and African drums. The question was posed to Mr Nikhil Dally, London-based gamelan teacher and player, and the following section is based on his response.

It is relatively easy to start children off in gamelan music. The basic technique of striking an instrument which has similarities to classroom instruments is usually quickly grasped. After a two-hour workshop the children can perform (admittedly with errors and lack of finesse) a piece of gamelan music: not something composed or simplified for children but a real piece of music from another culture; not something resurrected from the past but a piece of music belonging to a vigorous and popular tradition which still plays a significant part in Indonesian life. The children have the opportunity to play on genuine instruments which are objects of beauty and which, in ensemble, create a world of sound very different from any found in Western Music. The gamelan offers an ensemble experience ideally suited to children of mixed abilities because the less able can be given simpler parts to play, supported by other group members playing the same melody of rhythm, while a challenging part can always be found to stretch those children who have ability. Participation is not hindered by inability to read conventional notation as gamelan music is not written down but is learned by memorising basic principles and melodic patterns. Gamelan players must remember parts and reproduce them in the performance and they must listen carefully to the ensemble around them, responding to aural signals in the music which may keep the pulse of the music steady or which may accelerate or decelerate the pulse. Such challenges will particularly develop musical memory and aural awareness. The players must be aware of their individual parts and the parts played by others, and participation in gamelan performance (which is not conducted) develops skills vital to all types of ensemble playing. The memorisation of melodic patterns through singing rather than just copying on instruments further develops aural perception. Other benefits developed through gamelan work include extension of concentration, control of dynamics and awareness of texture and timbre. Understanding of form is developed by performing music based on structures not usually found in Western music. Growing familiarity with the tuned instruments will help children not to regard non-Western scales as 'out of tune'. A 'sort of gamelan' can be constructed out of classroom instruments, and this can be a valuable exercise, but without the rich timbre and the unique tuning of the genuine instruments the resulting music will be much less impressive than the real thing, and rather than just trying to recreate a gamelan in the classroom teachers could encourage pupils to use gamelan techniques in general classroom composition.

The great majority of teachers who have taken classes to gamelan workshops have been agreeably surprised at the way in which their pupils have responded to the venture. There are publicly accessible and well-established gamelan teaching centres in London, Manchester, York and Glasgow, and at least another two dozen gamelans are established around the country. The Music Education Service at the London South Bank Centre can give information about gamelan centres, and Gamelan teachers will also visit schools to do workshops.

## Some Conclusions

The schools chosen have, each in their own way, found a workable solution to the questions underlying the statements made in the introductory section of this article:

Which world musics?
How much world musics?
How are world musics to be presented?

The strategies in these five schools have been established more by evolutionary responses to the personnel and environments of the schools rather than by planning edicts. Schools lacking a world musics strategy or even a world musics input may at this stage not have time for a strategy to evolve and may have to take immediate decisions about how to start.

Teachers questioned for this article indicated that a workshop either in or out of school for pupils and teachers or for teachers unaccompanied by children, is very worthwhile; the significant factor in 'worthwhile' inevitably being finance weighed against educational outcomes. In one school there was a serious discussion to justify the cost of a proposed class visit to a gamelan workshop. The visit was eventually approved and took place. The teacher and children gained so much from the experience which they brought back into the school that afterwards the head teacher conceded that the financial outlay was fully justified.

Although a teacher can, for instance, learn enough from the published books and recordings about Indian music to introduce it to children, there is no substitute for demonstration and tuition by an expert who will present not only the music but also the added fascination of its style and trappings. A good workshop can inspire pupils and teachers to launch into new musical worlds with confidence and enthusiasm rather than timidity and suspicion, and will ensure that basic errors and misconceptions do not take root in the first stages. Schools organising or participating in major intercultural events (see Case Studies 3 and 4) have also gained lasting benefit to their music from such initiatives.

A number of educational authorities and institutions around the country arrange world musics workshops for teacher, pupils or both. The Commonwealth Institute, for example, run a highly successful series of workshops in Kensington and will organise similar events anywhere in the country. Its Key Stage 2 workshops are particularly well subscribed. (The Commonwealth Institute, incidentally, attempts to mail details of its programmes to every school in the country.) The London South Bank Centre also offers a wide range of services. Some county authorities are now running innovative programmes to promote intercultural study. The East Sussex Education Authority can be cited here as having a vigorous policy in which world musics are presented as part of a broad and balanced intercultural experience. This authority has purchased several sets of gamelans, steel bands and sets of African drums and Indian instruments for use in schools; and specialist teachers are regularly employed to teach them in schools. The projects were initially aimed at secondary schools but are now spreading into junior schools. Mary Cadogan, Projects Co-ordinator for East Sussex County Music Education reports that the successful practical experience in non-Western musics gained by pupils has more than justified the initial expense involved.

A less exciting way to start is to dip into one of the well known published music courses. The staff in school Case Study 1 felt that the Silver Burdett scheme suited their general needs in music and purchased it. It also served their world musics needs. Silver Burdett 7-9 and 9-11 books include work on music from Korea, Mexico, China, Hawaii, Indonesia, Japan, Nigeria, Zaire and Trinidad. The work presented often includes singing, instrumental work, composing and listening activities, all supported by sound tapes and visual aids. There are similar and significant world music elements in other published schemes such as Oxford Primary Music (Key Stage 2) and Novello's 'Let's Make Music'. A full investment in one of these schemes needs careful consideration and one would certainly not contemplate buying in a complete package of teachers pack, set of tapes, sets of pupil's books and other visual aids just for its world musics content. However, for starters the teacher's pack alone will be a very useful resource of examples and ideas.

For schools wishing to develop world musics through assemblies or topics on festivals and ceremonies, there are several helpful books, but three in particular could be mentioned: Barbara Cass-Begg's *A Calender of Festivals*, June B Tillman's *Light the Candles* and Jean Gilbert's *Festivals*. Between them, the books provide a good collection of singable songs from all over the world, performance and classroom instrument accompaniment suggestions and information about the festivals. Jean Gilbert's book gives suggestions for music lesson developments and also has an accompanying tape. This brings us to the observation that song collections are still being published without accompanying tapes. There are many non-specialist teachers, eager to develop music activities in their classes who have neither the theoretical knowledge to work out from a score the melody of a song, nor the practical skills to provide an accompaniment for it. While fully accepting that accompaniments are not always necessary or even desirable, tapes of songs are a great help to some teachers who therwise would not even know 'how the tune goes'.

Although there are plenty of available recordings of musics from all over the world, many music teachers have difficulty in finding exactly what they imagine is suitable for their needs. Comments from some teachers that they would welcome a publication with tapes, teaching plans and visual material suggest that there is surely room on the market for a publication at Key Stage 2 level which treats the musics most commonly introduced in junior schools: African, Caribbean, Chinese, Indian, Indonesian, Japanese, Jewish and South American. The W.O.M.A.D. Foundation has produced very useful comprehensive packs in their series, 'Exploring the World's Music'. The series currently includes packs on the musics of West Africa, Indonesia, the Caribbean and India. Although these are written for use in secondary schools, junior school teachers may well find both the tapes and teaching content to be valuable. W.O.M.A.D. are currently preparing a similar series specifically for Key Stage 2 work. Institutions such as the W.O.M.A.D. Foundation, the Commonwealth Institute and the several education intercultural centres run (mostly on inadequate budgets) by county authorities are all useful sources of resource information and some of them will loan instruments and artefacts to schools.

It is significant that each of the schools selected as case studies has a long-standing positive attitude to either music or interculture or both. Schools with neither have far to go. Teachers and pupils with a good background of musical activity and experience are obviously better placed to explore world musics than those without. Pupils unable to confidently perform on-beat and off-beat clapping in simple duple time are unlikely to manage syncopations and irregular rhythm patterns: those with little experience and confidence in singing songs of their own culture will find unfamiliar melodic shapes (and sometimes foreign words) to be daunting: those lacking a reasonable background in basic concepts in music will be deficient in both the understanding and the language needed for appraisal of the musics they hear: those unaccustomed to active listening will not suddenly upgrade their awareness when presented with unfamiliar music. Schools aiming to develop their work in world musics will find that their ventures into new areas are most worthwhile and productive when underpinned by a groundwork of well-organised week-to-week general music curriculum work.

## Bibliography

Cass-Beggs, Mary (1983) *A Calendar of Festivals.* London. Ward Lock

Gilbert, Jean (1983) *Festivals.* London. Oxford University Press

Gilbert, Jean and Davies, Leonora (1989) *Oxford Primary Music, Key Stage 2.* London. Oxford University Press

Hinkley, Prill and Martin (1992) *Let's Make Music: Music For All:1* London. Novello

Odam, G; Beethoven, J; Davidson, J; Nadon-Gabrion, C. (1989)
    *Silver Burdett Music Book 2 (7-9)*
    *Silver Burdett Music Book 3 (9-11)*
    Silver Burdett and Ginn

Tillman, June B (1991) *Light The Candles.* Cambridge. Cambridge University Press

W.O.M.A.D. Foundation (1994)
    *Exploring the World of Music Series*
    *The Music of West Africa*
    *The Music of India*
    *The Music of the Caribbean*
    *The Music of Indonesia*
    London. Heinemann

The writer is very greatful to the considerable number of people who have so willingly given him their valuable time and their valued information.

## Glossary

balalaika:    Russian folk instrument of the lute family with long neck and triangular body

dholki:    double-headed barrel-shaped drum from North India

didjeridu:    Australian aboriginal instrument which is a long hollowed out tube

drone:    a note or notes sounded continuously in a piece of music, usually as a form of a accompaniment

gamelan:    Indonesian ensemble consisting mainly of tuned percussion instruments, gongs, drums, but including some stringed and wind instruments

koto:    large Japanese zither with moveable frets

pentatonic:    strictly a five-note scale but generally used to describe the particular pattern given by the black notes on a keyboard

raga:    a type of note-pattern used as a basis for improvised composition in Indian music

sitar:    large long-necked lute of the classical tradition in Indian music

# 6 Music of the Caribbean: The Steel Band

*Wendy Brett*

Imagine my surprise and horror, when being shown around the Music Department on interview, on discovering that the school was the owner of a set of Steel Pans! As I knew nothing about Steel Pans my first reaction was to panic, my second, to allow the current Year 11 group to continue playing until the end of the term and then to find another use for the pans! Four and a half years later the Steel Band groups are flourishing, financially self-supporting and in great demand at local events

Any knowledge I have on Steel Bands is, as in many cases, self taught along the way. I am aware that other music staff who teach Steel Bands work in a variety of ways, whichever one works for them as individuals.

Steel Band music is a relatively new style of music, originating from the island of Trinidad during the 1940s. Information tells us that there was a surplus of oil drums left on the island which the Americans had discarded at the end of the Second World War. After the end of the war the supply of oil drums then continued from the island's own industry of petroleum based products.

As this was a very inexpensive way of making music, the first real interest came from the poorer population of the island, with an acceptance that this would continue. But as Steel Bands became more popular the Government gave its support and large companies on the island formed their own bands. Gradually Steel Bands spread to the other Caribbean islands and then to other countries.

The original style of music played in Trinidad was calypso music but you will find that the Steel Band sound is remarkably adaptable to almost any style, giving its own individual sound.

The tradition of Steel Bands has continued in Trinidad, and many of the local bands compete for a place in the famous festival held in Trinidad and Tobago every year. Of course, in England we associate Steel Bands with the Notting Hill Carnival and it is in this area that many bands are situated. New bands are being formed, mostly in schools, with music teachers, like myself, teaching them and it is rare to find two bands close to each other.

The instrumentation of a Steel Band depends very much on the manufacturer and how the individual makes them. My pans were originally from the Notting Hill area of London. I have been unable to trace the exact location and so the pans are now in the care of a Caribbean gentleman who lives in Kent, Mr Mike Contant. It is to him that I am obliged for much of what I have learnt about Steel Bands along the way.

My present band consists of two ping-pongs, (tenors) a double-second and single second (otherwise known as guitars), the cello and the bass. The set of bass pans consist of six pans, with three notes on each pan and are all played by one player. The cello consist of three pans, three quarters the size of the bass pans, again played by one player. The remainder of the pans now decrease in size, starting with the double second, a set of two pans, the single second and the two ping-pongs which are known as leads, being individual pans, each requiring one player. The single second was specially made for us by Mike Contant to enhance the middle of the band and made in the same pattern as the other pans.

The beaters are made from pieces of doweling with rubber wrapped tightly around one end, covered again tightly in foam rubber. Although my beaters are replaced every time the pans are tuned, it is very useful to be able to recover the beaters yourself. Large rubber bands and foam rubber are readily available, held in place by adhesive tape and will prolong the life of the beaters. Currently we are trying out a new set of beaters made from metal rods covered with rubber and foam. We have already noticed that these beaters give a much brighter sound than the wooden beaters, so the choice will come down to personal preference.

The tuning of the pans was my first major problem and I had great difficulty in locating a skilled person to come and tune them. It seems that the usual practice is for the person who made them to continue to maintain and tune them. As this was not possible, I managed to persuade Mike Contant, to at least come into school once and, having seen the pans, he has agreed to continue to tune them. It is an expensive business to keep them tuned, presently £160 per visit, and as the pans are in constant use they frequently need tuning. For the Steel Band to remain in use, it has to be self supporting and can only be used for the curriculum whilst this continues.

The Band members have recently rubbed down and re-painted the pans and I do any other maintenance that is required. For playing outside, it is wise to invest in a set of tent pegs to prevent the pans blowing over in the wind. Also water-proof covers for the music and a set of pegs. We are all quite adept at chasing music across fields!

My latest acquisition is a set of specially made cases for the five smaller pans, to prevent damage to the notes whilst in transit.

The National Curriculum has encouraged us to widen our own knowledge of world music. Having a set of Steel Pans in the school has brought a new dimension to Calypso music. Unfortunately, all too often the pupils only want to mess around assuming they will be able to play them immediately. They quickly find out that it is not so easy to produce the finished sound that they hear on CD, or at a live performance! Ideally, I would wish to use the pans in every topic, wherever composition is required. In reality only the GCSE pupils have this opportunity. I see the Steel Pans in the same way that I see orchestral instruments, which need to be treated with care and attention. Would we just hand out a trumpet, oboe or double bass to any pupil who asks?

My scheme of work for Year 9 incorporates music of the Caribbean. All pupils learn to play at least one simple tune on the pans, with some even working on composition. The results of their compositions have an improved musical content compared with using traditional classroom instruments. Only a limited number of pupils can use the pans, so who do you select to use them and why are their compositions much improved? Is it attraction of something different, live, real instruments, an accepted 'cool' instrument, a link to calypso, reggae music? Whatever the reason it is an area to continue to explore.

The G.C.S.E pupils are often involved in the extra curricular groups and have a good musical knowledge of the pans, having worked on technique and style. Some arrange and write for the band, using this for both composition and performance in their G.C.S.E exam.

Whilst studying Indian music this year, my Year 11 G.C.S.E pupils were set an assignment to compose a piece 'in the style of' Indian music using similar techniques to the traditional Indian music we had heard. After much trial and effort using keyboards to create as near authentic sounds as possible, most decided to use the pans. Gaining confidence this encouraged them to experiment with improvisation. The results were amazing. This also encouraged some of them to try some simple composition in different styles for the band.

Many Junior and Infant schools are trying to incorporate more music into their chosen topic, some schools allocating a weekly lesson in music, where staffing allows. With a much more structured requirement, the schools are looking for ways of enhancing their musical input by live music, bringing in activities that the staff are unable to offer. It is in this role that the Steel Band has become involved, running workshops. The workshop is either for a particular class or year group usually finishing with a concert for the rest of the school. The first time I took the Band out was to work with a

Year 5 class. Their enthusiasm and interest was overwhelming and we spent a very productive hour together, but how would I cope with the infants and would they be able to understand what I was trying to teach them? I need not have worried as the infants almost lead the girls of the band and myself along!

The workshops are both a learning and a practical experience, all learning to play something by the end of our visit.

The Band always starts with a traditional calypso song and I encourage the children to clap along in time with me. I talk about the island of Trinidad, the way of life, the climate, the people, and we imagine sitting on a golden beach, under a palm tree eating ice cream listening to calypso music. Cue for music!

We discuss that the pans start life as oil drums and that in this country we often see them used as dustbins. The various anecdotes from the children at this point are often very funny!

The concept of the small pans playing the high notes, down to the large pans playing the lowest notes is very visual and easily accepted by the infants. This concept extends to the different notes on the pans, the larger the dent the lower the note, the smaller the dent, the higher the note. The difference in the size of the largest/lowest note on the bass to the smallest/highest note on the ping-pong and the difference in pitch between the two, is both easy to see and hear. Although some understand that sound is made from vibrations, as this can't be seen on the Steel Pans, explanations in this area has caused confusion, so I now leave this discussion until the Junior School! It is now time for the pupils to play the pans themselves and the success of this is dependent upon the girls in the band. A group of six at a time, one per part, are taught to play a short phrase. Individual tuition takes place on how to hold the beaters, hitting notes in the middle of the dent, how to make the sound 'ring' rather than deaden it and after approximately five minutes we are ready to try to put all the parts together. Some need more help than others, yet some show a natural musical talent and are able to keep in time on their own. Again, the musical results in a very short time are most rewarding.

Approximately four years ago I heard an infant group play at The National Festival of Music for Youth at the South Bank in London. The music they played was very simple and involved children swapping in and out of the group that was playing, allowing up to about twelve children to play in total. They played without any inhibitions, giving a most refreshing performance. For my own interest I would like to work with a group of infants over a number of weeks, to see just what they can achieve at this age.

The most frequent use of the pans at school is in the extra curricular activities and so the Steel Bands have to take their place along with all the other activities the department offers. Unlike the school windband, it is possible to open membership of the Steel Bands to any interested pupil, as no previous experience is necessary. The initial interest to join a Steel Band is so great that I could give up my usual teaching and just give tuition on the pans all day, every day. The number of bands I run at the school is governed by the number of days and lunch times that I have available in a week. I encourage a group of friends to form a band as they are more likely to be reliable and less likely to fall out!

There are some occasions when a member might leave but there is always someone else waiting, ready to fill the gap. The commitment required from them is the same as any other band or choir I run and they must arrange to practise on their own during the week.

It is probably impossible to identify all the positive benefits the pupils gain from having a Steel Band at the school. Many are recognisable on the surface but some will not come to fruition until many years after leaving school. Obviously the benefits to the school of going out into the community brings its own rewards, but what are the rewards to the pupils?

My school is situated in an area where we have a very mixed catchment, some pupils giving up instrumental lessons due to lack of support and encouragement at home. The Steel Band is different. Rehearsals and practice can only be done at school, and, if needed, it is me who encourages pupils to continue, when they might otherwise have given up. Some of the 'characters' that have become involved, do so because they enjoy music and have a natural ability which has never been tapped before. They feel on equal terms with everyone else in the group, and behaviour and academic problems are left for the school day. As these characters become more involved and accepted by the other pupils, many of their social problems are reduced. Their confidence is improved because they can play as well as the other members of the group. The initial immediate success motivates them to continue and often these pupils are less inhibited than their peers who have instrumental lessons. Standards within the groups are high as they are continually 'on show', representing the school at so many events, and this is an accepted part of membership of the bands.

How do I teach the pupils to play the Steel Pans? Initially I had to listen and watch the group of girls who were playing when I arrived at the school. At that time my role was very limited; they had their repertoire, they just required a member of staff to accompany them to concerts. The group had plenty of music so I was able to stand back and watch and work out what the future held for the Steel Band.

I have always felt that to play by ear, by repetition seemed to be the accepted way to teach but to do this I had to feel confident myself, to know the music, to know all the pans, to be able to demonstrate, to feel uninhibited when playing. As I did not have any of these skills I found myself relying on my previous training and decided all I could do was to rely on the skills I had and see what happened.

The music is written out using capital letters. A space indicates a roll, / above a letter a short note, usually a quaver. Bar lines, double bar lines, repeat signs are used in the traditional way but surprisingly time-signatures were not evident. An example, 'Mango Tree' is given at the end of the chapter.

As the music has become increasingly more difficult with frequent changes of time, we have found it necessary to add time-signatures, especially when working with pupils who are traditionally trained.

When a new group comes for the first time, I spend the first few minutes explaining about the pans, the notes (each note has its letter name painted on it), how to hold the sticks, produce different sounds, and the pattern of the notes. I use 'Frere Jaques' to start each group, not only because each line is repeated but also, especially on the ping-pong, it teaches, in F major, the notes that are most commonly used. Each part is taught separately, giving a few minutes to practise and then we put it all together. For pupils without any previous group or band experience this is the most difficult part, as I now want them to play their notes and in time with everyone else. I count them in, wanting them to play their first note on the first beat of the bar. Just this activity can continue for quite some time. Five out of six players will strike the note together but one will be either early or late, then someone else will miss the note and so it goes on until we eventually progress to playing two notes together, then three, until we can play the whole of the first line over and over again. To add interest we try varying the tempo but always aiming to keep together by listening to each other. This is now the time to move on and to finish the song, keeping quavers in time on the ping-pong, adding minims in the other parts and explaining that notes do not always move together, so they must stick to their own part and not follow the tune. I also introduce the written notes explaining the signs and symbols they will have to understand.

This may sound quite an uninteresting way to teach but I can guarantee that the pupils really enjoy themselves. The missed notes, not being able to find the note and dropped sticks all help to create this sense of enjoyment. The sense of achievement they have at the end of their first practice, being able to play a recognisable tune, making it sound musical and having some technique, is far more than they expect. What other group of instruments can you start with from scratch and perform a recognisable tune within an hour?

By the following week the pupils have forgotten where some of the notes are but quickly remind themselves and practise together sorting out how they are going to start and finish together, playing at different tempo, trying to add dynamics, whilst hitting the correct notes.

It is now time to consider playing in a round! Not only is this musically satisfying but it also encourages the ping-pong players not to become too reliant on each other and enables them to play independently in different pieces. I'm sure you can imagine some of the results!

How each group progresses from here is determined by the make-up of the group and their own musical ability. Some groups need intensive help, others work out the music for themselves and only ask for help if something doesn't sound right or they can't work out a rhythm.

At the time of writing this I have two particularly musical groups who have been together for four and two years respectively. All the girls in the senior group took G.C.S.E. Music and musically have achieved more than any other group I have worked with before. The other group are not far behind and ideally I would like to enlarge the band and join both the groups together.

Over the last two years we have increased the repertoire and experimented with many different styles of music. The traditional Calypso style tunes just play themselves and by playing a Calypso carol this took us into the area of Christmas carols. After having success in this style we decided to experiment with any style that we enjoyed. Even the classics have not escaped; Beethoven and Handel may be turning in their graves but our audiences have given their approval. We are currently experimenting with music from the shows, to be followed by music from the 50s and 60s. Pop to children's songs: styles to suite all tastes.

Printed music for Steel Bands is not available and so writing arrangements is another time consuming job. This has become easier since some of the players have written out simple four-part arrangements themselves and I am now asking friends who enjoy arranging and composing to experiment with ideas for the band.

By far the biggest role that the Steel Band has is its place in the community. Personally I believe this is because the Steel Band is something different. Whether this trend will continue in the future, time will tell but whilst there are so few bands around I am sure we will continue to be in great demand.

Throughout the summer term the bands are regularly playing at Church and Charity events, fetes for schools, and carnivals and this gives me the opportunity to raise funds to continue to maintain the band.

Since the implementation of the National Curriculum and OFSTED, liaison with our feeder schools has become more frequent. Junior schools are incorporating as many live musical activities as possible into their schemes of work and we have been invited to participate in Caribbean themes, music weeks and workshops. More recently we have played at Ladies Nights, the AGM of the local NSPCC, The Salvation Army and we are now preparing for a world musics course, to demonstrate and give 'hands-on' experience to Infant and Junior teachers.

Whilst recently talking to Mike Contant I was interested to learn from him that the population on Trinidad is now very multi-racial and with a wide variety of musical backgrounds all having an influence on each other. Whatever their roots, once Trinidad has become their home, Steel Band music is part of their culture. I am told that the charm of the music comes from the charm of the island itself. After such a difficult and uncertain musical start on the island, Steel Bands became accepted and created an unrivalled interest. The island came alive to the music and has continued to develop from that time, showing no signs of this trend abating.

The bands hold communities together and encourage generation after generation to continue the skill of playing. Friendly rivalry is still part of the Steel Band competitions but they do take their music seriously, aiming for the highest honour of playing in the Island festival every other year.

Why do I continue to run the Steel Bands?

It is no longer just the pleasure I get from working with the children especially having played outside in all possible weathers, from over-powering heat, to howling wind and rain or even snow! I have to admit that the sound of the Steel Band has really charmed me and the possibility of introducing so many different styles of music makes it very interesting. I think the element of challenge is still there, and I want to continue to find out just what is musically possible. Of course, anything that interests and involves the pupils and broadens their experiences I will use to encourage the best from them. The positive comments and help from our audiences encourages us to continue, plus the support from the band members, parents, and my own family.

As long as the band can involve pupils from all walks of life and the full range of academic abilities in musical activities, I will continue to give it my time and support. It also gives me great personal satisfaction to show the critics that there are many happy, well motivated, self disciplined young people who will give up their time to enhance the lives of others. The music of the Steel Band may not be a traditional style of music in this country, yet it has encouraged many young people to become more involved in musical activities and to discover many previously unknown musical styles, and so where else should we begin this process but in our schools.

# Mango Tree

### Ping Pong

A   C G E C | D〰 F〰 | B G F D | C〰 E〰 |

     C G E G | F〰 A〰 | G A C ÁC〰〰 ‖

### Guitar/Single Second

A   E  E E | F〰 D〰 | D  D D | E〰〰G〰 |

     E  E E | F〰 D〰 | E F E ÉE〰〰 ‖

### Cello

A   G C G | F A F | D G D | E G E〰 |
     E E | D D | B B | C C〰 |

     G C G | F A F | G F G ÉE〰〰 |
     E E | D D | E A E ÓC〰〰 ‖

### Bass

A   C G G | D A D | G D F | E C G |

     C G C | D A D | G G G | C G C〰 ‖

# 7 Performing Groups in Schools: A Case Study

The Dagarti Arts Residency at Frogmore Community School

*Malcolm Floyd with Susan Darke and John Tucker*

One difficulty often faced by schools who want to integrate work from a variety of cultures is ensuring that students get an accurate and authentic view. This is a fundamental reason for inviting culture-bearers into schools; and because it takes time to get to grips with new ideas, materials and ways of working, residencies of various lengths are seen by some as the most effective way of incorporating this work. This chapter looks at one particular residency, describes the event from preparation to conclusion, and assesses its effectiveness.

In December 1993 the group 'Dagarti Arts' was in residence for a week at Frogmore Community School and three primary schools. 'Dagarti Arts' are based in London, and perform traditional works from Ghana. Dagarti Arts were selected for this because of the nature of the cross-media cultural experience they shared with students, which was felt to be particularly suited to the integrated way 'Creative Arts' was delivered at Frogmore Community School. It was the third time that the group had been in residence at the school. Previous visits in 1991 and 1992 had been solely for Frogmore itself, and aimed mainly at years 9 to 11. The 1993 residency concentrated on work with students in years 5, 6 and 7. Bringing back the same group was a decision made because of the positive previous experiences of staff and students. It was also considered to be easier to progress from the known, from where there were established links, and for which there was staff interest.

For the 1993 residency the aim was both to engage in significant inter-cultural work, and to be part of an outreach scheme to involve as many students of the Frogmore/Yateley area as possible, as part of a mixed primary and secondary Arts Festival, giving a higher profile to the schools involved, and to build links with 'feeder' schools.

Invitations to become involved were extended to 10 schools in the area, including independent schools. Four schools eventually took part; Frogmore Community School, who hosted the event, Newlands Primary School, who have considerable experience in inter-cultural work, Potley Hill Primary School who are also experienced, and have done much collaborative arts work with Frogmore, and Charles Kingsley Primary School, for whom this was a relatively new venture. A Committee was formed from members of these schools. From this committee three individuals were given specific responsibilities:

1.  a)  Initial liaison with the group.
    b)  Finding sponsorship.

2.  a)  Administration and organisation of programme.
    b)  Detailed liaison with group.
    c)  Liaison with other schools, negotiating with
        internal management systems

3.      Publicity and advertising.

The cost of the residency was funded by Yateley Arts Festival, Southern Arts, individual schools, and performance revenue (this last produced just over 10% of the total amount required).

Liaison started about six months before the event. There were three preliminary meetings when two members of the Dagarti Arts Group came for discussion, which entailed much negotiation and compromise on both sides. It was noted by teachers that the professionalism of the group made it easy to establish an effective workable programme. Difficulties with liaison were related to time. Although person 2 was given some time for Community Art based work, it was less than the time required for the number and length of phone calls required. Without the time allowance liaison would have been very problematic.

Accommodation for the group also proved difficult to arrange. In the end two members of the company stayed with a teacher from Frogmore School, and four stayed in 'Bed and Breakfast' places. However, it was eventually felt that this had given the company freedom, and opportunities to work in ways they found appropriate.

For Frogmore Community School the residency was the culmination of half a term's work in the Creative Arts departments. Some experience had been gained by teachers in previous residencies, so they felt able to tackle the whole project successfully. Below are summaries of some of the schemes of work in Music and Drama and a report from a Frogmore School Artist-in-Residence who worked with two schools.

## Music Scheme of Work: African Music

In preparation for the Dagarti Arts residential workshop for Year 7 pupils, the following areas/subject matter was covered in a seven week block of time, approximately one hour to each week:-

1.      Rhythm: square notation in developed form for more accurate notation of rhythms. Familiarity with half beat rests, occasional reference to syncopated rhythms.

2.      Polyrhythms, using notation or improvised in group/class work.

3.      Number circling: one clap on each circled number. For example, (1) 2 (3) 4 5 (6) 7 8. Different number totals used, e.g. 1 - 7 or 1 - 5.

4.      Accents: how they make music 'come alive'.

5.      Call-response: Leader (initially teacher led) chorus. Chorus could have fixed or variable response.

6.      African songs, often reflecting call-response technique, or the theme being based around typical village life.

7.      (Time allowing): Minimalism: an introduction to how the minimum amount of material could be used in effective, maximum outputs.

At all times, the necessity for repetition is continually re-enforced.

## Drama Year 7

Scheme of work for approximately seven weeks leading to the Dagarti Arts Residency.

Discussion to find out what students know about 'Africa' - varied cultures, traditions of many different countries and states. Where this knowledge comes from - need to research and be accurate in order to create; respect and understanding for another culture very different from our own. Arts linked in that drama almost always linked with music and dance.

Three Weeks

1.      Tradition and Ritual

        Gesture and choral speaking to create mood and atmosphere.
        Passing a gesture around circle using an image associated with
        e.g. water, land, sun, moon, everywhere.

2.      In groups, work on a short sequence to include words and
        movements.

3.      Use of narrator and chorus to tell a traditional story; e.g. Fire and
        Forest land (Zaire). Group work on a presentation of the story.

        Mime, dialogue and. story teller.  Possible use of drum beat etc.

Four Weeks

4.      The Lost Valley. Exploration project from 'Drama Structures'.
        (Linked more with an undiscovered area - lost people etc.)

**Dagarti Arts - Tile Panels Project** with Year 6 from Potley Hill
Juniors and Year 7 from Frogmore Community School. Completed
December 1993.

This was my first project as Artist-in-residence at Frogmore. Both the
schools would be working with members from the Dagarti Arts Dance
Company in separate workshops where they would learn to play Ghanaian
instruments and perform dances and songs. The project would end in a
public performance which would involve all the children and others from
Newlands Primary School and Charles Kingsley C.E. Primary School.
        As the children would be working together in groups I decided that
making a tile panel with each year would be an interesting way of portraying
the given theme : fishing communities.
        The first week I introduced the children to the fishing theme and
explained that they were going to all make one tile each which would in
some form tell a story.
        They then had to think of a story amongst themselves which would
relate to a Ghanaian fishing community. Once they had thought of their
stories they then had to draw it as a panel of 20cm by 50cm (10cm x 10cm

each tile). This proved quite difficult at first but eventually each group managed to draw out their story over the ten squares. Then each child was allocated a square. This was to be the design that would become a tile. The designs varied from different stores, i.e. ten different actions, one per tile, to one large picture covering ten tiles.

Once the tiles were rolled out, children sketched their designs into the clay. This had to be accurate as many of the children were working in pairs with their designs and in most cases the designs overlapped into neighbouring tiles.

Once the drawings were completed in the soft clay, the children then began to build up the clay into various forms and shapes in relation to their designs.

This gave the tiles a 3D surface. The children rolled small pieces of clay into 'sausage shapes' and stuck these onto their tiles, outlining many of the sketches, like - boats, fish, men and nets. This was the last stage in the actual making of the tile, the next stage was the decoration.

I wanted to keep the decoration as simple as possible to avoid overcrowding on the finished piece. They painted the tiles with slip and used a few glaze stains to add on to brighten them up.

The tiles were then biscuit fired, then the children glazed them with transparent glaze, these were then refired.

Once the panels were finished they were displayed in the school reception area. They received a very good response from the staff and the pupils and on the whole I felt that the project was a success. The children really enjoyed working in the clay, they all worked well together in the groups. The Dagarti Arts residency finished off the whole project spectacularly. All the children were involved in some way or other and felt that they all learned a great deal, not just about clay but also about working with each other and working together as a community.

In addition to these, the Dance work done was based on videos of performances by two other groups; 'Adzido' and 'Irie'.

It is quite possible to see how each area links to the overall theme and intention of the project, with many interesting, creative and challenging ideas. However, while there is a clear overt intention to demonstrate integration of creative areas, its outworkings are not always so apparent. It may be that this is inevitable as soon as areas are approached as discrete entities. The alternative might be for all teachers involved to develop skills in all areas, in the way the students are expected to, but the time for training to facilitate that may not exist.

During their week's residency Dagarti Arts worked with each school for one day, and students were selected from those workshops to spend more time with the group on the final day, leading to the evening performance. 10 to 12 students were selected from each primary school, and 15 to 20 from Frogmore School. There was reassurance for many students through the preparatory work, and this also enabled a feeling of continuity, rather than perceptions being of a one-off event, with no link to life or school. The essence of the project was:

> A fishing community celebrates the fishing season offshore and on land with storytelling using song, dance and music. The themes for the students' work were Time, Chores, Travel, Action and Atmospheres.

The title for the complete piece was *Nuba-Sier* (fishing season celebration), which consisted of the following sections:

1. *Yekyela-Solong* :   story and dance
2. *Ing ye-yaa* :   rites dance
3. *Adava* :   solo
4. *Wuldrum* :   rhythms and chant
5. *Bari* :   cleansing dance, solo
6. *Zunyarbo* :   fishing dance
7. *Napoo* :   celebration dance, duet
8. *Sami* :   rain dance

The media would be live drumming, percussion, songs and chants. The students concentrated on studying:

1. *Yekyela-Solong* :
6. *Zunyarbo* :
7. *Napoo* :

Each workshop session was led by two or more members of the group, with any school staff joining in with the children. The general pattern for a session was:

1. Learn the rhythm/beat pattern.
2. Learn the dance step.
3. Learn how to 'travel' with the step.
4. Learn the extended pattern using the step.

The evening performance had a first half of students and Dagarti Arts showing the work completed during the residency. The second half was a complete performance of Nuba-Sier by the full company of Dagarti Arts, with students joining in all the songs they knew.

How did everyone react to the residency? Teachers thought it was extremely successful, generating much energy, excitement and enthusiasm, amongst student participants and the audience. Within the school the event was seen as very successful, with *almost* all comments being positive; the main problem being that more areas wished they could have been involved, although timetable restrictions were the principal obstruction to that. The performance itself was summed up as 'moving'.

The Headteacher at Frogmore wrote:

> The work of Dagarti Arts at Frogmore undoubtedly enriched the educational experiences of both the student body and staff. It raised awareness in the local community of the worth and relevance of extending the cultural experiences of the pupils. The skills, knowledge and understanding of the Dagarti Arts team has enabled us to provide both cross-curricular opportunities for the student body as well as develop cross-phase liaison with primary and infant schools. An arts programme based around a whole cultural experience really does bring the music, dance, art and drama to life as well as provide a very practical historical and geographical context. I found that the student body were extremely challenged by the various aspects of the learning and the end focus of a performance created a fitting climax to a comprehensive programme of study.

Dagarti Arts themselves felt it had been a very successful residency in fulfilling all objectives, with a lot of effort from all involved; parents, students and teachers, and that the whole experience had been enjoyable. On a personal level they had also felt very well looked after and appreciated the letters and drawings they received from students after the week in Frogmore.

As for the children's perceptions, below are summaries of comments made by 70 of the Year 7 students on a questionnaire completed nine months after the residency.

## What did you enjoy most?

Music:        The different music ... making foreign music ... the music is fun ... the singing ... listening to all of the music ... the music they played ... learning complex rhythms

Instruments :  Playing the instruments for dancers ... playing an African instrument ... listening to all the different instruments played together ... playing the drums

Dancing:      Learning different dancing ... learning different type of moves and skills ... the little dances became the steps were easy to learn

Story Element:    Taking part in a story ... learning dances with a story to it

Performing:   Performing in front of the parents ... the performance

Culture/Content:
              Learning about African music and people ... the way they taught us some ways of life in Africa ... learning about their culture

Challenge:    Although it was hard work it was fun, and the people were really nice ... there were so many things to learn ... it was unusual ... taking part ... it was different from our usual work ... it was a totally new experience for me

Group's Qualities:
              They put a lot of effort in it to make it fun for us. I liked the way they tried to involve every student ... they were very friendly ... playing the music with them ... when they taught us the dances they looked like they were really happy

**The items commented on most were:**

| | |
|---|---|
| Dancing | 24 comments |
| Playing instruments | 17 |
| Music | 14 |
| New Dances | 13 |
| New music | 12 |
| Performing in front of others | 7 |
| Everyone joining in | 7 |
| Story element | 6 |
| Group's qualities | 6 |
| Culture and content | 5 |
| Listening to the whole group | 4 |
| Fun | 4 |
| African/foreign music | 4 |
| Singing | 3 |
| Complex rhythms | 2 |

**What did you enjoy least?**

Music: The singing because I didn't understand the words I was singing ... the music because I had the little instruments ... when they played the music ... the singing because I couldn't say them right ... the singing at first but in the end it was OK

Instruments: Playing the instruments-because it was hard to learn the notes

Dancing: Taking part in the dancing ... that we had to dance around (it was fun though) ... the dance as I always got it wrong ... some of the dancing they did ... dance, I think it was because it was unusual and I had never tried it and I was a bit wary

Performing : Showing it to other people ... having to show our pieces of work to the rest of the class ... the nervousness before the show

Group's Qualities:
The jokes and stories, I didn't think they were funny

Waiting:  Waiting for my turn to dance ... waiting to see if I was picked ... sitting around waiting to take part ... watching other people play the instruments when I did not get a chance to play them

Preparation and Follow Up:  Writing about it ... all the talk about it

Costumes:  Mine was very baggy

Nothing:  I didn't really not enjoy anything ... there was nothing boring or least enjoyed ... nothing because it was such fun and we all had a really good time

**The items commented upon most were:**

| | |
|---|---|
| Dancing | 14 |
| Singing | 9 |
| Nothing | 8 |
| Performing before others | 8 |
| Music | 5 |
| Being nervous | 5 |
| Costumes | 4 |
| Waiting | 4 |
| Not playing the instruments | 3 |
| Written work | 2 |
| Noise | 1 |
| Waiting for selection | 1 |
| Playing instruments | 1 |
| Dancing in small groups | 1 |
| Length of the day | 1 |
| Jokes | 1 |

**It is worth noting the items that occur in both lists:**

Dancing, Performing in front of others, Music, Playing instruments.

This serves to make the point that it is a virtually impossible task to find an activity that will satisfy all completely. It is also possible, however, to pick out items that might be adjusted for future occasions: Performing in front of others, Being nervous, Costumes, Waiting, Written work.

## What was learnt about Ghanaian music?

Repetition:     It needs repetition (7 comments) ... nearly all the same (2) ... didn't have to be exactly the same all the time (1)

Instruments:    Types of instruments (17) ... mainly percussion instruments (1) ... not just played on drums (2) ... instruments are often handmade (4) ... can be played on any instrument (1) ... you don't need electricity to make good music (2) ... drum is used to show movement (1)

Rhythm:         Rhythms including polyrhythms and accents (11) ... is not only about the beat (1) ... fast (1)

Links :         Mostly linked to stories (6) ... links with dance (6)

Value :         It's more interesting than people dancing in funny costumes (3) ... fun (4) ... more complex than I thought (1) ... can be played by anyone (2)

Difference :    It was different from 'our' music (8)

This seems to show a high degree of understanding and learning through the complete project, including preparation and the residency itself.

## What was disliked about Ghanaian music?

Repetition:     It went on with the same drone (1) ... all the same (16)
Instruments:    It doesn't use electric guitars (1) ... some instruments didn't suit music (1)

Links :         Jumping around (1) ... the dances (because you looked silly) (2) ... song doesn't go with the dance (1) ... linking dance to music (1)

Nature of Music:

Weird singing (2) ... started slowly and got faster (1) ... the use of patterns in the music (1) ... it got louder and then got quieter (1) ... bit slow (1) ... fast: (3) ... you have to keep time really well (1) ... too loud (1)

Difference/Difficulty:     A bit strange (1) ... it's hard (6) ... it's different (2) ... needed jazzing up (2) ... I didn't understand (4)

It is interesting to note the elements discussed in Ghanaian music that were disliked: Repetition, Instruments, Links with other arts, Difference.

The main problem appears to be use of repetition, and the perceived difficulty of the music. It can also be observed that most of the dislikes are voiced by very small numbers of children. It is perhaps put into perspective by the comments made by the students on the Dagarti Arts group and the whole experience which follow.

## Comments on Dagarti Arts Group and Performance

Really good ... music was always on beat and time ... brilliant ... great fun ... good and funny ... clever dancing ... excellent. They taught me a lot and I learned a lot .. funny, lively and exciting ... they made us feel that we were all ready with what we were doing ... they combined the dance, music, songs and fun ... they were caring and made us a part of the goings on ... they really enjoyed their work ... Dagarti Arts worked hard with us and were patient ... they were great teachers ... they made the learning fun and exciting ... can they come again? They are very talented at their work ... many parents walked away with smiles on their faces and I don't think the performance could be any better ... I think a good 9 out of 10 as they put up with us for a long time and their show was very good ... (59 positive comments).

It was OK ... I don't think they had enough instruments ... it was a bit confusing ... it was a shame that not everyone got in the main performance ... (5 negative comments).

This contains many comments that would delight everyone involved in organising the project, and several that could be dealt with on any future occasions .

For comparison a summary is included of the responses to the 1992 residency, which involved Year 9 students, in which items also mentioned in the 1993 survey are marked *.

## 1992 Questionnaires (64 Responses)

| Most Enjoyed: | | | Least Enjoyed: | |
|---|---|---|---|---|
| * | Dancing | 42 | * Nothing | 18 |
| | Singing | 20 | * Singing | 8 |
| * | Drumming | 6 | * Learning Instruments | 7 |
| | Missing lessons | 6 | * Dancing | 5 |
| * | Playing instrument | 5 | * Being tired out | 5 |
| * | Performance | 4 | Repetition | 4 |
| * | Fun | 4 | Singing alone | 2 |
| * | Music | 3 | Bit boring | 1 |
| | Everything | 3 | Acting | 1 |
| * | Good rhythm | 2 | Can't understand words | 1 |
| * | Seeing something new | 1 | Being 'picked on' | 1 |
| * | Feeling part of their culture | 1 | | |
| | Happy atmosphere | 1 | | |
| | Beat | 1 | | |

### Group's Qualities

Positive: 53          Negative: 6

Again we see an overwhelmingly positive appraisal of the experience.

It seems appropriate to finish this review of the children's views by quoting two letters that were sent to the Dagarti Arts group after the visit.

2nd December 1993

Dear Mario, CK, Mannie, Chancy and Evia

Thank you very much for the lovely day working with you. The rhythm of the music made me want to dance about and when I was allowed to dance the music just carried me along. I especially liked playing the drums. When I found out that I was chosen to play in the concert I was really happy. I never thought that it would be me.

It was much much better than I thought it would be and it was the best experience I have ever had on a class trip. I liked hearing and trying to remember the names of all of the instruments the only one I can remember is Gymbay.

I am looking forward to seeing you on Friday and meeting all the other children taking part.  I think that this will be one of the very rare performances that I don't lie awake at night worrying about!

I really enjoyed the dance because it was fun to do and I liked it when the girls refused the boys.

I am getting my family to buy tickets so that they can feel the catchy rhythm of the music too.

6.12.93
Dear Dagarti Arts,

I think the drums are brilliant and all the instruments are very exciting. Thank you for teaching us dancing.

I liked the story about the fishing festival and the song about the chief's wife. I liked playing the drums I know what it feels like to be a drummer it really hurts your hands after a while. I would like to live in Africa.

With significant appreciation expressed by students of the residency as shown in both surveys (1992 and 1993), it should be possible to identify and assemble the constituent parts of this success. The following diagrams are an attempt to do this:

**1. The choice and combination of activities:**

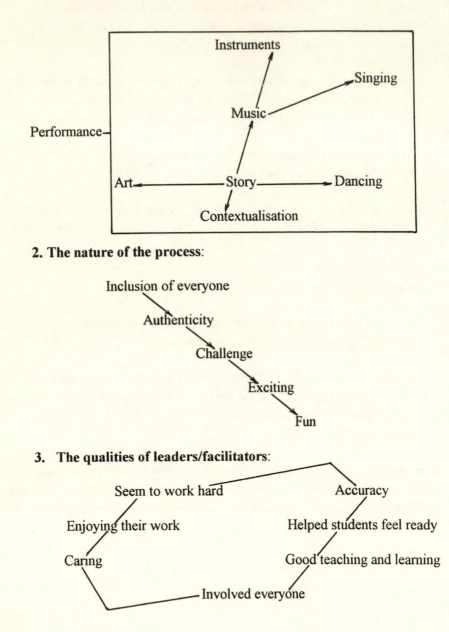

**2. The nature of the process:**

Inclusion of everyone

Authenticity

Challenge

Exciting

Fun

**3. The qualities of leaders/facilitators:**

Seem to work hard            Accuracy

Enjoying their work        Helped students feel ready

Caring                Good teaching and learning

Involved everyone

Furthermore, this was something that worked because of the preparation which, as was seen earlier, involved:

- Setting aims for residency (intercultural arts development, outreach)
- Choice of group (based on own and others' experiences )
- (Self) selection of participants
- Establish method of organisation (committee)
- Find funding
- Set up administration
- Organise publicity
- Set up liaison with groups
- Allot tasks to named individuals
- Liaison with group members on specifics
- Draw up schemes of work for preparatory sessions
- Lead into activity.

This is, of course, not the only possible model, but it is at least one that has been tested and found to be successful.

The prime requirements for setting all this up are time and commitment from staff involved, and there are already plenty of demands on these. But the responses we have seen from students involved are remarkably close to unanimity in their enthusiasm, and we have seen the evidence of growing understanding of, and respect for, another world culture. If these are the outcomes and achievements then perhaps all the effort is well directed and valuable.

# Directions for Music Education in Africa

*Mepal oloitiko isirat lenyena*
A Zebra does not despise its own stripes
(Maasai proverb)

We are used to thinking about the multi-cultural nature of modern Britain, but this is the situation in many other countries. These also have to make decisions about the way in which music education may be influenced by the nature of society, and also how it might be employed in an attempt to influence that same society. It would have proved unwieldy within the scope of this book to try and look at the whole world, so we have chosen to look at one continent, Africa, and two countries, Ghana and Kenya, who are faced with a colonial inheritance, and strong indigenous musical traditions. What decisions are these countries making about World Musics while not despising their own musical 'stripes'?

# 8 Music Education in Ghana: The Way Forward

*James Flolu*

## Educational Reforms and Music Education in Ghana

The year 1987 was a watershed in Ghana's educational system: the old system of schooling gave way to the new structure of education. This has necessitated radical innovations in both the structure and content of the country's educational system. The total period of schooling at pre-university level has been reduced from 17 to 12 years, while university education increases from 3 to 4, or 5, years. New subjects, syllabuses and textbooks have been introduced, and older ones revised.

Under the new structure often referred to as the 6-3 - 3-4 system of education, Ghana has

a) a nine-year Basic Education Programme consisting of six years Primary and three years Junior Secondary schools;
b) a three-year Senior Secondary (including other technical and vocational institutions); and
c) a four-year University or Tertiary education.

Music education has been at the centre of these changes. Yet music educators find themselves in an awkward situation. While there is little disagreement on the content of the music syllabus for Senior Secondary Schools (SSS) at the basic level, conflicting opinions and objectives between the curriculum planners on one hand, and the music teachers on the other, have dominated the debates on the place of music in the new system of education.

After a general review of the status of music in the current educational system by music teachers attending the 'Orientation Course for Senior Secondary School Teachers' at Obuasi in January 1991, it became clear to them that unless they revised their strategies, music faced the threat of becoming neglected and being abandoned by SSS students. Some music teachers had already been warned by their heads of being made redundant in view of the insufficient number of Junior Secondary School (JSS) leavers who had registered to study music at SSS level. Up to the present few Senior Secondary Schools are offering music. The appointment of a music teacher in most schools is justified by his or her ability to teach other subjects, and/or to maintain a school choir.

Although it was apparent that the standard of the SSS music syllabus was high compared with that of the JSS, it was generally agreed that the absence of competent music teachers in the JSSs was responsible for the low enrolment. Subsequently, participants - mostly diplomats and graduates - expressed the view that a recommendation be made to the Ministry of Education to post qualified music teachers to the JSS in order to prepare the ground for the study of SSS music.

Some also suggested that music should be made a compulsory subject for all SSS students, thus sharing the same view with Okafor (1991) on music education in Nigeria.

The current wisdom behind World Bank educational projects in African countries is that 'investments in primary education yield a higher social rate of return than investments in secondary education' (Samoff, 1993: 202). Acknowledging that effort at higher levels of the educational system has been misplaced may not readily attract a consensus among educators. It is, however, quite reasonable to assert that, despite government and educational policy statements regarding the importance of basic level (elementary sector) education, attempts at curriculum innovation in music education in Ghana have been extraordinarily timid.

Music education in Ghana needs to be completely re-structured in order to bring it in tune with the realities of the environment and to make new and innovative ideas naturally assimilable to its life. As Carl Orff says,

> Just as humus in nature makes growth possible, so elementary music gives to the child powers that cannot otherwise come to fruition. It is at the primary school age that the imagination must be stimulated and opportunities for emotional development which contain experience of the ability to feel and the power to control the expression of that feeling must be provided.
> Orff, 1978: 245)

What we have at the present has been repeatedly criticised and shown to be unsatisfactory. In 1973, Offei, building on analytical data of folk music, argued that elementary music education should be made the spring board of the entire structure. Other Ghanaian writers have made similar suggestions. Although the problems have been continually pointed out, to date, no firm proposals have been made on how to introduce any variety in the singing lessons at the elementary level, and in particular how to make use of the musical resources of the environment.

## Music in Cultural Education

Since the 1960s attempts have been made to adapt the content and methods of education in Ghana to suit local needs and environments. The teaching of Ghanaian culture has been stressed. Thus the Cultural Studies Programme was developed in 1987 for Primary and Junior Secondary schools, and in 1988 for Teacher Training Colleges. Music, Dance, Drama and Folklore and Religious Knowledge are regarded by the Programme as basic components of Ghanaian culture. The planners take the view that these would:

> encourage the use of proverbs, essay writing, public speaking, riddles, tongue twisters, appellations (praise names etc.), poems and rhymes, etc. The pupils would be made to realise the richness of our musical heritage. Functionally, the music of our society reveals a great deal about beliefs and sentiments; often it is difficult to separate music from dancing and drama in a socio-religious context.
> (CRDD, 1987: 1)

Both the objectives and the content of the three syllabuses are the same, although they are more explicitly stated at the Secondary and Teacher Training College levels. The general course objectives of the JSS syllabus are that the pupils should be able to:

1. understand that culture is a way of life;

2. appreciate a great deal of the basic customary behaviour, also to accept relevant modifications as time goes by;

3. be in tune with a culture which is Ghanaian and can stand the test of time;

4. appreciate the way our people worship in relation to other religions.

5. develop the awareness that music permeates our way of life.

For Teacher Training Colleges two further objectives have been added; namely, to 'give students a better understanding of the nature of man and his environment' and 'enable them to appreciate the languages spoken in the community' (1988: 2).

From the above, ten objectives have been developed to enable the pupils to:

1.  identify types of music performed on different occasions, for example, dooring (the first time a new born baby is brought out of the birth room and shown to the public), marriage, puberty, death ceremonies, and so on;

2.  write out some rudiments of music, for example, note values, time values, the rhythm - the accent, kinds of time, grouping of notes and the construction of scales;

3.  indicate various rites in connection with ceremonies, for example, birth, puberty, marriage, death (emphasizing religious and social aspects);

4.  identify performing arts of the community, for example, music, drumming, dancing and drama (including patriotic songs);

5.  identify the social structure of Ghanaian society (that is to say the family set up);

6.  visualize the roles of the various Ghanaian social structures (for example, family kinship, clans etc);

7.  identify the traditional system of government;

8.  compare and contrast traditional and political systems of governments;

9.  list the main religious groupings within Ghanaian society;

10. differentiate between the various religious beliefs.

The only differences between the above objectives and those listed for the Teacher Training Colleges occur in number 2 where it reads, 'to read, perform and compose simple music for the occasions mentioned in item 1', and with the addition of an eleventh one, namely, 'to equip students with basic methodology in order to be able to teach the objectives outlined above' (1988: 3)

## Music in Contemporary Ghana

A recognizable fact is that developments in Ghana's musical culture have been more rapid and multifarious in the last three decades than in any other period; however, a full description of the situation is beyond the scope of this chapter. Whereas some of the types of folk music performed in the past are no longer performed - or where they are, not for exactly the same purposes for which they were in the 1950s and 1960s - others have changed completely in both structure and instrumentation.

In most cases the creation of new dances leads to a gradual displacement of existing ones. Often the new music incorporates the rhythm and songs of its contemporaries, leading to invigorating and captivating elements which tend to be more attractive. In Northern Eweland, for instance, *Dedeleme, Totoeme, Gumbe, Tudzi* and *Akpese* have been dominated by *Boboobo*, which can now be described as Northern Ewe national recreational music. In its formative years the bass drum, adapted from the elementary school band by *Tudzi* and *Akpese* remained its (the *boboobo's*) master drum until the *Boboobo vuga* was introduced. The *donno* (hourglass drum) has replaced the *pati*. The songs are not entirely indigenous like those of other Ewe dances; they are usually based on a blend of Western melodic patterns and traditional Ewe idioms reflecting its recency. Even so, the Boboobo continues to adopt musical ideas from modern forms of popular music; the conga, for example, comes from the dance band. We now hear of Funk and Reggae Boboobo. Some bands use the trumpet, instead of the bugle with which Boboobo music is associated, the bugle itself having replaced the whistle in Akpese, the immediate precursor of the Boboobo. Boboobo rhythms are now widely used in the Christian churches which hitherto had treated it with hostility. For its part, the Boboobo has adopted church music - hymns - and this has made it more acceptable to Christian practices.

Similar developments can be noticed in Ghanaian Highlife. It is becoming increasing difficult to distinguish between the highlife and Gospel band music in terms of structure and instrumentation; the only noticeable difference being the use of Christian religious text in the latter's case. Furthermore, some Gospel band musicians have been borrowing heavily from fine art music, and gradually developing a distinct choral art form; the use of a large chorus supported by dance band musical instruments is relatively modern.

The incorporation of traditional forms of music into church activities has brought about new forms which are neither Western nor purely traditional. A typical example is the music of the church youth bands, popularly known in the Volta Region as *Kantata* bands. The songs lean towards Western idioms but the rhythm of the drums presents a very complex picture. However, it is easy to hear a mixture of *agbadza* (Anlo community dance), *atsyiagbekor* (Anlo warrior dance drama) and *yeve* (cult music of the Anlo) rhythms. The fact that the drums are also of Anlo origin supports this supposition. Practically, even though Kantata music can be classified as a distinct musical type, the repertoire of the bands is very wide. During a performance a band may decide to improvise on other musical types of the community, depending on the nature of the occasion and the kind of audience involved. This habit has recently been in vogue due to the gradual removal of the barriers between church music and indigenous Ghanaian music.

The attempt at integrating traditional music into Christian worship has been more radical in some churches. The *gyile* (xylophone) now functions as the church organ among the Catholic churches of Northern Ghana. Frequently too Dagare seasonal songs are sung at church to the accompaniment of the *gyile*. While in the Catholic churches in Ashanti, special *nnwonkoro* (a recreational dance of Ashanti women) songs have been composed and sung at various stages of the mass, in Eweland, *ampoti* (warrior calls) have been adapted. In some churches Biblical texts are frequently substituted where indigenous words are considered unsuitable for Christian worship. When attending important church ceremonies the Moderator of the Evangelical Presbyterian church walks to the rhythm of *atumpan* drums, resembling the appearance in public of an Ewe paramount chief.

There is a long tradition of singing Western sacred anthems in the orthodox churches, a practice associated with the high level of Western formal education; however, the Musama Disco Christo Church (MDCC), a relatively new Christian sect, has a membership which is dominated by illiterates and uneducated persons. The current Head Prophet holds a Teacher's Certificate, compared with the PhD and Professorial status of the main church leaders. Nevertheless, looked at objectively, the music in the MDCC demonstrates a truly Ghanaian attitude to art music. No doubt traditional religious music is at the root of worship, structurally arranged to mark specific stages of the ceremony, though not without aesthetic considerations. The presentation of an art song during worship and the organization of choir rallies and competitions are common to all the churches, but the taste for Western sacred anthems and art music compositions of the Ghanaian 'masters', and a desire to achieve the highest level of musical excellence, are perhaps strongest in the MDCC. Artistic and aesthetic values are placed at the forefront and are manifest in the organisation of the 'Annual Choir Competition'. It is worth pointing out that people with little or no formal music education have a very strong taste for music generally considered to be technically challenging. The absence of a keyboard, or of orchestral instruments, does not inhibit the pursuit of this ambition. Excerpts from Handel's *Messiah* and Haydn's *Creation*, have been given 'a cappella'. Some critics have rightly considered the practice as an incomplete presentation of these scores. However, any observer would be amazed at how, for example, a conductor could dramatize the long instrumental links with hand gestures, with the singers making their entries so accurately and without panic, a practice students under formal music training would never attempt. Such musical sensitivity never goes without public applause.

This discussion of church musical activities is only intended to throw light upon current happenings. In the presentation of short compositions, whether Ghanaian or Western, it is fashionable for choirs to repeat them or find a suitable place for repetition even though it may not be indicated by the composer. In some cases, a solo, duet, or quartet may sing the whole piece or portion to be repeated before others join in again. This is an adaptation of the call and response style. It is usual for some conductors to ignore the composer's repetition marks and repeat the music from where, to them, is more artistically exciting. Furthermore some more elaborate pieces may be accompanied with Western instruments, often a keyboard where available, or, more frequently, with traditional percussion instruments. In other words, unless in competitions, in which case some limitations may be imposed as general rules, many singers and conductors have the tendency to add something of their own to the music to suit their interest and the purpose of the occasion: it is recomposition in performance. Although, by definition, this is not 'ethnic' music, the presentation - such as in the case of the MDCC - may conveniently be described as an ethnic approach to art music.

Another dimension of the ethnic approach can be discerned in the activities of Kofi Ghanaba (Guy Warren), the virtuoso Ghanaian drummer. When he first performed Handel's 'Hallelujah Chorus' on a set of *fontomfrom* drums at the Arts Centre in Accra, the immediate reaction from some music scholars was that he was making a mockery of 'music'. Yet that performance attracted - as his performances usually do - more than four times the number of the audience who would attend a concert presented by the National Symphony Orchestra, even if it was playing the same music. Ghanaba later toured Europe with 'Hallelujah Chorus' as the principal item on his concert programme list. Perhaps he attracted a great number of people for two reasons: familiarity with the drums; and the excitement of hearing and watching the drums in a new and different context from what they have been used to. There can be no doubt that something novel and original arises from Ghanaba's desire to give his own meaning to the music of 'the masters'.

Increasing knowledge of Western music theory and analytic technique has enabled Ghanaian composers to combine Western musical forms and chord progression with traditional African idioms in choral art music composition, producing what has become variously known as Western-derived African music, hybridised or syncretic music. Amu's 1933 'Twenty-five African Songs' is usually regarded as a useful pointer to the new musical endeavours to be followed by the works of Phillip Gbeho (composer of the National Anthem), Nketia, Nayo, Ammisah, Ndor and their students. Both Western and traditional Ghanaian instruments have also been fused in the larger forces, such as symphony orchestras, producing a tonal colour distinct from that of Beethoven or Mahler. Take for example, Kenn Kafui's 'Kale' (Bravery), a symphony written in the style of Ewe traditional military music, which uses indigenous sacred drums; and countless similar compositions of students graduating from the Universities and the National Academy of Music. N. Z. Nayo, conductor of the National Symphony Orchestra, is now regarded as the leading orchestral music composer, and his latest 'Volta Symphony' (employing a large variety of traditional instruments) has been widely acclaimed as a typically 20th century African composition. What are the implications of these developments for music education in Ghana?

## The Prospects of Creative Music in Ghanaian Education (toward a systematic philosophy of music education in Ghana)

Because both the Curriculum Enrichment and Cultural Studies Programmes - and indeed other attempts at reforming music education in Ghana - have been wrongly perceived as signifiers of the fight for cultural independence, they have resulted only in magnifying the existing gap between African music and Western classical music in schools. The crucial question is, can music teaching in Ghana not be based on African resources without necessarily continuing to be Western oriented and still share uniformity with the education systems of other countries? If not, why not? If yes, how?

The provision of effective music education should be put back into the wider context that encompasses national values, beliefs and objectives. Based upon current church musical activities the overall attitudes of Ghanaian choirs, the increasing number of musical groups and associations emerging from the hospitals, factories and government offices, this would seem to suggest that there is a growing interest in art music and, consequently, a demand for challenging pieces; a recognition of a distinction between music in social context and music in artistic context. The Cultural Policy of Ghana has among its objectives to 'act as the impetus for the evolution of a national culture from the plural cultural make up of our state, in a blend that acknowledges the vitality of each individual component culture' (CNC, 1990: 4). With regard to the arts, the policy states that:

> The State shall preserve, promote and establish conducive conditions for creativity by encouraging the establishment of strong national professional associations for artists, authors, dramatists, films makers etc. and shall promote and encourage the establishment of writers' clubs, art clubs, creative centres, for encouraging creativity and popularising the arts.
> (CNC, 1990: 11)

It goes on to say:

> The State shall guarantee freedom of artistic expression, institutional and infrastructural provisions for housing and developing the arts, and promote competitions, expositions and talent hunts in all the arts; it shall also see to the protection of traditional, natural contexts for aesthetic expression (p. 12).

Elsewhere in the document it is recommended that a National Gallery be established

   a. to serve as repository for artistic creations since the birth of the country as a nation,

   b. to promote the creative genius in Ghanaian artists, and

c. to promote research, art education and appreciation. (p. 14)

In the light of these recent developments, it is important for arts educators also to consider the need to increase social awareness and patronage for proper artistic appreciation. However; more thought has to be applied to the traditional settings in which African folk arts are practised so that presentation in modern theatres does not distort completely the original artistic elements and values inherent in them. Much effort is needed to establish a medium through which the skills and ideas of traditional artists, arts organisations, educational institutions, and architects are brought together to design theatre houses which are sympathetic to the African environment, able to sustain, captivate and increase the participatory level of the Ghanaian public, as well as provide innumerable opportunities for attracting the interest of the foreign audience.

Creating a national culture is an inter-ethnic task, which calls for cooperation with specialists from other arts - drama, dance, fine art and craft - as well as with other agents, politicians, cultural officers, writers and publishers. Also, uniting the diversities of indigenous cultures is an artistic task. It is a creative activity which involves the process of 'selection and rejection', 'thinking and making', 'reflection in action'. What is being sought is a national arts culture and all the arts must contribute to this selection from the 'socio-cultural group's stock of valued traditional and current public knowledge, (artistic) conceptions and experiences...' (Bullivant, 1981 cited in Hoskyns, 1992: 98). True national cultural education, however, begins only when students confront the complexities of intercultural relationships and of the resulting artistic and aesthetic problems. The study of music in culture should therefore be aimed at enhancing people's feelings, critical and creative thinking, and imagination in music and art in order to reinforce the public's capacity for change and promote growth in our artistic and aesthetic sensitivities.

Inevitably, with the introduction of the Cultural Studies Programme, the need for a completely new attitude toward music teaching is being recognised. Despite its flaws, the Cultural Studies Programme tries to confront the reality of diffraction in African culture. The syllabus presents us with the collisions and contradictions of perspective. It is up to music educators to make musical sense of it, because it is no longer a matter of the coexistence between Western music and traditional African music in schools and colleges.

To appreciate the value of African folk music and the power it exerts on its listeners we must begin not by prettifying its social and cultural factors and comparing it with an 'illusionary prestigious' Western classical music, but by putting it independently in its own emerging artistic context. Looking at it as folk music versus art music rather than as indigenous music versus western classical music could give a better sense of direction. It is by understanding the influence of development on indigenous music itself and the resulting musical styles that we can best discern the creative impact of ethnic music on contemporary Ghanaian society.

Music education's task today lies not just in making children interested in folk music but in how its practice can help them to develop a positive and responsive attitude to music and art of all kinds. As Ross (1984: x) has argued, the challenge is to help students 'establish firm and sensitive ties between their formative feelings and the materials and artifacts which they encounter'. Accordingly. the 'function of arts in general education is to give children - by whatever means and in whatever medium - experience of the sacred and of the numinous. Not by information but by experience' (Ross, 1984: x; c.f. Paynter, 1982: 24). Education becomes meaningless if it fails to provide students with an understanding of their experiences. 'By the same token, music education fails if it does not help them understand their musical experiences' (Tait, 1992: 532).

According to Omibiyi (1972), music education in Africa should be able:

1.  to alter the attitude of African school children from one of cultural inferiority to that of cultural relativism.

2.  to develop a musicianly enlightened public.

3.  to provide a strong foundation of music education for future African music specialists.

There is some agreement between these views and those of the Ghana Music Teachers' Association (GMTA), adapted from the US:

GMTA shall conduct programmes and activities to build:

A vital musical culture,
An enlightened musical public . . .[and]
A Comprehensive music programme in all schools (GMTA, 1992: 20).

Music education must now focus on music as an aspect of the national culture. Its aim should be to develop in the future generation the productive, perceptual and reflective abilities in art, in order to enable them to contribute to national artistic excellence through the medium of music. It should consider as part of its goal the creation of a 'musical heritage' derived from current practice, which will meet the challenges of the modern world, and which will facilitate a continuous development of children's musical abilities to the highest level possible. Class music should provide opportunities for all children to be exposed to and be encouraged to play with a wide and infinite variety of musical instruments and music's raw materials. The music education programme should be based on the following three interwoven objectives.

First, to build a strong desire in children to continue to participate in music actively and creatively.

Secondly, to nurture the ability of critical listening through improvisation and composition, performance, appreciation and enjoyment of music.

Thirdly, to enable them to develop the initiative and understanding on one hand, and the desire and admiration on the other, for creativity and artistic activities in general and in music in particular.

In addition, helping learners to understand the distinction between music generally intended for specific purposes (say dance, party, wedding, shopping, worship, drama) and music intended for purely artistic purposes can enhance their understanding of artistic phenomena. The development of the courage, dedication and capacity to search for the best means of expressing one's musical intentions should receive a great deal of attention.

There is an urgent need to reconsider the musical needs and capabilities of children and rekindle interest in the ideas and practices which we know of, but which had previously been excluded from our tactics. How can school music enrich the musical experiences and contribute to the development of the creativity of children? As John Paynter says;

All conscious musical experience is concerned with adventures of feeling, imagination and invention. These features link composing, performing and listening. and should presumably be given some prominence in music education (1992: 13).

Classroom composition is a high ideal. It is being practised in Britain and other European countries. And at least one study has demonstrated that Ghanaian secondary school students have the interest and capacity for classroom improvisation and composition, and music teachers showed some enthusiasm (Fadlu-Deen, 1989). However, no one has taken up the challenge. Yet the natural resources for it seem even more diverse in Ghana than in places where it has already taken root, and could even be introduced earlier than has been identified. Nevertheless, the circumstances in which classroom composition is being carried out in Europe and elsewhere are completely different from the Ghanaian situation. It would be futile to introduce such an activity in Ghanaian schools without first preparing the ground for it. Resources could be wasted if they are not guided by a meaningful purpose or if they are thrown into a vacuum.

To begin with, it requires an investigation of the social-cultural environment, the available infrastructure, the socio-economic situation, and the opportunities for harnessing human resources. A good seed also needs an equally rich soil and care in order to thrive. The question is whether the current classroom conditions and facilities are adequate to ensure success and continuity, and whether teachers are prepared or have been properly trained for it. A good educational principle can become faulty if it is introduced at the wrong time or to the wrong group. 'Time lost and opportunities neglected in early education can only be compensated for later on with great difficulty' (Meyer-Denkmann, 1977: 2). Therefore, some care is needed in finding a suitable starting point.

Providing an effective link between the home and the school will help to sustain the rate of the children's musical development. The primary task of the music teacher, therefore, is to consolidate the children's experience of their own music before they can successfully be taught the music of others. In this way the necessary basis for creativity, adventure, and imagination will be established so that new ideas and practices can be easily incorporated in the future.

Because of the natural interest in music, children possess a corpus of skills with which they can begin to explore the tonal resources of their surroundings; Coral Davis has warned recently that the tendency to base music education on the sequential model of development without further investigation into what young children are actually capable of doing 'may lead us to offer them an impoverished curriculum' (Davies, 1992: 47). For example, most of the instruments available to Ghanaian children are those they have constructed themselves, or are objects they have 'found' and adapted for musical reasons, and therefore are capable of manipulating very competently. (See Flolu 1994 for a detailed description of Ghanaian children's musical resources). School music can easily draw ideas and inspiration and proceed from the natural instincts of experimentation and inventiveness, with which the children are endowed. The success of the educational programme can be assessed by the contribution it makes to the development of these innate capabilities of children.

## Which Local Musical Resources?

Currently the most pervasively influential argument about instrumental music is based on the ever mounting pressure on schools to be more 'Ghanaian' in character. The playing of traditional Ghanaian instruments in schools has been advocated with the axiom that they are easy to acquire because they can be purchased locally. This is a logical argument. However, three factors work against their full use for academic purposes. First, experience shows that no school can afford them in sufficient quantities that would enable the majority of pupils to have access to them. Secondly, not enough is understood about how they should be used in the classroom for tuition and what exactly is expected of students. And thirdly, their absence on the list of examinable instruments in the West African based G.C.E. '0' Level Music Syllabus demeans their status in the eyes of both students and teachers who might have the interest and potential. In the present circumstances is it really worthwhile continuing to pay lip service to the use of indigenous musical instruments? Perhaps the time has come for us to tackle the issue from a more realistic point of view; as Cockburn (1987) has said, not too infrequently, when we look critically for solutions to most of our problems, we soon realise that they lie in bed with us every day; naturally, culturally and socially.

Children's instruments are made with local and natural materials, at very little or no cost; their use in schools would hardly make any substantial demand on the educational budget. They are simple and easy to handle. Most of them can be made any time they are needed, in so far as the local materials and resources make it possible, and indications are that the natural habitat and its resources will be intact for several decades.

Considering the enthusiasm and accuracy with which Primary and JSS pupils learn and perform traditional music, given the opportunity at school to continue to explore materials appropriate to their age and interests, some amazing results will be achieved. The need is for a strong basic education system which places emphasis, at elementary level, on children's music, instruments, and suitable 'found' sounds as the starting point of music education.

## A Musicianly and Integrated Approach

Real music making occurs outside the classroom and the school, but inside the community; music exists in our culture because it is created and recreated. Its teaching should also be seen as a process of musical creation. However, class music cannot be organised in exactly the same manner as people are seen to be involved with musical activities within the community.

Schools are artificial institutions designed by society to explore, analyze and criticise our culture in a special way. This critical and analytical function of the schools is expected to yield innovative results for the enrichment of culture (Swanwick, 1988: 117-118). It is, however, the things which go on outside the classroom that inform, challenge and supplement what is possible within the classroom, what teachers have to think about, and the extent of their achievements and failures. It therefore requires some ingenuity to cause students to experience and apprehend things they do at home in a different and unique way when they go through the same processes at school.

Essential aspects of Africanness in music making include the aural-oral and practical approaches. Indeed traditional African music itself has survived not because of the development of written notation but in spite of it. Music is a practical activity. Listening, observation and participation constitute the reciprocal dimensions in the development of musicianship. Musical memory and aural skills are not tested separately: they are demonstrated in the learner's attitude to music; musical analysis is an integral feature of music composition. The teaching of the rudiments and theory of music are also the making of music, and that is the ethnic essence. This oral ability, as illustrated earlier, enables Ghanaians to learn and perform with much ease art music of other cultures without knowledge or reference to written notation, though the music may be adapted to the performers' resources and interests.

In our discussions on music in Ghana, we noted the influence of the music of other cultures on indigenous Ghanaian music. All these, beyond the artistic aspiration, also portray the natural Ghanaian sense of choice and accommodation of external values found to be useful. In fact, Ghanaian culture is a hospitable one; or at worst, a greedy one. Naturally, it is a culture which is ready to absorb elements from any source - Western,

Arabic, Oriental and other African - in order to brighten its canopy, while at the same time strengthening its roots so as to be able to carry any additional load. That is why exclusive selection is no longer practicable. What could be musically and artistically beneficial is free borrowing from all the musical traditions we are now exposed to in order to develop a system which would provide insight into the legacies inherited from our former colonial masters. The task is for us to define an educational agenda which will synthesize indigenous culture and traditional orality with the literary and scientific resources of modern formal education. It is here that the ethnic attitude has practical relevance for music teaching and could be integrated into creative education. We shall call this a musicianly and integrated approach.

This would mean the application of the creative principles of ethnic music making to the education of children in the art of music. It should be a practical, inter-ethnic and inter-artistic approach to music teaching. Taking as its starting point the natural roots of the musical culture, we pursue musical learning and teaching with an exploration of the interrelationships of the creative elements in various ethnic music and its effluent styles. The underlying principle here is that no ideas must be rejected simply because they are foreign. They should be adapted and recreated according to Ghanaian resources. What is important for school education is to establish a firm grounding among children in this aural-oral and practical approach to the promotion of general musicianship as preparation for musical literacy in later years.

Opportunities should be created for young children to establish an understanding of musical form and structure. Utilising the creative impulse of children they should be encouraged to try out new musical structures by taking elements from various musical styles and putting them into new sound contexts. Through this, their insight into the process of structural organisation in music will be increased; their overall capacity for artistic creativity and musical imagination will be better enhanced.

The vital objective is not so much the learning of a particular music or type of music; rather, the stress should be on nurturing in children the ability to respond to music with ingenuity and thoughtful activity, and to develop in them the interest in experimenting and exploring new possibilities. The principle should be that, music is being made, and the primary goal is to seek ways of fostering a continuous growth and development of the indigenous creative attitude in children.

Before we tackle the classroom possibilities, it may be useful to tabulate the resources of this system.

| | |
|---|---|
| 1. Children's Music and Games | Children's Musical Instruments |
| 2. Indigenous Music | Indigenous music from other communities |
| 3. Traditional Pop | Highlife and Dance Band music |
| 4. Hymns, Spirituals and Gospel Music | Latin and Afro-American Pop |
| 5. Ghanaian art music | Art music from other nations |

By making children's musical resources the base, the teacher draws on and is informed by, ideas from the environment.

## Suggested Practical Activities

The practical classroom possibilities are enormous. What is being suggested here is not to replace the existing practices in connection with music and cultural festivals. We should focus on activities that could go on in the music classroom, during the two 35 or 40 minute lesson periods a week. Such festival celebrations should, however, be supplemental to classroom activities and be used as avenues for broadening children's musical and artistic experiences.

In the performance of both cradle songs and musical games, for example, a theme is introduced and the process is enlarged through addition, improvisation and extemporisation. In *kangbe* (Ewe children's game of stones with singing), for example, children may be encouraged to suggest new introductory activities: by varying the signal for attack, the rhythm of the movement of stones will automatically change. The stone may be hit on the floor twice, thrice, instead of once, or vice versa, as may be desired. This will also affect the rhythm of accompanying songs. The game does not have to be played with stones all the time. Children may substitute/add other instruments and objects; for example, paper drums, rattles, shakers, and stamped idiophones such as the bamboo band. Instead of hitting or stamping on the floor, suitable objects - *akaye* (gourd container rattle) and similar rattles - may be shaken, or swung. This will generate varying textures while at the same time call for a modification in the name of the introductory signal: 'bell, bell' (*dawuro, dawuro*), or 'rattle, rattle' (*akaye, akaye*) 'bamboo,

bamboo' (*mpamprom mpamprom*); in the appropriate local language this will be rhythmically exciting. Instrumental music playing should be integrated with all the suggested activities. *Asara* (scraped idiophone), for example, could be suitable for introducing the game. The reed pipes and bamboo flutes which are usually played in hocket fashion may also be tried.

Activities from two or more different games may be fused. For example, while one group of children play *kangbe*, a second group, in an outer circle, play *tsolotsolo* (a game of songs and clapping) or *atiee yaye* (a similar game with anti-clockwise movement). In this way, not only musical elements are being combined, but also layers of different patterns of movement and rhythm will be generated. The integration of music and movement is a natural activity among children and it is important that classroom lessons give it a creative dimension. This will challenge children's creative ability and will stimulate their imagination in linking movement and drama with aural activity.

An additional possibility is a third circle of instrumentalists playing the accompanying songs on bamboo flutes, papaw stalks, and so on. Again, it is possible to rotate musical leadership from singer to singer, singer to instrumentalist, and player to player. Of course, the choice of activities will depend on the basic principles of each game.

Another way of exploring the fusion of music, movement and drama is through the use of folk tale musical activities. Here, short stories and those related to the day to day experiences of children are most suitable. Children should be encouraged to make up their own stories and suggest stages when music and dance or drama can be  introduced. The celebration of a festival, church anniversary or a funeral ceremony, may be retold in story form with music depicting the various stages. Stories may also be based on life at home or some major activities of the school. Ideas from traditional dances should be incorporated. Stories can be mimed to the accompaniment of music and dance. The triologue between the bugle, master drum and dancers in *boboobo* could appropriately represent three different characters in a story; similarly, that between the *gyile*, singers and dancers in *Bawa* (a social dance of the Dagaaba of Northern Ghana) or the *atsyiagbeko*. These may be fused with ideas from concert bands. One child may suggest a story and the class will propose the accompanying musical activities. Special background sound effects may be created to accompany the narration. Musical ideas can also be abstracted from the story. Small group work should be encouraged. Below is a short story which illustrates one possibility.

Once upon a time, the King requested all the *asafo* in his kingdom to clear the forest and prepare the land for the new yam season. The forest covered an area of seven miles square and consisted of several big trees which needed to be felled. Heavy and sharp axes were required. So, the King went to a blacksmith to order a new set of tools. The blacksmith worked day and night, without any sleep, but it took him seven days to complete the job.

It is said that to ensure that the blacksmith completed the job on time, the King would send his servants to visit the blacksmith's workshop, and to come to report to him (the King) the progress of work. There were three servants who were not allowed to address the King in words, except by music and dance.

(A *glitefenoha* (verification) music can be introduced at this stage. It might use three different instruments to represent the three servants. If there should be some background music it could be provided on *dawuro, frekyiwa, gankogui* and/or other bells).

It is also said that it took the asafo another seven days to fell all the trees. Each day they went to work, the sound of chopping the trees echoed in surrounding villages and towns: 'kaka dzo kaka, kata dzo; kaka dzo kaka, kata dzo.

To show appreciation the King invited all the asafo and their wives to his palace for entertainment They ate, drank and made music. (What would this music be like?
 The sound and rhythm of 'kaka dzo kaka kata dzo' could become a central figure for improvisation.
Appropriate Dance and dramatic movements could be added).

Teachers should explore the integration of ideas from different musical types. There are three levels to this approach. First, is that within one ethnic tribe ( *nnwonkoro, asaadua* and *adowa* - Akan dances, or *bawa*, *takai* and *nagla* - Northern Ghanaian). The second is between music and dance of different localities; for example, between Akan and Ewe, Ewe and Ga-Adagnme, or Northern Ghanaian, Ewe and Ga. It is possible to combine the *adowa* bell pattern with that of *agbadza* and a tune in *nnwonkoro* with a rhythmic figure selected from *kpanlogo* (a neocolonial dance of the Ga for mixed group), boboobo, and so on. The third level involves integration between indigenous music and other modern, popular and art forms for example, *bosoe* (Fante traditional popular music), *nnwonkoro* and highlife. These can be appropriately distributed and rotated among groups of voices and instruments. Here is an example of a basic arrangement:

| Instrument | Dances |
| --- | --- |
| Rattles | agbadza |
| Flutes | adowa |
| Strings, e.g Kolgo | nnwonkoro |
| Drums/Bamboo band | kpanlogo |

The specific elements chosen, and the pattern and order of entries, will vary according to the particular group. This structure may be extended and altered to generate varying textures. For example, themes may be shifted, or exchanged between instruments to produce a longer cycle of musical events. Let us see how this could work within a five movement structure:

### First Movement

| *Instrument* | *Dances* | *Elements* (patterns, phrases, etc.) |
| --- | --- | --- |
| Rattles | Agbadza | axatse and gankogui |
| Flutes/Voices | Adowa | a tune |
| Strings | Nnwonkoro | tontonsansaen |
| Drums | Highlife | Conga |

### Second Movement

| *Instrument* | *Dances* | *Elements* (patterns, phrases, etc.) |
| --- | --- | --- |
| Rattles | Highlife | Conga |
| Flutes/Voices | Agbadza | axatse and gankogui |
| Strings | Adowa | tune |
| Drums | Nnwonkoro | tontonsansaen |

### Third Movement

| *Instrument* | *Dances* | *Elements* (patterns, phrases. etc.) |
| --- | --- | --- |
| Rattles | Nnwonkoro | tontonsansaen |
| Flutes/Voices | Highlife | Conga |
| Strings | Agbadza | axatse and gankogui |
| Drums | Adowa | tune |

## Fourth Movement

| _Instruments_ | _Dances_ | _Elements_ (patterns, phrases, etc.) |
|---|---|---|
| Rattles | Adowa | a tune |
| Flutes/Voices | Nnwonkoro | tontonsansaen |
| Strings | Highlife | Conga |
| Drums | Agbadza | axatse and gankogui |

## Fifth Movement

| _Instrument_ | _Dances_ | _Elements_ (patterns. phrases. etc.) |
|---|---|---|
| Rattles | Agbadza | axatse and gankogui |
| Flutes/Voices | Adowa | a tune |
| Strings | Nnwonkoro | tontonsansaen |
| Drums | Highlife | Conga |

Notice that the fifth movement is a repetition of the first. Each movement could be treated as a single unit or the whole structure may be taken as a long piece with subsections. Rests and varying elements could be introduced at some stages. But the length of pauses and the number of cycles in each movement depend upon the preferences of the group involved. Any movement could be taken as the beginning, but the cyclical effect should be maintained with dovetail entries.

Along the same line, dancing could be introduced at appropriate stages, but the steps will depend on what is taken to be the master instrument or the main theme in each movernent. It is important that students are encouraged to invent new dance movements, by alternating and combining foot steps, hand signs and other body and facial gestures from various idioms.

The fact is that children are not composing new rhythms or tunes; they are merely drawing new relationships between originally unrelated elements; combining them in novel ways thus deriving new meanings from them. This sort of activity is a route to innovation and originality. If well selected and coordinated the result could be an entirely new music. Here also, the choice of elements depends on some coherence and what the class finds interesting. However, more of the recreational musical types should be used. This is because they are simpler and also their forms and structures are usually open: a successful presentation depends upon the creative improvisation of the performer(s).

Instrumental music playing should begin with what the children usually play on the instruments. Then other music will be adapted to the instruments. Children are to explore with new tonal colours and textures. The combination of plucked string instruments, with pipes and mirlitons and various groupings can be employed in the playing of traditional as well popular school songs.

There will be several limitations in terms of the capabilities of children's instruments, especially if they are employed in the playing of adult music. We must expect that any attempt to play more formal compositions may lead to 'distortions'. The purpose of playing such music is not to make an accurate presentation of 'that music' but to encourage children to explore and improvise on the artistic elements in the music they hear or play. With this attitude, the playing of any music will not be restricted by lack of 'authentic' instruments. In fact few or no basic schools have a complete set of instruments to present the full score of much of the existing instrumental music compositions. Moreover, even if they can afford it, very few basic schools have electricity to be able to use the electronic equipment and instruments to play pop and highlife music, for instance. Yet it is not a reason to exclude their performance from the programme. The *kolgo* (two-stringed instrument) and other plucked strings could suitably be employed as guitar whilst papaw stalks and similar objects could do well for wind instruments.

Whatever the music is, both rhythm and melodic instruments should be used, children responding to the music with what is at hand. Melody may be sacrificed for rhythm, and harmony for tone colour and texture. The overriding objective is to achieve some freshness and pleasure, and increase children's interest in instrumental music, whilst at the same time, developing in them a wide repertoire and fluency in handling musical material. Interest in improvisation and composition is being inspired.

The class should be encouraged to make up their own instrumental preludes, interludes or accompaniments to the songs they sing or are taught at school. Does the character of a particular song suggest an instrumental introduction? Which combination of instruments, melodic, percussion or mixture? Which type of idiom will be suitable, highlife, *agbadza*, or *adenkum*? These are some of the questions which may come to mind. Whereas Dosoo's 'We are all involved' is usually sung or played to marching rhythms, Amu's 'Yen Ara Asase Ni' is accompanied with highlife. It is possible to experiment with other idioms for varying effects. The class can try out several alternatives and choose the most musically interesting. Take, for example, Amankwa's 'Maye Kom'. Sing it first to highlife, then to Gospel band, reggae, or funk. We could also sing it to other indigenous rhythms, *apatampa* (Fante traditional music), *bosoe*, or *gebolo* (traditional recreational music of Ewe women).

Usually, the bamboo band goes quite well as rhythmic accompaniment to songs in highlife or other popular idioms or songs which require dance or some form of body gestures. Wind instruments, such as flutes. are suitable for more serious music. Borrowing and mixing ideas from different styles is possible here too. For example, *gankogui* and *axatse* patterns in *agbadza* - along with those of *adowa* and highlife - are so commonly employed today that they can be regarded as national rhythms and not just those of one music or tribe. One can hear choral compositions written in other traditional idioms rendered to the accompaniment of *agbadza*. However, experience shows that it is not so much the ability to play horizontally the rhythm of *axatse*, for instance, as the abilities to coordinate shaking, hitting (on thigh) and patting (with the palm) and keep this motif in time with other instruments, singing, and dancing for a relatively long period within a proper performance context. And this should be the concern of music teachers. Rattles made from cans and tins, and those collected from plants could be used for class lessons.

To pursue the foundation for improvisation we may adapt the pattern of follow-up or progressive rhymes. Divide the class into two or more small groups of pairs, singers and instrumentalists with players imitating the singers, phrase by phrase. Both solo and chorus imitations should be employed. Poetry may also be integrated. A verse is recited and instruments try to respond musically. *Asara* and other concussion instruments could be very effective in this sort of activity. This idea can also be extended to involve pairs of instruments, between a wind and a string, or a melodic and non-melodic instrument.

Now, teachers and composers will be faced with the challenge of making up and composing simple music for the various instruments for use in class. School bands can be reintroduced with a careful selection and combination of children's instruments. The *atenteben* combined with other bamboo flutes and melodic instruments could be suitable. When children know that there is music for their instruments at school, the construction of more instruments will be especially exciting. Almost certainly they will receive support and assistance from parents

Small group and solo performances on melodic as well as percussion instruments should begin as early as possible. Teaching should now focus on performance techniques and building up the players' artistic, musical confidence. It would be good to encourage the development of proficiency on an instrument in which the student is interested. The *atenteben*, *kolgo* and *xylophone* are good starting points but others should also be fully utilised.

Those interested in drumming could pursue the skill on selected master drums. For example, the *sogo* player should work toward the mastery of the repertoire of dances in which *sogo* functions as a principal instrument in Ewe culture. This will also involve the acquisition of a wide range of sonic mnemonics and burden texts associated with *sogo*. The interrelationship between the *sogo*, *kidi* and the dancer is one that could provide ideas for spontaneous creativity, and students should be encouraged to make up their own texts.

To work towards improvisation in drumming, there should be a conscious effort to equip children with the various techniques of linear and stress diversification by which timbral differentiation can be achieved. These may involve muffling the drumhead, beating on the centre or near the rim of the drum, combining beating the drumhead and beating on the drum shell, drubbing, patting or bouncing the hand on the drumhead, striking it with the fingers or with open or cupped palm or fist, with or without stress and so on (see Mensah, n.d: 8). In all these, paper and rubber drums could be employed for classroom purposes.

The vocabulary of varying pitch and timbre is the same on all other drums. Emphasis should be placed on how to combine these snippets and other drum strokes (for example see Kwami 1989) as improvisatory techniques within proper performance contexts.

The atumpan drummer should be familiar with, first, the contexts in which the instrument functions as a speech surrogate, secondly, its dance idioms and thirdly, how drum poetry is integrated into dance music. *Atumpan* playing in schools should emphasize:

1.  the skill and technique of playing

2.  the speaking nature of the drums

3.  the language of the drums (which, like any other form of poetry, is different from ordinary speech)

4.  the techniques of composing appropriate drum poetry

5.  group instruction rather than of selected pupil drummers

6.  composing and performing with special texts, appellations, praises and proverbs in various Ghanaian languages including English.

The *donno* (hourglass drum) is another important instrument, both as speech surrogate and dance drum. It could be treated in the same way as the *atumpan*.

Listening and analysis can also be organised as practical lessons. These should be supplemented and intensified by singing and playing. For most children there is nothing like listening for listening sake. The purpose should therefore be clear and functional. Children can be asked to look for ideas that they will want to extract them for use in other class activities - such as composition and improvisation. In this way, discriminatory listening can more easily be enhanced. Picking a rhythmic motif, a theme, or an instrumental figure, from a highlife, or a piece of art music, depends on attentive listening. This may lead to the development of preferences. For, if a piece of music has only little excitement to offer, or lacks musical thought-provoking qualities, it will not be up to the teacher to point these out, although much of the children's understanding depends upon the teacher's own organisational ability.

With regard to art music compositions, we may adapt Nketia's (1978) classification of choral musical styles as a starting point, although from an analytical point of view a more comprehensive study is now required to fully cover modern trends. Nketia groups contemporary choral music compositions in Ghana along five models - Amu, Traditional, *Yaa Amponsa*, Highlife and Other forms. The distinctions are blurred, as one composition may belong to more than one group. For instance. it would be difficult to separate *Yaa Amponsa* (which gave birth to Highlife) from the Highlife itself. The Amu model may be confusing since Amu's compositions span all five categories. Teachers should endeavour to identify new criteria and develop their own models. This will help them to provide exciting samples for their students.

Practical listening and analysis can also involve pop and highlife music. For example, examining the instrumental and rhythmic differences between Funk and Reggae, Reggae and highlife, Afro Rock and Gospel Band. It would be interesting to compare the works of various Ghanaian pop musicians, such as E. T. Mensah, Jewel Ackah and Charles Amoah; Onyina, Kakaiku and George Darko. The interrelationship of indigenous and pop music could be explored.

Traditional religious music and music associated with kingship should also be used. There is all the evidence that such categories of music are as equally evocative artistically as they are ritually. So, it would be educationally futile as it is socially offensive, to exclude such music from the school curriculum. Teachers should be encouraged to play recordings to their students, and help them to develop a positive attitude toward them.

Religious music provides wide perspectives for establishing connection between sonic structure and organisation of ritual art. *Yeve*, for instance. has about nine movements which are intended to depict various characters of the gods. The whole performance also illustrates the stages of the worship, from invocation of the spirits, appearance of the gods in public, communication with the spirits, and so on, to the point when the gods finally retire. Then there is a special finale to round off the whole proceedings. This finale is usually a medley of several pieces so artisically knitted that it can last for hours without the slightest moment of boredom. *Yeve* music thus provides another scheme for the integration of culture, art and aesthetics. The use of religious music could therefore help school students to better apprehend the cultural dynamics of the community as critics, artists and revisionists. This structure of religious music can also be adapted to the process of story telling as well as serve as a frame-work for the musicianly and integrated approach to the teaching of Cultural Studies.

There should be comparative analysis of various religious musics, for example, between *akom* and *yeve* or *trovu* (cult music of Northern Eweland) and *klama* (traditional religious music of the *Ga Adagnme*) as well as religious and other musics of the community. Artistic elements can be derived and re-combined in classroom composition/improvisation.

The ideas presented in this chapter represent an attempt at making music education in Ghana African oriented. In particular, we encourage the adaptation of the ethnic educational practices to modern classroom music teaching. In a broad sense, traditional African education is that natural - social, cultural and political - growth that arises from the acting and interacting with the environment, individuals and groups of society. The ways of life and living are transmitted from the older to the younger. Adults become the symbol of life, just as they may become the symbol of decay. Creativity and education are not part of daily discussion, they occur as a matter of course, as part of the whole gamut of the enculturation process within which the acquisition of vocational skills, social and moral values and attitudes are secreted. The young are prepared and encouraged to display independence, initiative, and creative imagination in all aspects of life - sex, cooking, warfare, and vocation.

African education is practical, aural-oral and informal. Despite the introduction of the writing culture of the West, listening and observation interwoven by memory remain the key elements of acquiring the basic skills of social adjustment. Tribal and family history, taboos and rites, and the codes necessary for sustaining society - all codified in proverbs, riddles, epics, and poetry - continue to be transmitted orally. Knowledge is thus in people's heads not in books. Teaching is by example, not by precepts; and learning is by doing, not by reading. This practical-orality of African civilisation is still vigorous and cannot simply be dismissed.

We agree with Kwami (1989) that 'the traditional context is the best environment for a student of African music' (p. 24). School education can improve its own methods by drawing ideas directly from this environment. Thus by preferring the more western regimental (bar-to-bar) approach to the village oral-cum-gestalt system, our approaches fall prey to the fallacy of the more analytical and technical the teaching process, the more educationally valid and prestigious is the subject. Whether music that is composed within an oral tradition can be properly fitted into the intricate analytical system of the written culture of the West, is a contentious issue. It would be too simplistic to say that traditional African music - no matter how challenging it is - makes the same demand on the African ear as Western classical music on the European. Equally debatable is whether this is essential for its educational import. The issue is: why do village traditional musicians continue to produce more competent musicians than the western type school system? The musicality of the teaching process is essential for ethnic musicians and this must not be underrated. Rural wisdom still strives and could be profitably exploited for the improvement of formal music education.

It is hoped that when practical activity in music making is made firm at the basic school level, formal study of other composed music and musical instruments will be tackled with much more interest.

## Bibliography

Centre for National Culture, (1990) *The Cultural Policy of Ghana.* Accra. Ministry of Education and Culture

CRDD. (1987) *Suggested Cultural Studies Syllabus for Junior Secondary Schools (1-3) Years*. Accra. Ministry of Education

CRDD. (1988) *Suggested Cultural Studies Syllabus for Three-Year Post Secondary Teacher Training Colleges.* Accra Ministry of Education

Davies, C. (1992) 'Listen to My Song: A Study of Songs Invented by Children Aged 5 to 7 Years' *British Journal of Music Education*, Vol 9 No. 1 March (19-48)

Fadlu-Deen, K. C. S. (1989) *New Roots: Affirmation and Innovation in Music Education for West Africa with Special Reference to Sierra Leone and Ghana*. D.Phil Thesis. York University

Flolu, E. J. (1994) *Re-tuning Music education in Ghana: A Study of Cultural Influences and Musical Developments, and of the Dilemma Confronting Ghanaian Music Teachers*. D.Phil thesis. York University

GMTA. *Handbook for the 1992 Meeting of the GMTA*. Winneba. National Academy of Music

Hoskyns, J. (1992) 'Music Education and a European Dimension'. *British Journal of Music Education*, Vol. 9 Cambridge. Cambridge University Press (97-102)

Meyer-Denkmann, G. (1977) *Experiments in Sound: New Directions in Musical Education for Young Children*. Adapted for use in English Schools by E. & J. Paynter. London. Universal Edition

Nketia, J,. H. (1978) *'The Typology of Contemporary Ghanaian Choral Music'*. Institute of African Studies, Legon. Pamphlet Box

Okafor, R. C. (1991) 'Music Education in Nigerian Education' *Council for research in Music Education*. No. 108 Spring 1991 (59-68)

Omibiyi. M. (1972) *Folk Music and Dance in African Education.* Yearbook of the International Folk Music Council

Orff, C. (1978) *Carl Orff: The Schulwerk*. translated by Margaret Murray. New York. Schott Music Corporation

Paynter, J. (1982) *Music in the Secondary School Curriculum: trends and developments in class music teaching*. London. Cambridge University Press

Paynter, J. (1992) *Sound and Structure*. Cambridge. Cambridge University Press

Ross, M. (1984) *The Aesthetic Impulse*. Oxford. Pergamon Press

Swanwick, K. (1988) *Music Mind and Education*. London. Routledge

Tait, M. (1992) 'Teaching Strategies and Styles' in R. Colwell 1992 (ed.) *Handbook of Research on Music Teaching*. New York. Schirmer Books

# 9 Promoting Traditional Music: The Kenyan Decision

*Malcolm Floyd*

In April 1982 the President of Kenya, Daniel arap Moi, appointed a team of six Kenyan musicians to the Presidential National Music Commission:

> To undertake a detailed study and make recommendations on the preservation and development of the rich music and varied dance traditions of our people (Omondi 1984 :v).

They presented their findings in January 1984 in the 'Report of the Presidential National Music Commission'. This chapter looks at the historical background that led to the setting up of the Commission, and, after 10 years, assesses the intentions of the Report, with specific reference to formal education, and developments in achieving its aims. My observations are based primarily on a seven-year period of residence in Kenya from 1982 to 1989 and on brief visits in 1990, 1991, 1993 and 1994, teaching music at all levels in the Kenyan education system, and being involved in the many changes that occurred.

The Commission was set up to consider:

1.    The effecting of Music and Dance Education at all levels.

2.    A systematic collection, preservation and dissemination of traditional music and dance of Kenyan peoples.

3.    The increase and popularisation of occasions of music performance, both in rural and urban areas.

4.    Ensuring that music which is made available to the public either through radio and television or public places such as festivals, public gatherings and churches is of content and quality that is compatible with the cultural values of our nation.

5.    Catering for and safeguarding the interest of our musicians.
      (Omondi 1984: vi, 211)

The members of the Commission spent their time travelling throughout Kenya to make 56 visits, to consult nearly 2,000 musicians, educators, and other interested parties. The Report consists of 647 chapters containing comment, discussion and 360 specific proposals. It would be the task of a much larger essay to evaluate each proposal, so I shall confine myself to examples of the proposals which are designed to enhance traditional music through educational policy. These include:

75(d)     That music syllabi should emphasise the theory and practice of traditional African music which is relevant to the child's environment. This, however, should be done with the full awareness that there is a great deal of cross-cultural interaction in the present age. (Ibid: 147).

80(b)     That music teachers of noteworthy talents should be commissioned immediately by the Ministry of Education, Science and Technology to write for Music teaching. (Ibid: 147).

80(e)     That traditional musicians should be made use of in schools, either as subordinate staff or simply as tutors. In the latter case they could be rotated so as to serve several schools. (Ibid: 148).

85(b)     That music and other cultural subjects in schools must be examinable in the same way as any other subject. These should be included in the General Paper in the Kenya Certificate of Primary Education (KCPE). (Ibid: 149).

What led the Kenyan government to this direct involvement in strengthening the role of traditional music in all sectors of society, and particularly through formal educational processes? Let us consider first the nature of Kenya's population. There are at least 42 distinct socio-linguistic groups, linked to three of Africa's great language families - Bantu, Cushitic and Nilotic - with important Arab influences at the coast, descendants of immigrants from the Indian sub-continent, and a small number of Kenyans of European (predominantly British) extraction. In percentage terms this can be seen in summary below, (adapted from Barrett : 1982):

**Figure 9.1: Example of Population Distribution**

| Group Name | Language | % of Population | Position by size |
|---|---|---|---|
| Kikuyu | Bantu | 20.1 | 1st |
| Luo | Nilotic | 13.3 | 2nd |
| Somali | Cushitic | 1.9 | 16th |
| Indo-Pakistani | | 1.1 | 19th |
| European | | 0.4 | 29th |

The largest group of each linguistic affiliation is shown. All other groups are similarly affiliated, but not necessarily mutually intelligible.

Bantu and Nilotic groups provide the great majority of Kenya's population, and each is large enough to present a distinct identity. The Somali, although a relatively small group, has influence through its strong representation in the armed forces, and the need to maintain a strong political interest in keeping the Somali-populated North Eastern Province as an integral part of Kenya. The presence of Indo-Pakistani citizens in Kenya is widespread, both as large communities in cities, and as small groups and individual families in rural areas. The permanent European population consists mainly of farmers, whose families settled in colonial times and their descendants who have taken on a wide range of entrepreneurial and professional roles. Their influence is seen in the colonial legacies of language, education, administration and religion. This all goes to show a population that is extremely diverse, in cultural, social and linguistic terms.

A further element in Kenya's make-up is its history as a colony. It was created initially as a British 'sphere of influence', in co-operation with Germany and Italy, thus dividing Eastern Africa into large tracts by economic acquisitiveness and military strength. (Mungeam: 1978: 2) Education was a controversial issue almost from the beginning, particularly with regard to the indigenous population:

> Apparently the only object the Church Missionary Society's representatives here have is to educate and Christianise the heathen - about the advisability of which a good many people are sceptical. (Ibid: 231)

The Commissioner for Education in 1906 considered Industrial Education (training for a trade) to be the only essential requirement for Africans:

Without it he will....fail to derive the full benefits of schools; and
after his school days are over there is grave danger of his lapsing
to those conditions from which he has for a time been uplifted.
(Ibid: 234)

J R Orr, Director of Education in 1912 wrote:

...native education has hardly begun. The government is strongly
opposed at present to any save industrial education, which will be
carried out extensively by Government schools and grants to
Missions. ( Ibid: 250-251)

By 1921 ideas had begun to develop, as seen in the 'Departmental
Instructions governing native education in assisted schools'. The list of
compulsory subjects includes literacy in the vernacular, Swahili  and
English, and Mathematics. The list of optional subjects included History,
Geography, Physical Exercises, and most significantly for our present
study, singing (Ibid: 272) The development of music  education continued
following a predominantly English pattern up to the late 1970s. Schools
used the syllabus of the Cambridge Overseas 'O' level certificate, until the
syllabus of the Kenya Certificate of  Education (KCE) was developed. The
Cambridge Music 'O' level had no African music element, and was almost
exclusively taken by formerly British expatriate schools. There are,
however, examples of Kenyan musicians who managed to rise through the
system to the highest levels of musical training. The KCE had most of the
material of the 'O' level, with the addition of questions about Kenyan
traditional music.

When the Presidential National Music Commission was set up there
were, therefore, syllabi which included traditional music as integral to the
course.

Primary Schools were not neglected; in 1975 the Ministry of
Education published a syllabus in Music for them. It included among its
National Goals 'Respect and Development of Cultural Heritage'

Education should respect, foster and develop Kenya's rich and
varied cultures. It should instil in the youth of Kenya an
understanding of past and present culture and its valid place in
contemporary society. It should also instil in the youth a sense of
respect for unfamiliar cultures (Ministry of Education 1975:vi)

This is followed by the aims and objectives of music teaching:

> Collection, promotion and preservation of African music. Its value
> should be understood and it must be authentic and suitable for
> Primary Schools - geared to encourage creativity in pupils' minds.
> (Ibid)

How did this make itself apparent in the work to be covered?

Figure 9.2 shows the specifically Kenyan content:

**Figure 9.2 Primary School Music Syllabus (1975)**

| Level | Section | Work required |
|---|---|---|
| Primary 1 | (e) | Learn the Kenya National Anthem |
| Primary 2 | (d) | Continue learning the National Anthem |
| Primary 3 | (i) | Continue learning the National anthem |
| Primary 4 | (c) | Traditional Dances |
| | (i) | The National Anthem in KiSwahili and English, and how to behave when it is performed |
| Primary 5 | (b) | Traditional Dances |
| | (d) | Learn to play simple Traditional Instruments |
| | (e) (iii) | The National Anthem (in parts) |
| Primary 6 | (b) | Traditional Dances |
| | (e) | Traditional Instruments |
| | (s) | The National Anthem (in Harmony) |
| Primary 7 | (b) | Traditional Dances |
| | (e) | Traditional Instruments |
| | (f) | Ensure that the National Anthem is thoroughly learnt |

(Ibid: 1-4)

The introduction of requirements can be tabulated thus:

**Figure 9.3**    Primary 1    National Anthem
                2
                3
                4       Traditional Dances
                5         Traditional instruments
                6
                7

The remainder of time-tabled music was to be taken up with singing, in up to four parts, music literacy, elements of theory, and music appreciation. Of course, in reality much of the singing was of traditional songs, but there was no specific requirement that it should be.

Secondary Schools before the Commission had a syllabus with an element of traditional music. This element is indicated in Figure 9.4, which indicated the type of questions in the examination for the Kenya Certificate of Secondary Education (KCSE), taken after four years study.

## Figure 9.4 KCSE Music Syllabus

Paper 1 (Aural)
*   1.   Rhythm - repetitive drum pattern
    2.   Rhythm - 8 measures in simple time
    3.   Rhythm - 4 measures in compound time
    4.   Melody - 4 diatonic measures
    5.   Intervals - 2 diatonic examples
    6.   Cadences - 4 examples in Western Classical style

Paper 2 (Written)
    1.   Analysis, melodic writing and harmony
*   2.   African melodic analysis
    3.   Continuation of a melody
    4.   Elementary harmony
*   5.   Prescribed African recordings
    6.   Prescribed Western works
    7.   Prescribed Western composers
*   8.   General musical knowledge - Western and
         traditional - essays
*   9.   General musical knowledge - Western and
         traditional - meanings

Paper 3 (Performance)
    1.   Western instrument/voice
*   2.   African instrument/voice
(* indicates traditional elements)

These syllabi show an underlying interest in disseminating 'the rich music and varied dance traditions' of Kenya, but only in the vaguest terms at the Primary level, and in very limited and prescriptive terms at Secondary level.

The Paper 3 (Performance) African element was most commonly realised by a small number of specially learnt traditional songs. The number of Secondary schools taking such exams was remarkably small; in most years less than 10 out of over 1,000 schools entered candidates.

It would of course be a gross misrepresentation to say that this was the only traditional music going on in schools before President Moi set up the Commission. The tradition of (usually competitive) Music Festivals was started in pre-Independence times, and has developed into an enormous national network. All sorts of music are included, but it must be admitted that the traditional music performances are of the highest calibre across the country. The selection process is rigorous, going through competition at school, Zone, District, Province and National level. The vast majority of schools, Primary and Secondary, are involved in, and prepare very thoroughly for, these festivals, and the number of locations demands a lot of travelling, which also assists the dissemination of traditional music.

The other main feature that affects Kenyan society, and its view of traditional culture, is the rapid and vigorous process of acculturation. The highest levels of technology can be found, and Western 'popular' cultural forms are spread through radio, television, audio cassette, video and satellite. The output of traditional music and dance is very limited, amounting to about one hour a week on television (Kenya Broadcasting Corporation), mainly aimed at students, and up to two hours a week on radio, though there can be rather more on the KiSwahili and vernacular services. The material includes modern compositions in traditional styles, and Christian songs based on traditional musical patterns.

To summarise at this point; we can observe that the Presidential National Music Commission was dealing with a country that had a multi-ethnic population, a colonial history and education policy, an ambiguous set of developments in music education, and a hi-tech acculturation process being enthusiastically adopted as widely as possible. How far were the Commission's proposals new departures, and how far were they reiterations of existing practice? Figure 9.5 shows the links between the 1984 proposals, and syllabi already in existence:

## Figure 9.5 1984 Proposals and existing Syllabi

| 1984 Proposals | | Existing Syllabi/Examination |
|---|---|---|
| 75(d) | (emphasise theory and practice of traditional African music...with full awareness...of cross-cultural inter-action) | Primary 4-7: KCSE 1(1); 2(2,5,8,9) |
| 80(b) | (music teachers...be commissioned...to write for music teaching) | |
| 80(e) | (traditional musicians should be made use of in schools...) | (Primary 4-7: KCSE 3) |
| 89(b) | (music must be examinable in the same way as any other subject) | KCSE 1(1); 2(2,5,8,9);  3 |

( ) indicates where best practice was already following this injunction, but was by no means generally happening.

What, then, are the new elements?

75(d)  Awareness of cross-cultural interaction is emphasised, and taken to mean intra- as well as inter-national. The intention is to develop understanding and acceptance of groups beyond one's own through their cultural expressions.

80(b)  The singling out of Music Teachers as potential authors of text books is significant. Most previous texts had either been imported (mainly from the United Kingdom) or written by Europeans holding senior music posts in Kenya.

80(e)   This is looking to ensure authentic music and performance practice, moving away from the 1975 syllabus's demand for 'sweet sounds' (Ministry of Education 1975:1) towards sounds appropriate to the cultural context of a particular performance.

89(b)   The examination process is brought into Primary music, in addition to the existing Kenya Certificate of Education (KCE) (later to become the Kenya Certificate of Secondary Education:KCSE). The Kenya Certificate of Primary Education (KCPE) is the demanding set of examinations at the end of Primary School education. It appeared with the dramatic re-structuring of Kenyan education in 1985, to replace the previous Certificate of Primary Education (CPE) which was essentially an examination in literacy, numeracy and humanities related to Kenya.

In 1985 the pattern of 7 years Primary; 6 years Secondary; 3 years Tertiary was adjusted to become 8 years Primary; 4 years Secondary; 4 years Tertiary with the principal intention being to make Primary education fuller and more complete, involving Agriculture and Business Studies, in addition to Music, as this was the full extent of education that many Kenyans could expect.

To consider proposals 75(d) and 80(b) it is most revealing to look at the publication patterns of music texts from 1971 to 1993. 1971 because that was when the first significant music texts were published in Kenya, and 1993 because the production of books has continued well into the decade after the Commission's Report. I have collected 20 texts, most of which are designed specifically for schools, others contain material that could be used, at least by teachers. (The list of texts can be found in Appendix A). It is possible that some material has not been included, but it is reasonable to assume that this collection is a fairly full and representative sample. The texts have been searched for traditional songs, and information about traditional instruments, being two representative requirements of the Report. The range of ethnic groups covered has also been indicated, to see what 'cross-cultural interaction' has been facilitated. Figure 9.6, opposite, indicates texts containing traditional songs, showing the number of songs given for each ethnic group which appears at least once in any text.

**Figure  9.6   Range of songs in texts**

| Text Group | SoK | TMS | SGT | LM | FMK | 5OKF | LLM | MM | ETS |
|---|---|---|---|---|---|---|---|---|---|
| Ki | 40 | 20 | | 1 | 10 | 20 | 32 | 10 | |
| Luh | | | 2 | | 1 | 9 | 10 | 4 | |
| Kam | | | 2 | | | 2 | 1 | 1 | |
| Gu | | | | | | | | 1 | |
| Mi | | | 2 | | 1 | 2 | 4 | 2 | |
| Me | | | | | | 2 | 2 | | |
| Em | | | | | | | 1 | 1 | 18 |
| Ta | | | | | 2 | | | | |
| Sw | | | | | | 1 | 1 | | |
| Luo | | | 1 | | | 8 | 9 | 4 | |
| Kal | | | | | | | 1 | 2 | |
| Kip | | | | | 1 | 4 | 7 | 2 | |
| Na | | | | | | 1 | 3 | 1 | |
| Po | | | | | | 1 | 1 | 1 | |
| El | | | | | | | | 1 | |
| Sab | | | | | | | 1 | | |
| Tu | | | | | 1 | | | 1 | |
| Sam | | | | | | | | 2 | |
| So | | | | | | | | 1 | |
| Bo | | | | | | | | 2 | |

(For group abbreviations see Appendix B)

Figure 9.7 indicates the total numbers of songs, the number of ethnic groups represented, the number and names of groups represented uniquely in individual texts, and the percentage of songs from the single largest group, the Kikuyu, and its related societies, the Embu and Meru.

**Figure 9.7**

| Text | No. of songs | No. of groups | No. of unique groups | Name of unique groups | % Kikuyu, etc |
|------|------|------|------|------|------|
| ETS | 18 | 1 | 0 | 0 | 100% |
| LLM | 73 | 13 | 1 | Sabaot | 43.8% |
| LH | 1 | 1 | 0 | 0 | (100%) |
| MM | 38 | 17 | 5 | Gusii Somali Elgeyo Samburu Boran | 28.6% |
| FMK | 17 | 7 | 1 | Pokomo | 58.8% |
| SoK | 40 | 3 | 0 | 0 | 100% |
| SGT | 7 | 4 | 0 | 0 | 0% |
| TMS | 20 | 1 | 0 | 0 | 100% |
| 50KF | 50 | 10 | 0 | 0 | 44% |

What observations can immediately be made?

Only nine out of the 20 texts contain any songs at all.

Three texts contain songs only from the Kikuyu/Embu/Meru group.

The other texts have a proportion of K/E/M songs often larger than their proportion of the population.

Two texts (LM:SGT) have very small numbers of songs compared with the other seven texts.

Only four texts contain songs from more than five groups.

Figure 9.8, opposite, gives an idea of the range of traditional instruments mentioned by each text. Only general categories are given, and are indicated thus:

A - aerophone
C - chordophone
I - idiophone
M - membranophone

# Figure 9.8    Traditional Instruments mentioned in texts
(For group abbreviations see Appendix B)

| TEXT GROUP | LM | MIEA | TMIK | FMK | MI | MMK | MMP | TMK | S6MC | MCS4 | BM | RM | GM | MM |
|---|---|---|---|---|---|---|---|---|---|---|---|---|---|---|
| Ku | C | C | AC | ACIM | ACM | C | C | | C | AI | AC | | AC/M | A |
| Ki | ACM | C | ACIM | AIC | ACI | | AC | ACI | C | AI | A | AC/IM | A/CI | AC |
| Kam | A | | ACIM | ACM | ACM | | M | | C | A | AC | AC/IM | AC/IM | AC |
| Gu | | | CIM | ACI | C | | C | | | I | | CIM | A/CI | |
| Mi | A | AIM | ACIM | ACIM | ACIM | AI | AIM | | C | AI | A | AC/IM | AC/IM | AIM |
| Luh | AC | ACIM | ACM | ACIM | ACIM | AM | ACM | CIM | C | AI | AC | AC/IM | AC/IM | ACIM |
| Me | | | AM | C | CM | M | | | C | | C | | C/IM | |
| Em | A | | IM | CIM | ACM | M | | | C | | C | | C/IM | A |
| Ta | | | M | ACIM | I | | | | | | | | | |
| Luo | AC | C | ACIM | ACIM | ACI | C | AC | C | C | AI | | AC/IM | AC/IM | AC |
| Kal | AC | | ACIM | AC | AC | | C | | C | A | AC | AC/IM | A/CI | A |
| Po | | | AC | ACI | AC | | | | | I | | M | C | A |
| Tu | | | AI | AI | | A | | | | | | AI | A | A |
| Sam | A | | | A | A | | | | | | | | | |
| So | | | M | AM | | | | | | | | | | |
| Bo | | | I | | | | | | | | | | I | |
| Ma | | | I | AI | CI | | | | | | | | | |

The observations that follow from this are:

14 out of the 20 texts contain information about traditional music.

Most texts show a fair range of instruments across a reasonable spread of socio-linguistic groups.

Only one text (TMK) has information on fewer than five groups.

It also needs to be observed that of the 20 texts only three (FHK:LM:MM] contain both songs and information on instruments [although LM has only one song]. The background of the authors is shown in Figure 9.9:

## Figure 9.9 Socio-linguistic Backgrounds of Authors

| Group | Number of texts |
|---|---|
| Kikuyu | 9 |
| English/American | 5 |
| Ugandan | 2 |
| Kamba | 1 |
| Embu | 1 |
| Luhya | 1 |
| (Various) | 1 |

What conclusions can be drawn from this information? There is certainly sufficient material for a good study of traditional instruments, and several texts would be sufficient in themselves. There is also a fairly wide range of song material (which is perhaps the most accessible element of a culture), but only a few texts contain enough variety to be useful as cross-cultural sources. Several ethnic groups are represented by only one song in any text, and other groups can be identified who are not represented at all, for example the Maasai.

This may be due, at least partly, to the cultural backgrounds of the authors, and although all of the authors have music teaching experience (with the possible exception of ETS) that needs to be combined with further research, and the involvement of practising musicians throughout Kenya, to provide resources that cover the full range of musical experiences throughout

Kenya. This is also an issue with regard to some non-African cultures found in Kenya. For example, while European songs are available, often of English origin, there are virtually no examples of Arab, or Indo-Pakistani songs.

To turn to proposal 80(e), it is clear that in the 10 years since the Report, many schools have been involving traditional musicians in one form or another. In some they are visiting specialists, in others they are friends and relatives of staff or students, and some are employed as 'subordinate' non-teaching staff (groundsmen etc.). No research has been done yet on the growth of this aspect of music teaching and its effectiveness, and so it is not appropriate at this stage to make any conclusions. It does, of course, mean that where it happens students are exposed to expertise and authenticity in one culture (usually their own), in addition to a wide range of other cultures from within Kenya and beyond via texts.

For proposal 89(b), it is necessary to remember the context of the change to the 8-4-4 system, which brought examinations in a much wider range of subjects to the Primary School pupil, including Music, and required changes to the examinations at the end of Secondary education. Syllabi were rushed out in the mid-80s for the new system, but 1992 saw the issue of revised syllabi, and it is those we shall draw on to assess the progress in implementing the Commission's Report.

In Primary Schools we find in the 'National Goals'

> Respect and Development of Cultural Heritage Education should respect foster and develop Kenya's rich and varied cultures. It should instil in the youth of Kenya an understanding of past and present culture and its valid place in contemporary society. It should also instil in the youth a sense of respect for unfamiliar cultures. (Ministry of Education 1992:vi)

This is of course identical to the equivalent 'National Goal' in the syllabus of 1975 (Ministry of Education 1975:vi). It was an admirable goal, and deserves to maintain its place, but it points to the Report being about finding better ways to achieve the goal, rather than about proposing a better goal. Figure 9.10 shows the specifically traditional elements in the revised (1992) syllabus for Primary Schools;

## Figure 9.10 Revised Primary Music Syllabus (1992)

| Standard (Grade) | Section | Work required |
|---|---|---|
| 1 | 1.11 | The Kenya National Anthem. |
|  | 2.1 | Develop an appreciation of folk music. Develop respect for and positive reaction to other people's cultures. |
|  | 3.1 | Collect and use songs and singing games. Collect and use musical instruments. |
| 2 |  | As Standard 1 plus |
|  | 5.11 | Play a musical instrument (in some schools this will be a recorder or other Western instrument). |
| 3 |  | As Standard 2 |
| 4 |  | As Standard 2 plus |
|  | 10.ll (iii) | Singing; Patriotic/national songs |
|  | 12.1 | Compare songs and dances in traditional, popular and contemporary styles. Collect and preserve traditional songs, dances and musical instruments. |
| 5 |  | As Standard 4 plus |
|  |  | Types of songs and their social use. |
| 6 |  | As Standard 5 |
| 7 |  | As Standard 5 |
| 8 |  | As Standard 5 plus |
|  | 24.11 (b)(ii) | Types of folk dances, the role of costumes, ornaments and make-up in songs and dances. |

The sequence of requirements is given in Figure 9.11.

**Figure 9.11**

| Standard | Work required |
|---|---|
| 1 | National Anthem<br>Appreciation and respect<br>Collection and use |
| 2 | Play an instrument |
| 3 | |
| 4 | Collect; Preserve; Compare |
| 5 | Social role |
| 6 | |
| 7 | |
| 8 | Dance and costume |

(drawn from Ministry of Education 1992a)

The most invigorating element is the intention to involve the child in the cultures around them. This manifests itself in the 'collect and use' requirements from Standard One, which becomes 'collect and preserve' in Standard Four. There is also a significant appreciation of music within its cultural context leading to an eventual picture that links aspects as shown in Figure 9.12.

**Figure 9.12 Music and Cultural Context**

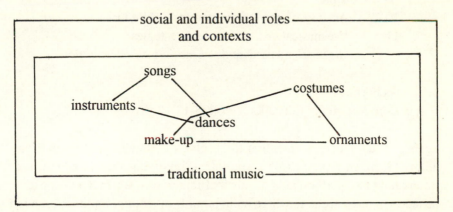

This contact with traditional music also has the potential to increase the involvement of local musicians in schools as advocated in proposal 80(e).

The Secondary School syllabus is notable for the nature of its continuity from the Primary School syllabus, and for having several concepts and skills in common. Figure 9.13 outlines the requirements:

**Figure 9.13 Revised Secondary Music Syllabus (1992)**

Form   Section   Work required

1        2.11      A study of music from two of African, Western and
                   Oriental
         3.1       Develop an appreciation of folk music.
                   Develop respect for and positive reaction to other
                   people's cultures.
         3.11      Performance of a dance (Af/We/Or)
                   Play two instruments from each of two; (Af/We/Or)
         4.1       Compare song in traditional, popular and contemporary
                   styles.
                   Collect and preserve traditional songs, dances and
                   musical instruments.
         4.11 (a)  Collecting folksongs and dances.
              (b)  Collectinq instruments.
              (c)  Visits to/participation in      (i) national days
                                                   (ii) cultural festivals

2.       As Form 1 (with specific topics changed)

3.       As Form 1 plus
         10.12     Analysis of music from two (of Af/We/Or)
         11.1      Use musical instruments and costumes
                   Organise and participate in music-making activities

4        As Form 3
(drawn from Ministry of Education 1992b:5-12)

Again we can notice the intention to involve the student actively in living
cultures through a process of assimilation involving the collection, use,
preservation and performance of musical materials. We may also observe
the repeated reference to the three main strands of cultural tradition found in
Kenya (African, Western and Oriental), and the interesting requirement that
two of the cultures must be studied.

    Ten years on from the Commission's Report, what conclusions can
we draw about Kenya's cultural identities, the role of the Presidential
National Music Commission, and the adjustments to formal education
policies in music that have resulted from the Commission's report? The

Commission was clearly aware of the presence of many distinct socio-linguistic groups; of a colonial history which had had a particular impact on educational policy; of an acculturation process which was particularly strong and highly regarded. There had, however, been a cultural element to National Goals in Education since at least 1975, within which music was valued as a cultural strengthener, within its social context. What did change was the desire to consider methods more carefully and thoroughly, in terms both of content and progression. Syllabi become more fully developed after the Commission's Report and show continuity through the stages of education. There is a significant change from 'learning about' to 'being involved in' traditional music, and this is reflected in the new examinations, KCPE and KCSE, where specified development of skills and understanding is planned, and there is a strong link with existing performances of traditional music, whether formal or informal. It can also be observed that the number of groups represented in texts is growing, particularly with regard to their instruments, although there is room for more detailed information, and a wider range of songs. There has been progress in the integration of Kenyans of Oriental (Indo-Pakistani) origin but this is not yet represented in school music texts.

The authorities in Kenya seem to have shown a remarkable interest and involvement in maintaining and developing the cultural traditions of the population, to strengthen individual feelings of identity to a particular group, and positive appreciation of others. It will be intriguing to see this work itself out in practice over the next decade.


## Appendix A

## Music Texts in Kenya: 1971 - 1993

BM      Wahome, John Kamenyi (1991) *Beginning Music*. Nairobi. Jesmisik Cultural Books Ltd

ETS     Mwaniki, HSK (1986) *Embu Traditional Songs and Dances*. Nairobi. Kenya Literature Bureau

FMK     Senoga-Zake, George (1986) *Folk Music of Kenya*. Nairobi. Uzima Press

GM      Wanjala, H N (1990) *Gateway Primary Revision Music*. Nairobi. Longman Kenya

LLM     Miller, Annetta (1987) *Let's Learn Music*. Nairobi. Baptist Music Publications

LM      Wahome, John Kamenyi (1971/1984) *Learning Music.* Nairobi. Uzima Press

MCS4   Amunga, Wahu (1991) *Music Course for Standard 4*. Nairobi. Muziki Wetu Publications

MI       Wahome, John Kamenyi (1986) *Musical Instruments*. Nairobi. Jemisik Cultural Books

MIEA    Hyslop, Graham (1975) *Musical Instruments of East Africa*. Nairobi. Nelson Africa

MM     Floyd, Malcolm     (1985) *Music Makers Standards 7 and 8.*
                                (1989) *Music Makers Standards 5 and 6.*
                                Nairobi. Oxford University Press

MMK    Senoga-Zake, George and Eldon, Kathy (1981) *Making Music in Kenya*. Nairobi. Macmillan Kenya

MMP    Gichimu, Chege (no date) *Music for Modern KCPE Pupils*. Nairobi. Chege Gichimu

RM     Floyd, Malcolm (1985/1990) *Revision Music for Standard 8*. Nairobi. Oxford University Press

SGT     Hyslop, Graham (1971) *Since Singing is so Good a Thing*. Nairobi. Oxford University Press

SoK     Kamenyi, John W (no date) *Songs of Kenya*. Nairobi. Equatorial Publishers

TMIK    Kavyu, P N (1980) *Traditional Musical Instruments of Kenya*. Nairobi. Kenya Literature Bureau

TMS    Wahome, John Kamenyi (1974) *Traditional Music and Songs*.
       Nairobi. East African Literature Bureau

S6MC   Karanja, Njoroge J (1990) *A Standard 6 Music Companion*.
       Limuru. Companion Publishers

50KF   Kenya Conservatoire of Music (1984) *50 Kenyan Foksongs*.
       Nairobi. Kenya Conservatoire of Music

## Appendix B

1.   Socio-linguistic groups mentioned in the text with their abbreviations.

[B    Bantu         C    Cushitic    N    Nilotic]

| | | | | |
|---|---|---|---|---|
| Bo | Boran C | | Me | Meru B |
| El | Elgeyo N | | Mi | Mijikenda B |
| Em | Embu B | | Na | Nandi N |
| Gu | Gusii/Kisii B | | Po | Pokot N |
| Kal | Kalenjin N | | Sab | Sabaot N |
| Kam | Kamba B | | Sam | Samburu N |
| Ki | Kikuyu B | | So | Somali C |
| Kip | Kipsigis N | | Sw | Swahili B |
| Ku | Kuria B | | Ta | Taita B |
| Luh | Luhya B | | Tu | Turkana N |
| Luo | Luo N | | | |
| Ma | Maasai N | | | |

This does not indicate the complex links, relations and incorporations which exist among groups.

## Bibliography

Barrett, David (ed) (1982) *World Christian Encyclopedia*. Nairobi. Oxford University Press

Kenya National Examinations Council (1984) *Past Examination Papers for Kenya Certificate of Education, vol 4*. Nairobi. KNEC

Kenya National Examinations Council (1987) *KCSE Regulations and Syllabuses 1989-1990*. Nairobi. KNEC

Ministry of Education (1975) *Kenya Syllabus for Primary Schools: Music*. Nairobi. Jomo Kenyatta Foundation

Ministry of Education, Science and Technology, (1986) *Syllabuses for Kenya Primary Schools: vol. 2*. Nairobi. Jomo Kenyatta Foundation

Ministry of Education (1992a) *Primary Education Syllabus vol. 2*. Nairobi. Kenya Literature Bureau

Ministry of Education (1992b) *Secondary Education Syllabus*. Nairobi. Kenya Literature Bureau

Mungeam, G H (1978) *Kenya: Select Historical Documents 1984 - 1922*. Nairobi. East African Publishing House

Omondi, Washington A. (Chairman) (1984) *Report of the Presidential National Music Commission*. Nairobi. Republic of Kenya

## Resources

*Penye mafundi, hapakosi wanafunzi*
Where there are experts there will be no lack of learners
(Swahili proverb)

This part looks first at published materials designed for use in schools. The reviews aim to pinpoint where they would be useful, and considers their strengths and weaknesses from a range of viewpoints.

The survey of the Higher Education situation is included in this part because it seems that this should be regarded as a resource, and perhaps ought to be encouraged to make itself more active in this role. It may be that this chapter will indicate useful contacts and potential connections.

# 10 Materials for Schools

*Rosemary Davis, Malcolm Floyd, Kathryn Howard, Anthony Noble, Tina Parry-Jones, Ann Tann*

This chapter contains reviews of books and other materials designed for use in schools. We have relied on publishers to send samples they consider appropriate on the whole, although occasionally we have suggested other items which look as if they might be helpful. A panel of six then reviewed them, and made comments and suggestions. Where they felt insufficiently expert they did not review particular texts, most frequently when it was outside their teaching experience. Similarly, where there was an element of personal interest in a publication no review was given.

Each review starts with a description of the material, and then suggests Key Stages which could use it. It shows if the material is considered interesting, appropriate and authentic, as far as that can be judged. It then goes on to comment on some possible uses, and whether there is scope for the development of work from the material, and if this is indicated in the material, or if it relies on the interests and skills of teachers. It goes on to ask if there is sufficient background and support information to enable the greatest use of the material. It indicates if the material can be used by children, teachers who are not specialist musicians, and specialist music teachers. There is then a section with suggestions for further provision, with ideas for improving the material in any later editions. At the end of these comments and suggestions a category is given by each reviewer, these are:

A    Very suitable or usable material, with very few difficulties or problems.

B    Mainly suitable and usable material, which might need some adaptation.

C    Would require a fair degree of adaptation, but contains useful elements.

D    Could not be recommended under any of the categories above.

In addition, panel members have indicated material they particularly liked with a '*'. One star is given for each panel member who selected an item.

The panel have a wide range of experience in schools, across all Key Stages and beyond, with children of varying abilities, in a range of settings in Britain and overseas. We have also included a teacher in training, to include the opinions of those new to the profession.  The materials looked at are listed below:

| Publisher | Title | Author |
|---|---|---|
| A & C Black | Look Lively Rest Easy | Helen East, Jane Ray |
| A & C Black | Mango Spice | Yvonne Connolly et al. |
| A & C Black | The Singing Sack | Helen East, Mary Currie |
| | | |
| Boosey & Hawkes | African Celebration | arr Stephen Hatfield |
| Boosey & Hawkes | Nukapianguaq | arr Stephen Hatfield |
| Boosey & Hawkes | Niska Banja | arr Nick Page |
| Boosey & Hawkes | Siyahamba | ed Doreen Rao |
| Boosey & Hawkes | Bohemia to the Balkans | Andrew Watts |
| Boosey & Hawkes | Caneuan Cymru | arr Margery Hargest Jones |
| Boosey & Hawkes | Songs of Ireland | arr Margery Hargest Jones |
| | | |
| Camb. Univ. Press | Light the Candles | June B Tillman |
| | | |
| Faber Music | Folksongs from Africa | arr Malcolm Floyd |
| Faber Music | Folksongs from the British Isles | arr Ronald Corp |
| Faber Music | Folksongs from the Caribbean | arr K. Bolam & P. Gritton |
| Faber Music | Spirituals from the Deep South | arr Ronald Corp |
| Faber Music | Folksongs from Eastern Europe | arr Ken & Jean Bolam |
| Faber Music | Folksongs from the Far East | arr Peter Gritton |
| Faber Music | Folksongs from India | arr Peter Gritton |
| Faber Music | Folksongs from Ireland | arr Ronald Corp |
| Faber Music | Folksongs from North America | arr Ronald Corp |
| Faber Music | Folksongs of the Sea | arr Ronald Corp |
| Faber Music | Inside Music I and II | David Carter |
| Faber Music | The Music Factory | Jonathan Rayner |
| | | |
| J M Fuzeau | Music of the World | Michel Asselineau et al |
| | | |
| Heinemann | Music Matters | M Metcalf, C Hiscock |
| Heinemann | Music of the Caribbean | Michael Burnett |
| Heinemann | Music of India | Gerry Farrell |
| Heinemann | Music of Indonesia | Gordon Jones |
| Heinemann | Music of West Africa | Trevor Wiggins |
| | | |
| Oxf. Univ. Press | Festivals | Jean Gilbert |
| Oxf. Univ. Press | Indian Music | Leela Floyd |
| Oxf. Univ. Press | Jamaican Music | Michael Burnett |
| Oxf. Univ. Press | The Steel Band | John Bartholomew |
| Oxf. Univ. Press | Oxford Primary Music | J. Gilbert, L Davies |
| Oxf. Univ. Press | Music Round the World | K & V McLeish |
| | | |
| Schott & Co | Aural Matters | David Bowman et al |
| Schott & Co | Sound Matters | David Bowman, Bruce Cole |

# shows positive response    ? shows possibility of positive response

| | |
|---|---|
| Title: | **Look Lively Rest Easy** |
| Author: | Helen East, Jane Ray |
| Publisher: | A & C Black |
| Price: | £ 7.95 (Book & Cassette) |
| ISBN: | 0 7136 3330 1 |

Description:

This book contains 31 'stories, songs, tricks and rhymes to rouse and to relax', with a cassette containing performances of all 31 activities. The material comes from a wide range of sources.

Suitable Key Stages:     1 [#]   2 [#]   3 [  ]   4 [  ]

Material is:   interesting   [#]

appropriate   [#]

authentic     [#]

Possible uses:

As stories first with music added, and for class and group work in English, Drama and Music.

Scope for development:

Plenty of ideas are suggested, although further extension may depend on specialist input or the imagination of individual teachers.

Background and support information:

There is useful material on many of the activities, but not all, and some teachers might like rather more.

Could be used by children:     [#]

non-specialist teachers:     [#]

specialist teachers:     [#]

Suggestions for further provision:

Colour pictures would add to the appeal of the book, and there is scope to include more ideas for composition and instrumental work.

Overall recommendation:

B B - C C          *

Title:     **Mango Spice**
Author:    Yvonne Conolly, Gloria Cameron, Sonia Singham,
           Chris Cameron, Vallin Miller, Maggie Ling.
Publisher: A & C Black
Price:     £ 7.99
ISBN:      0 7136 2107 9  Book
           0 7136 2110 9  Cassette

Description:

A landscape format spiral-bound book with cassette, containing 44 songs (20 of which are performed on the cassette). A range of ideas for accompaniment is given

Suitable Key Stages:     1 [#]  2 [#]  3 [?]  4 [ ]
Material is:  interesting   [#]
              appropriate   [#]
              authentic     [#]

Possible uses:

Group and whole class work. Extracurricular groups would find material here as well, especially for part singing. Much of this would be very popular with children.

Scope for development:

Close harmony 'a cappella' singing, and ideas for composition work.

Background and support information:

There is a good amount of this, which is interesting, and includes suggestions for cross-curricular work

Could be used by children:     [?]
     non-specialist teachers:   [?]
        specialist teachers:    [#]

Suggestions for further provision:

'Real' pictures would encourage its use at KS1, and recordings of all the songs would bring it fully to the non-specialist.

Overall recommendation:

A - B B B        *

Title:        **The Singing Sack**
Author:      Helen East, Mary Currie
Publisher:   A & C Black
Price:        £ 8.99  Book
ISBN:         0 7136 3115 5  Book
              0 7136 5638 7  Cassette

Description:

A landscape format spiral-bound book with accompanying cassette. There are 28 song-stories from a wide range of countries. All the songs are performed on the accompanying cassette.

Suitable Key Stages:     1 [#]  2 [#]  3 [ ]  4 [ ]
Material is:   interesting   [#]
              appropriate   [#]
              authentic      [#]

Possible uses:

For class story time, in assemblies, for performance based work, and for drama sessions.

Scope for development:

There are some suggestions in the book, but it would be possible for individual teachers to adapt and extend the material in various ways.

Background and support information:

Some information is given, but there may well be teachers who would appreciate more about the context and cultural backgrounds of the songs.

Could be used by children:        [#]
    non-specialist teachers:       [#]
       specialist teachers:        [#]

Suggestions for further provision:

Pictures would be helpful in using the material. Ideas for performance development would also be useful.

Overall recommendation:

                    B B - C C      *

Title:          **African Celebration**
Author:         African Folksongs arr. Stephen Hatfield
Publisher:      Boosey & Hawkes
Price:          £ 1.95

Description:

Five part treble voices unaccompanied.

Suitable Key Stages:      1 [ ]  2 [?]  3 [#]  4 [#]
Material is:   interesting   [?]
               appropriate   [#]
               authentic     [?]

Possible uses:

Choirs, some classroom use, and ideas could be adapted for composing activities. The arrangements are effective, if demanding, and at times paying too much homage to Western perceptions of such music.

Scope for development:

Few ideas are given, but the imaginative specialist or choir trainer would see possibilities.

Background and support information:

Some information on pronunciation and suggestions for performance are given, but little on social or cultural context.

Could be used by children:      [#]  high ability
   non-specialist teachers:      [ ]
       specialist teachers:      [#]

Suggestions for further provision:

Some recordings are available, but not as part of this publication. This might prove useful. Greater support information would be valuable.

Overall recommendation:

A - B  B - C

Title:      **Nukapianguaq**
Author:     Inuit Chants arr. Stephen Hatfield
Publisher:  Boosey & Hawkes
Price:      £ 0.95

Description:

| |
|---|
| Four part treble voices unaccompanied. |

Suitable Key Stages:      1 [ ]  2 [ ]  3 [#]  4 [#]
Material is:   interesting   [?]
               appropriate   [#]
               authentic     [?]

Possible uses:

| |
|---|
| Choirs, some classroom use, and ideas could be adapted for composing activities. The arrangements are effective, if demanding, and at times paying too much homage to Western perceptions of such music. |

Scope for development:

| |
|---|
| Few ideas are given, but the imaginative specialist or choir trainer would see possiblities. |

Background and support information:

| |
|---|
| Some information on pronunciation and suggestions for performance are given, but little on social or cultural context. |

Could be used by children:      [#]  high ability
    non-specialist teachers:    [ ]
        specialist teachers:    [#]

Suggestions for further provision:

| |
|---|
| Some recordings are available, but not as part of this publication. This might prove useful. Greater support information would be valuable. |

Overall recommendation:

| |
|---|
| A - B B - C |

Title:         **Niska Banja**
Author:        Serbian Gypsy arr. Nick Page
Publisher:     Boosey & Hawkes
Price:         £ 0.95

Description:

SAAB or SSAA. Piano duet accompaniment.

Suitable Key Stages:      1 [ ]  2 [ ]  3 [#]  4 [#]
Material is:  interesting   [?]
              appropriate   [#]
              authentic     [?]

Possible uses:

Choirs, some classroom use, and ideas could be adapted for composing activities. The arrangements are effective, if demanding, and at times paying too much homage to Western perceptions of such music.

Scope for development:

Few ideas are given, but the imaginative specialist or choir trainer would see possiblities.

Background and support information:

Some information on pronunciation and suggestions for performance are given, but little on social or cultural context.

Could be used by children:     [#]  high ability
         non-specialist teachers:    [ ]
             specialist teachers:    [#]

Suggestions for further provision:

Some recordings are available, but not as part of this publication. This might prove useful. Greater support information would be valuable.

Overall recommendation:

A - B B - C

Title:        **Siyahamba**
Author:     Zulu Song ed. Doreen Rao
Publisher:  Boosey & Hawkes
Price:       £ 0.95

Description:

Three part treble voices unaccompanied.

Suitable Key Stages:        1 [ ]  2 [?]  3 [#]  4 [#]
Material is:  interesting    [?]
               appropriate    [#]
               authentic      [?]

Possible uses:

Choirs, some classroom use, and ideas could be adapted for composing activities. The arrangements are effective, if demanding, and at times paying too much homage to Western perceptions of such music.

Scope for development:

Few ideas are given, but the imaginative specialist or choir trainer would see possiblities.

Background and support information:

Some information on pronunciation and suggestions for performance are given, but little on social or cultural context.

Could be used by children:       [#]  high ability
    non-specialist teachers:      [ ]
        specialist teachers:      [#]

Suggestions for further provision:

Some recordings are available, but not as part of this publication. This might prove useful. Greater support information would be valuable.

Overall recommendation:

A - B B - C

| | |
|---|---|
| Title: | **Bohemia to the Balkans** |
| Author: | Andrew Watts |
| Publisher: | Boosey & Hawkes |
| Price: | Teacher's Book £5.95, pack of 10 Pupils' books £12.95, CD £9.95 |
| ISBN: | 0 85162 118 x |

Description:

This is a collection of projects for use in school, based on music from Eastern Europe. There is an accompanying CD.

Suitable Key Stages:     1 [ ]  2 [#]  3 [#]  4 [#]
Material is:   interesting   [#]
appropriate   [#]
authentic    [#]

Possible uses:

For class and group work in composing, performing, listening and appraising. It could be used for extra-curricular work.

Scope for development:

There are many ideas here for extension, and the combination of text and CD may inspire yet further ideas.

Background and support information:

A fair amount of information is given about the music, but there is very little to give a cultural context to the music.

Could be used by children:     [#]
    non-specialist teachers:     [ ]
        specialist teachers:     [#]

Suggestions for further provision:

More background information would be helpful, as would a video showing some of the dances.

Overall recommendation:

A A - B B

Title:          **Caneuon Cymru**
Author:         arr: Margery Hargest Jones
Publisher:      Boosey & Hawkes
Price:          £ 4.95
ISBN:           0 85162 080 9

Description:

A collection of 51 Welsh songs. Titles are also given in English with each song, but not in the contents list. There is an English Language version.

Suitable Key Stages:     1 [ ]  2 [#]  3 [#]  4 [ ]
Material is:    interesting     [?]
                appropriate     [#]
                authentic       [#]

Possible uses:

As with 'Songs of Ireland', for class singing, as an introduction to folk music, dealing with structure, balance and so on. The student's version (with melody and chords only) was particularly liked by several of the panel.

Scope for development:

Specialists would be able to develop, adapt and extend the material, though without much help from the book.

Background and support information:

The use of a different language could be useful, although there is no pronunciation guide in this edition. There is little other information.

Could be used by children:       [ ]
    non-specialist teachers:     [ ]
        specialist teachers:     [#]

Suggestions for further provision:

Ideas for classroom use, and sufficient support for those wanting to use these original versions.

Overall recommendation:

C C C - D

Title:        **Songs of Ireland**
Author:       arr: Margery Hargest Jones
Publisher:    Boosey & Hawkes
Price:        £ 9.95
ISBN:         0 85162 077 9

Description:

A spiral bound collection of 37 songs in English with piano accompaniments, and chord suggestions for guitar accompaniment.

Suitable Key Stages:     1 [ ]  2 [#]  3 [#]  4 [?]
Material is:  interesting  [#]
              appropriate  [#]
              authentic    [#]    accompaniments are perhaps
                                  too sophisticated

Possible uses:

Class performances, choirs, solo singing, sight singing, work on song accompaniments.

Scope for development:

Specialists would be able to develop and adapt the material, but few suggestions are given in the book.

Background and support information:

There is some useful information on the social context, but little on the music and performance practice.

Could be used by children:     [#]
         non-specialist teachers:     [ ]
             specialist teachers:     [#]

Suggestions for further provision:

More supporting information would be helpful, along with instrumental and other vocal parts suitable for school use. Some ideas for classroom inclusion would be valuable.

Overall recommendation:

B B - C C

| Title: | **Light the Candles** |
| Author: | June B Tillman |
| Publisher: | Boosey & Hawkes |
| Price: | £ 11.50 |
| ISBN: | 0 521 33969 3 |

Description:

A spiral-bound book containing 67 'songs of praise and ceremony' from a wide range of countries, in four sections; Festivals and Seasons, Special Events, One World, Songs of Praise.

Suitable Key Stages:     1 [#]  2 [#]  3 [#]  4 [ ]

Material is:   interesting  [#]

            appropriate  [#]

            authentic    [?]

Possible uses:

Assemblies, class singing, class and group work in music, and in cross-curricular topics.

Scope for development:

There are many suggestions for development and extension of the material.

Background and support information:

Support information is full, and clearly presented, although some more help on pronunciation would be helpful.

Could be used by children:     [#]

   non-specialist teachers:    [#]

     specialist teachers:    [#]

Suggestions for further provision:

A cassette of authentic performances would be useful, along with some performance ideas.

Overall recommendation:

A - B B - C

Title:          **Folksongs from Africa**
Author:         arr: Malcolm Floyd
Publisher:      Faber Music
Price:          £ 4.95
ISBN:           0 571 51230 5

Description:

| A landscape format book containing 22 songs, from around Africa. There is an intention to produce an accompanying cassette. |
| --- |

Suitable Key Stages:      1 [#]   2 [#]   3 [#]   4 [#]
Material is:   interesting   [#]
               appropriate   [#]
               authentic     [?]

Possible uses:

| For introducing African singing, performing with simple accompaniments, class, group, GCSE course work, and for a variety of projects. |
| --- |

Scope for development:

| There are ideas for performance, and specialists could devise composing strategies from the material. |
| --- |

Background and support information:

| There is a fair amount, but more would be useful for higher Key Stages. |
| --- |

Could be used by children:      [#]
    non-specialist teachers:     [?]
        specialist teachers:     [#]

Suggestions for further provision:

| A recording would be particularly useful, along with more ideas for classroom use. |
| --- |

Overall recommendation:

| A A - C C          * |
| --- |

Title:      **Folksongs from the British Isles**
Author:     arr: Ronald Corp
Publisher:  Faber Music
Price:      £ 4.95
ISBN:       0 571 51119 8

Description:

A landscape format book containing 27 songs from around the British Isles.
Faber intend to produce an accompanying cassette.

Suitable Key Stages:      1 [#]  2 [#]  3 [ ]  4 [ ]
Material is:  interesting    [#]
              appropriate    [#]
              authentic      [?] uncertain in several cases

Possible uses:

To enjoy songs of English heritage, for groups, class and assembly music,
for arrangement in GCSE course work.

Scope for development:

Nothing is suggested, so teachers would need to use their own imagination.

Background and support information:

There is a lot known about the contexts of many of these songs, but nothing
is explained here.

Could be used by children:      [?]
    non-specialist teachers:    [?]
      specialist teachers:      [#]

Suggestions for further provision:

Background information and performance suggestions would be helpful.

Overall recommendation:

B - C C C

Title:        **Folksongs from the Caribbean**
Author:       arr: Ken Bolam and Peter Gritton
Publisher:    Faber Music
Price:        £ 4.95
ISBN:         0 571 51374 3

Description:

A landscape format book containing 21 songs, with ideas for accompaniment. Material is drawn from around the Caribbean.

Suitable Key Stages:      1 [ ]  2 [#]  3 [#]  4 [#]
Material is:   interesting   [#]
               appropriate   [#]
               authentic     [#] except some accompaniments

Possible uses:

Introducing Caribbean style, performing with simple accompaniment.

Scope for development:

There are some useful ideas and possibilities for development, but more would be useful.

Background and support information:

Information is given, but rather more would be needed for Key Stages 3 and 4.

Could be used by children:        [#]
        non-specialist teachers:  [#]
            specialist teachers:  [#]

Suggestions for further provision:

More ideas for classroom use would be helpful, including some easier performance suggestions

Overall recommendation:

B - C C C

Title:        **Spirituals from the Deep South**
Author:       arr: Ronald Corp
Publisher:    Faber Music
Price:        £ 4.95
ISBN:         0 571 51371 9

Description:

A landscape format book containing 28 songs with simple accompaniments.

Suitable Key Stages:     1 [#]   2 [#]   3 [#]   4 [?]
Material is:   interesting    [#]
               appropriate    [#]
               authentic      [?]

Possible uses:

Introducing simple harmonic structures, pentatonic work with unusual songs, and to support work in other curriculum areas. Concern was expressed at using some forms of 'pidgin' English however.

Scope for development:

Little is suggested, but imaginative teachers would find extensions and activities.

Background and support information:

Very little is given, and it was felt that this is an area where more context would be highly desireable.

Could be used by children:        [#]
   non-specialist teachers:       [?] with cassette as an aid
      specialist teachers:        [#]

Suggestions for further provision:

Recordings, cultural background, and more interesting presentation.

Overall recommendation:

B B - C C

| | |
|---|---|
| Title: | **Folksongs from Eastern Europe** |
| Author: | arr: Ken and Jean Bolam |
| Publisher: | Faber Music |
| Price: | £ 4.95 |
| ISBN: | 0 571 51308 5 |

Description:

A landscape format book containing 28 songs from seven Eastern Europe countries, with simple accompaniments. All songs are given in English only.

Suitable Key Stages:     1 [#]  2 [#]  3 [#]  4 [ ]
Material is:  interesting   [#]
              appropriate   [#]
              authentic     [?] no original language

Possible uses:

Choir, class and solo singing, to support History and Geography work.

Scope for development:

Nothing is suggested, so individual teachers will need to use their imaginations.

Background and support information:

Again none is given, requiring research if these are to be used fully in schools.

Could be used by children:        [#]
   non-specialist teachers:        [?] if cassette were available
      specialist teachers:         [#]

Suggestions for further provision:

Recordings, background and performance information would be useful, with some songs in original languages.

Overall recommendation:

B - C C C

| | |
|---|---|
| Title: | **Folksongs from the Far East** |
| Author: | arr: Peter Gritton |
| Publisher: | Faber Music |
| Price: | £ 4.95 |
| ISBN: | 0 571 51203 8 |

Description:

A landscape format book containing 15 songs, principally from a range of cultures in Malaysia.

Suitable Key Stages:    1 [ ]  2 [#]  3 [#]  4 [#]
Material is:  interesting    [#]
        appropriate    [#]
        authentic    [#]

Possible uses:

For class, whole school, choir, solo-singing, GCSE course work, and to develop cultural awareness.

Scope for development:

There are some ideas within the text, and specialists will be able to develop further activities.

Background and support information:

There is a fair amount of information, but more would be useful for older children.

Could be used by children:    [#]
    non-specialist teachers:    [ ]
        specialist teachers:    [#]

Suggestions for further provision:

Recordings would be particularly useful for this unfamiliar material. Further ideas for classroom work, and illustrations would also be valuable.

Overall recommendation:

A - B - C C            *

Title:         **Folksongs from India**
Author:        arr: Peter Gritton
Publisher:     Faber Music
Price:         £ 4.95
ISBN:          0 571 51372 7

Description:

A landscape format book containing information on the principles of Indian music, and 20 folksongs.

Suitable Key Stages:        1 [?]  2 [#]  3 [#]  4 [#]
Material is:   interesting   [#]
               appropriate   [#]
               authentic     [#]

Possible uses:

Class and group work in composition and performance, and a valuable resource for improvisation work.

Scope for development:

There are many suggestions in this, and information on performance is helpful and clear.

Background and support information:

This is well handled, in sufficient detail while retaining clarity.

Could be used by children:     [?]
    non-specialist teachers:    [?]
        specialist teachers:    [#]

Suggestions for further provision:

Recordings and a pronunciation guide would be useful.

Overall recommendation:

A A - B - C           *

Title:        **Folksongs from Ireland**
Author:       arr: Ronald Corp
Publisher:    Faber Music
Price:        £ 4.95
ISBN:         0 571 51417 0

Description:

A landscape format book, containing 28 songs with simple accompaniments.
Faber intend to produce an accompanying cassette.

Suitable Key Stages:        1 [ ]   2 [#]   3 [#]   4 [#]
Material is:   interesting    [?]
               appropriate    [#]
               authentic      [#]

Possible uses:

For class, whole school, junior choirs, solos, to develop cultural awareness.

Scope for development:

Very little is suggested, but specialists would be able to develop activities
from the material.

Background and support information:

There is virtually no contextual explanation of the music, and little to aid
performance.

Could be used by children:      [#]
   non-specialist teachers:     [#] if cassette available
      specialist teachers:      [#]

Suggestions for further provision:

A teacher's support book with ideas for classroom performance, and
background information.

Overall recommendation:

A - B - C C

Title:       **Folksongs from North America**
Author:      arr: Ronald Corp
Publisher:   Faber Music
Price:       £ 4.95
ISBN:        0 571 51323 9

Description:

A landscape format book, containing 28 songs with simple accompaniments.
Faber intend to produce an accompanying cassette.

Suitable Key Stages:      1 [?]  2 [#]  3 [#]  4 [#]
Material is:  interesting   [?]
              appropriate   [#]
              authentic     [#]

Possible uses:

Class, choir, solo singing, and for arrangement work at GCSE.

Scope for development:

None is suggested, but specialists would be able to develop activities.

Background and support information:

There is virtually no helpful information.

Could be used by children:        [#]
    non-specialist teachers:      [ ]
        specialist teachers:      [#]

Suggestions for further provision:

More contextual and performance material would be helpful, and the
presentation could be rather more interesting.

Overall recommendation:

B B - C C

Title:        **Folksongs of the Sea**
Author:       arr: Ronald Corp
Publisher:    Faber Music
Price:        £ 4.95
ISBN:         0 571 51120 1

Description:

A landscape format book, containing 28 songs with simple accompaniments.

Suitable Key Stages:    1 [#]  2 [#]  3 [#]  4 [ ]
Material is:  interesting   [?] little is not already available
              appropriate   [#]
              authentic     [#]

Possible uses:

Class and group work, choirs, and to link with other curriculum areas.

Scope for development:

Little is suggested, but information can be drawn from songs to build up contexts.

Background and support information:

Very little is offered.

Could be used by children:      [#]
   non-specialist teachers:     [#] with support
       specialist teachers:     [#]

Suggestions for further provision:

Some more (authentic) ideas for performance, with greater cultural background.

Overall recommendation:

B - C C C

Title:       **Inside Music** I.Structures II.Music and Expressive Art
Author:      David Carter
Publisher:   Faber Music
Price:       £ 5.95 - book;  £ 12.95 - cassette
ISBN:        0 571 51087 6 Book I; 0 571 51234 8 Book II
             0 571 51235 6 Cassette

Description:

These are workbooks designed for GCSE students. Book I contains 24 projects on Repetition and Contrast, Textures and Contrasts, and Experimental Music and Structures. Book II contains 18 projects on Music and Visual Art, Music and Words and Music and Performing Arts. (There is an accompanying cassette.)

Suitable Key Stages:      1 [ ]   2 [  ]   3 [   ]   4 [#]
Material is:   interesting   [?]
               appropriate   [?]
               authentic     [#]

Possible uses:

There is a rather limited World Musics context, but there is potential for work in composing, performing, listening and appraising.

Scope for development:

There are many possibilities for development, but some might feel restricted to the process employed here.

Background and support information:

There is sufficient information, and an emphasis on dealing with the music itself.

Could be used by children:       [#] with help
   non-specialist teachers:       [ ]
       specialist teachers:       [#] in Music and other subjects

Suggestions for further provision:

Some more variety might be mentioned, both of material and methods of use.

Overall recommendation:

A A - B B

Title:      **The Music Factory** Teacher Resource Book
Author:     Jonathan Rayner
Publisher:  Faber Music
Price:      £ 19.95
ISBN:       0 571 51116 3

Description:

This contains 24 main activities, and has accompanying scores and
instrumental work-books. Work is in five areas: Rhythm and Metre, Pitch
and Melody, Harmony, Stucture and Form, and Timbre and Texture.

Suitable Key Stages:      1 [ ]  2 [ ]  3 [#]  4 [#]
Material is:   interesting   [#]
               appropriate   [#] World Musics not high, however.
               authentic     [#]

Possible uses:

For class and group work in composing and performing.

Scope for development:

There are many development possibilities and extentions.

Background and support information:

There is not much specifically World Musics supporting information, but
otherwise the material is managed well.

Could be used by children:        [ ]
    non-specialist teachers:      [ ]
        specialist teachers:      [#]

Suggestions for further provision:

Taped examples would be useful, along with more varied material.

Overall recommendation:

                    A - B B - C            *

Title:       **Music of the World**
Author:     Michel Asselineau, Eugene Berel, Tran Quang Hai
Publisher:  J M Fuzeau
Price:       £ 39.95  (CD version)
ISBN:       2 9052 1835 5

Description:

A teacher's guide, pupils' workbook, with 3 accompanying CDs. For each
musical example there is material on the relevant geography, the music itself,
performances, and sometimes historical accounts.

Suitable Key Stages:      1 [ ]  2 [ ]  3 [#]  4 [#] A level and beyond.
Material is:   interesting   [#]
               appropriate   [#]
               authentic      [#]

Possible uses:

As a resource for the teacher, for aural development, and as an example of
varied styles. The 'workbook' is the least satisfactory element of the
package.

Scope for development:

There are many possibilities for building up to quite extensive cross-
curricular projects.

Background and support information:

This is a particular strength of this material. It is particularly good to have
music from francophone sources.

Could be used by children:        [ ] older students
   non-specialist teachers:       [#] in various subjects
      specialist teachers:        [#]

Suggestions for further provision:

The translation is not always appropriate, particularly in the workbook. The
level aimed at is not always clear, it ranges from Year 7 level to HE
institutions, and this could be adapted.

Overall recommendation:

Teacher's Guide & CDs: A A   Workbook:  C D

Title:        **Music Matters**
Author:     Marion Metcalfe, Chris Hiscock
Publisher:  Heinemann
Price:       £ 81.50
ISBN:        0 435 81004 9

Description:

A ring-binder containing material in the form of 15 projects across years 7 to 9, with three cassettes. World Musics occur as integral parts of the projects, although the variety is limited.

Suitable Key Stages:      1 [ ]  2 [  ]  3 [#]  4 [?]
Material is:   interesting    [#]
                  appropriate   [#]
                  authentic       [#]

Possible uses:

This would prove very useful for group and class work. Although it is not cheap, the nature of the photocopiable materials makes it a valuable resource. There is not sufficient World Musics content to allow choice however.

Scope for development:

There is little opportunity to develop the World Musics, particularly in the fields of performing and composing.

Background and support information:

Little information is given about the cultural contexts of the World Musics content, although the musical links and differences are made clear.

Could be used by children:       [#]
    non-specialist teachers:       [ ]
        specialist teachers:       [#]

Suggestions for further provision:

A wider selection of cultures explored in rather more depth would add to what already exists

Overall recommendation:

A - B - C C                     *

Title:          Exploring the Music of the World
                **Music of the Caribbean**
Author:         Michael Burnett
Publisher:      Heinemann
Price:          £ 37.50
ISBN:           0 435 81011 1
Description:

| A ring-binder of material, with 2 cassettes, and a poster containing a range of pictures and maps. There is a range of musical styles explored. The contents include: |
| --- |

      Introducing the Caribbean    Jamaican Dance Music and Folk Songs
      Caribbean Music           Religious Music in Jamaica
      Jamaican Music

Suitable Key Stages:     1 [ ]  2 [?]  3 [#]  4 [#]
Material is:  interesting   [#]
              appropriate   [#]
              authentic     [#]
Possible uses:

| For class and group work, in composing, performing and listening, in general music classes and for GCSE (and arguably even beyond). |
| --- |

Scope for development:

| There are many ideas for development and other activities, with suggestions for further reading and listening. Some may be rather overcomplicated, however. |
| --- |

Background and support information:

| This is sometimes perhaps too detailed, and in other cases too vague, but generally the package is considered to provide at least as much as could be wanted. |
| --- |

Could be used by children:      [#]
    non-specialist teachers:    [#]
        specialist teachers:    [#]
Suggestions for further provision:

| A tighter structure would be useful in making the pack accessible. More pieces for performance would be valuable, as would a video showing performance practice in cultural contexts. |
| --- |

Overall recommendation:

| A A - B - C            * * |
| --- |

Title:      Exploring the Music of the World
            **Music of India**
Author:     Gerry Farrell
Publisher:  Heinemann
Price:      £ 37.50
ISBN:       0 435 81012 X
Description:

A ring-binder of material, with 2 cassettes, and a poster containing a range of pictures and maps. There is a range of musical styles explored. Contents include:

| | |
|---|---|
| Introducing India | Popular Music in India |
| Classical Musical Traditions | Indian Popular Music in the West |
| Music and Religion | |

Suitable Key Stages:      1 [ ]   2 [?]   3 [#]   4 [#]
Material is:   interesting   [#]
               appropriate   [#]
               authentic     [#]
Possible uses:

For class and group work, in composing, performing and listening, in general music classes and for GCSE (and arguably even beyond).

Scope for development:

There are many ideas for development and other activities, with suggestions for further reading and listening. Some may be rather overcomplicated, however.

Background and support information:

This is sometimes perhaps too detailed, and in other cases too vague, but generally the package is considered to provide at least as much as could be wanted.

Could be used by children:      [#]
     non-specialist teachers:   [#]
         specialist teachers:   [#]
Suggestions for further provision:

A tighter structure would be useful in making the pack accessible. More pieces for performance would be valuable, as would a video showing performance practice in cultural contexts.

Overall recommendation:

A A - B - C          * *

Title:        Exploring the Music of the World
              **Music of Indonesia**
Author:       Gordon Jones
Publisher:    Heinemann
Price:        £ 37.50
ISBN:         0 435 81014 6
Description:

A ring-binder of material, with 2 cassettes, and a poster containing a range of pictures and maps. There is a range of musical styles explored. Contents include:

|                          |                          |
|--------------------------|--------------------------|
| Introducing Indonesia    | Wayang Kulit and Kecak   |
| Indonesian Music         | Influences in Western Music |
| Gamelan Music of Bali    | Popular Music            |

Suitable Key Stages:      1 [ ]  2 [?]  3 [#]  4 [#]
Material is:  interesting    [#]
              appropriate    [#]
              authentic      [#]
Possible uses:

For class and group work, in composing, performing and listening, in general music classes and for GCSE (and arguably even beyond).

Scope for development:

There are many ideas for development and other activities, with suggestions for further reading and listening. Some may be rather overcomplicated, however.

Background and support information:

This is sometimes perhaps too detailed, and in other cases too vague, but generally the package is considered to provide at least as much as could be wanted.

Could be used by children:        [#]
    non-specialist teachers:       [#]
        specialist teachers:       [#]
Suggestions for further provision:

A tighter structure would be useful in making the pack accessible. More pieces for performance would be valuable, as would a video showing performance practice in cultural contexts.

Overall recommendation:

A A - B - C          * *

Title:        Exploring the Music of the World
              **Music of West Africa**
Author:       Trevor Wiggins
Publisher:    Heinemann
Price:        £ 37.50
ISBN:         0 435 81010 3
Description:

A ring-binder of material, with 2 cassettes, and a poster containing a range
of pictures and maps. There is a range of musical styles explored. Contents
include:

| | |
|---|---|
| Introduction to West Africa | Pitched Instruments |
| Rhythm | Music for Recreation |
| Music and Ceremony | Popular Music |

Suitable Key Stages:      1 [ ]  2 [?]  3 [#]  4 [#]
Material is:   interesting    [#]
               appropriate    [#]
               authentic      [#]
Possible uses:

For class and group work, in composing, performing and listening, in
general music classes and for GCSE (and arguably even beyond).

Scope for development:

There are many ideas for development and other activities, with suggestions
for further reading and listening. Some may be rather overcomplicated,
however.

Background and support information:

This is sometimes perhaps too detailed, and in other cases too vague, but
generally the package is considered to provide at least as much as could be
wanted.

Could be used by children:       [#]
     non-specialist teachers:    [#]
         specialist teachers:    [#]
Suggestions for further provision:

A tighter structure would be useful in making the pack accessible. More
pieces for performance would be valuable, as would a video showing
performance practice in cultural contexts.

Overall recommendation:

A A - B - C            * *

Title: **Festivals**
Author: Jean Gilbert
Publisher: Oxford University Press
Price: £ 10.95 Book; £ 10.52 Cassette
ISBN: 0 19 3212854

Description:

A spiral-bound book containing a wide range of materials for 13 festivals from a variety of cultures around the world.

Suitable Key Stages: 1 [#] 2 [#] 3 [?] 4 [ ]
Material is: interesting [#] but confusing at times
appropriate [#]
authentic [#]

Possible uses:

For celebrations, assemblies, and for general class and group work. Some of the material would be suitable for performance by whole schools.

Scope for development:

One of the panel suggested there was almost too much! There are certainly many ideas, with suggestions for cross-curricular links.

Background and support information:

Certainly there is enough to enable full and thorough understanding of a great diversity of human celebration.

Could be used by children: [ ]
non-specialist teachers: [?]
specialist teachers: [#]

Suggestions for further provision:

Colour photos and other illustrations would be helpful, and some clearer setting out in places. Suggestions for 'authentic' performance would also be welcomed.

Overall recommendation:

A - B B - C *

Title:       **Indian Music**
Author:      Leela Floyd
Publisher:   Oxford University Press
Price:       £ 4.25 Book;  £8.95 Cassette
ISBN:        0 19 321330 3

Description:

An informative book dealing with: India and its culture, Five Kinds of Music, Form, Instruments and Players, History of Indian Music. There is an accompanying cassette.

Suitable Key Stages:      1 [ ]  2 [#]  3 [#]  4 [#]
Material is:   interesting    [?]
               appropriate    [?]
               authentic      [#]

Possible uses:

In research projects, as a background to practical work, to initiate composition, to aid GCSE course work.

Scope for development:

Some ideas are given, but there could be more.

Background and support information:

This is really the main function of this book, and it is full and clear.

Could be used by children:        [#]
   non-specialist teachers:       [#]  in a range of subjects.
       specialist teachers:       [#]

Suggestions for further provision:

More practical musical examples would add to the value of this.

Overall recommendation:

B B B - C

Title:        **Jamaican Music**
Author:       Michael Burnett
Publisher:    Oxford University Press
Price:        £ 4.25
ISBN:         0 19 321333 8

Description:

An information book dealing with: Introducing Jamaica, Introducing Jamaican music, Religious music, Music for work and play, Dance music and Reggae.

Suitable Key Stages:      1 [ ]  2 [#]  3 [#]  4 [?]
Material is:  interesting    [#]
              appropriate    [#]
              authentic      [#]

Possible uses:

For research projects, for composing and performing activities by class and group.

Scope for development:

A range of ideas, questions and activities are suggested.

Background and support information:

This is a useful source of appropriate information.

Could be used by children:      [#]
    non-specialist teachers:     [#]  in a range of subjects.
       specialist teachers:      [#]

Suggestions for further provision:

More performance examples, and recordings.

Overall recommendation:

B B B B

Title:          **The Steel Band**
Author:         John Bartholomew
Publisher:      Oxford University Press
Price:          £ 4.25
ISBN:           0 19 321329 X

Description:

An information book dealing with: Trinidad and the Caribbean, Steel Bands in Trinidad, The pans, The arranger, and Starting a Steel Band.

Suitable Key Stages:    1 [ ]  2 [#]  3 [#]  4 [#]
Material is:   interesting   [#]
               appropriate   [#]
               authentic     [#]

Possible uses:

In research projects, composing and performing activities for group and class.

Scope for development:

Some activities are suggested, and more could be attempted.

Background and support information:

Much useful information is given.

Could be used by children:      [#]
   non-specialist teachers:     [#]
      specialist teachers:      [#]

Suggestions for further provision:

Recordings of performance would be useful, perhaps with a video.

Overall recommendation:

B B B - C

Title:        **Oxford Primary Music**
Author:       Jean Gilbert, Leonora Davies
Publisher:    Oxford University Press
Price:        £ 16.95 Teacher's Pack for Key Stage 1, and for Key Stage 2.
ISBN:         0 19 321263 3

Description:

The teacher's pack contains a teacher's book, activity sheets, a songbook and copies of pupils' books. An accompanying cassette is also available.

Suitable Key Stages:       1 [#]  2 [#]  3 [ ]  4 [ ]
Material is:   interesting   [#]
               appropriate   [#]  particularly the KS2 pack.
               authentic     [?]  to an extent.

Possible uses:

Class, group and individual work, and could be adopted as a school music course.

Scope for development:

There are many suggestions, but not for World Musics elements in any depth.

Background and support information:

There is good general supporting information, but little on World Musics.

Could be used by children:      [#]
    non-specialist teachers:    [#]
        specialist teachers:    [#]

Suggestions for further provision:

The inclusion of more traditional British folk songs would be helpful.

Overall recommendation:

AA-CC        * *

Title:       **Music Round the World**
Author:      Kenneth and Valerie McLeish
Publisher:   Oxford University Press
Price:       £ 4.95
ISBN:        0 19 321434 2

Description:

An information book linked to the 'Oxford First Companion to Music', and designed as an introduction or 'starter' book.

Suitable Key Stages:     1 [ ]  2 [#]  3 [#]  4 [ ]
Material is:  interesting   [#]
              appropriate   [#] Sometimes outdated
              authentic     [#]

Possible uses:

Research projects and general information for groups and individuals, to support cross-curricular topics.

Scope for development:

There are many suggestions, but not many for practical musical work.

Background and support information:

This is the main function of the book, and it leads enquirers to the more detailed 'First Companion'.

Could be used by children:      [#]
   non-specialist teachers:     [#]  in a wide range of subjects.
      specialist teachers:      [#]

Suggestions for further provision:

More musical examples would be useful, and several of the drawings would be better replaced by photographs.

Overall recommendation:

A A A - C

Title:          **Aural Matters**
                **Aural Matters in Practice**
Author:         David Bowman, Paul Terry, Mark Lockett
Publisher:      Schott & Co
Price:          £ 20.00 inc. 2 CDs; £ 5.95 + £ 3.99 (CD)
ISBN:           0 946535 22 1
                0 946353 23 X

Description:

A guide to aural perception development, with tests. 12 of the 112 tests use World Musics materials.

Suitable Key Stages:     1 [ ]  2 [ ]  3 [ ]  4 [#] A levels [#]
Material is:  interesting   [#]
              appropriate   [#]
              authentic     [#]

Possible uses:

Individual and group work for aural and stylistic analysis skills.

Scope for development:

There are many possibilities for development from this rich source of material.

Background and support information:

The World Music information is limited, but useful for this purpose.

Could be used by children:      [#]
    non-specialist teachers:    [ ]
       specialist teachers:     [#]

Suggestions for further provision:

More examples would, of course, be useful, and perhaps more work 'in practice', rather than 'in test'.

Overall recommendation:

A A - B - C          *

| Title: | **Sound Matters**  Music Book, Teacher's Manual, Cassettes |
|---|---|
| Author: | David Bowman, Bruce Cole |
| Publisher: | Schott & Co. |
| Price: | £ 8.95 book, £22.00 manual, £16.95 cassettes |
| ISBN: | 0 946535 13 2 |
| | 0 946535 14 0 |

Description:

This comes as various combinations of the Anthology, Teacher's Manual with Pupils' Questions, and two cassettes. 10 of the 71 examples are of World Musics.

Suitable Key Stages:  1 [ ]  2 [ ]  3 [ ]  4 [#]

Material is:  interesting  [#]

appropriate  [#]

authentic  [#]

Possible uses:

Listening material to develop and extend musical experience, from written and heard sources.

Scope for development:

Teachers will be able to develop material and ideas from what is given here.

Background and support information:

The World Musics content is not particularly well  supported, but this is a useful start.

Could be used by children:  [#]

non-specialist teachers:  [ ]

specialist teachers:  [#]

Suggestions for further provision:

Rather more supporting information, and more than one example of rarer musical material.

Overall recommendation:

A A - B - C

This review concludes with some general comments on the materials seen:

> I thoroughly enjoyed seeing so much material available of which I was completely unaware. As a non-specialist rather frightened of the whole concept of 'teaching music' I was pleased to see some material I feel 'even I' could use. RD

> There is a wide range of presentation styles, but very few books/packs contain good material that can be immediately used in the classroom. A narrow uninteresting picture of World Musics is sometimes painted, and there are materials that contain only one or two good examples.  KH

> There appears to be something of a 'band wagon' approach to World Musics. Consequently much of the  material is rather directionless. Most of the material is based on existing folk music, and ignores the essential role of improvisation in many World Music traditions. There is little on Arabic, South American or Native American music. AN

> I prefer the books providing ideas and extension work on composition, performing and listening activities which can be developed and modified to suit circumstances. I like World Musics to be included as part of musical exploration. TP-J

> I feel the presentation of many leaves a lot to be desired, as few made me 'sit up and look', and as a non-specialist I require more to keep me interested. AT

In conclusion, we would say that there is a great deal of useful material here to serve the inclusion of World Musics in school work, and there are some particularly good books. However, it may be that where there is not an enthusiastic specialist to find ways of using some of these materials effectively, this music may rest on shelves after initial excursions. We would also encourage publishers to consider producing recordings of as much of the music as possible, authentically where this is realistic. Compact Discs are also very useful as alternatives to cassettes, especially for ease of finding the right item without a lot of fuss.

All that said, we have been intrigued at what we have seen, and are busy making selections for own situations.

The panel were:

Rosemary Davis: since training at Bishop Otter College she has taught children aged seven to sixteen in England, South America, West Africa, and the Seychelles. She is presently teaching a year 3/4 class in a primary school, where she is also History and Geography Coordinator.

Malcolm Floyd: after study at London and Exeter Universities he has worked in junior and secondary schools and institutions of Higher Education both in England and Kenya.

Kathryn Howard: currently a third year student on a BA (Ed) course at a College of Higher Education, specialising in working with children at Key Stage 2.

Anthony Noble: studied at Trinity College of Music, and has recorded as performer and conductor. He is currently Director of Music at a Roman Catholic Grammar School, and Organist and Rector Chori of Farnborough Abbey.

Tina Parry-Jones: after graduating from Bulmershe College she has worked as an instrumental teacher and in secondary schools, and has also taught 'Kindermusik' (for children aged five to eight years). She is currently Director of Music at a comprehensive school.

Ann Tann: trained at Rolle College, and has since worked in infant, nursery and primary schools, mainly with Key Stage 1 children. In addition she has experienced working in Special Education, with the physically handicapped, and on the neurological ward at Guy's Hospital for three years. She is now teaching a Year R/1 class in a primary school.

# 11 World Musics in Higher Education

*Malcolm Floyd*

The interest shown in World Musics has been increasing in recent years. This is evidenced by the growing number of institutions including elements in their courses, and the appearance and recruitment of specialists in the field. There follows an overview of courses and interests at seventeen colleges and universities who responded to requests for information. They were among those selected because World Musics was included in their advertising or was given in summaries in year books and similar sources.

The material is divided into three main parts, dealing first with undergraduate courses, and then postgraduate work including taught MAs and research degrees. This is followed by a section containing additional information on areas such as staff and resources.

Following the information supplied by institutions there are tables which summarise the data, and finally a commentary.

There are certainly other institutions who include World Musics in their teaching, and it is hoped that they will contribute appropriate information for any future updates to be made to this review.

The colleges and universities included in this survey are:

Anglia Polytechnic University
Bangor: University College of North Wales
Birmingham Conservatoire
Bretton Hall College
Cambridge University
City University
Dartington College of Arts
Durham University
King Alfred's College of Higher Education, Winchester
Kingston University
London College of Music
London University: Goldsmiths College
London University: School of Oriental and African Studies
Manchester Metropolitan University: Crewe and Alsager Faculty
Queen's University, Belfast
Southampton University
York University

# Undergraduate Courses

## Anglia Polytechnic University   (Cambridge)
BA World Music Modules at Anglia Polytechnic University

Three modules at undergraduate level take a broad look at various non-western traditions and at European folk music. In the first year, the 'World Musics' module introduces a variety of musical traditions and describes musical structures, textures and ensembles in relation to their social contexts and functions.

The social significance of music in different cultures is developed in the module 'Anthropology of Music' which examines the ways in which music traditions are the outcome of social necessities, structures and priorities. Case studies examining teaching methods, the role of the musician and mythological or religious associations contrast the roles and functions of music in different cultures.

In conjunction with this the module presents some theoretical background describing ethnomusicological and anthropological methodology.

'Music in a Changing World' examines the acceleration of social and technological change in the twentieth century and the consequences for indigenous music traditions. The mass media, urbanisation and westernisation and questions of cultural identity and political change are examined through case studies. The products of cross-cultural exchange and fusion are considered, challenging the traditional categories of national, folk, art or popular music.

## Bangor:   University College of North Wales

Ethnomusicology at the University of Wales, (Bangor) has an emphasis on Welsh/Celtic Cultures, but world music, instruments and recordings are available for wider studies. The Department houses an Archive of Traditional Welsh Music (supported by the Arts Council of Wales) and the Peter Crossley-Holland collection of European folk instruments.

Courses are studied through formal classes, seminar discussion groups and practical sessions. All areas are offered in Welsh and English.

1.   Ethnomusicology and Organology
     Part 1  (First year) & Honours 1 (Second year)

2.    Music and Society: Music in Primitive Cultures available in Part 1
      (First year) & Honours 1 (Second year)
3.    Studies in Welsh Music I & II
4.    Harps, harpists and Harp Music
5.    Music of many cultures
6.    Irish & Scottish Folk Music
7.    Women in Welsh Music
8.    Men in Welsh Music
9.    Traditional Elements in Contemporary Welsh Music

## Birmingham  Conservatoire
BA  BEd  BMus

In multicultural Britain of the 1990s it is important for musicians to
understand and value the musical and cultural contribution of minority
groups to contemporary society as a whole. It is of particular significance to
the future of music education.

The aims of the unit are to develop a basic understanding of the
purposes and methods of ethnomusicology by studying different musical
systems of the world and the implications of those systems in terms of
human musicality, and to develop the student's awareness of the social
function of all music by studying a range of non-Western cultures.

The learning outcomes will be an elementary knowledge of the study of
ethnomusicology and a variety of non-Western musical traditions, eg.
Aboriginal Australian music, Japanese Court music, Native American music,
plus a more in-depth knowledge of one of the following four areas:

1.    European/Mediterranean Folk Music
2.    Indian Classical Music
3.    Sub-Saharan African or
      Latin American/Afro Caribbean Musics
4.    Indonesian Music (Gamelan)

Modules 2 and 3 are significant in their reflection of the cultural backgrounds
of large sections of contemporary British society, and Module 1 by virtue of
its geographical proximity. The rationale behind Module 4 is slightly
different - although there is no sizeable Indonesian population in the UK the
study of gamelan music during the last decade has assumed a crucial role in
music education and is identified as one of the key areas of non-Western
music in the National Curriculum.

As well as these units in ethnomusicology there are a variety of non-Western ensembles that students can be part of and be assessed as part of their degree:

Javanese Gamelan
Indian Classical Music
Indo-Jazz Music
African and Latin Drumming Groups
Folk Music Ensembles

**Bretton Hall College** (University of Leeds)
BA (Hons) Contemporary Music

There will be a compulsory short course introducing ethnomusicology in the first year. Also, an optional five week course (a "project" taught full-time for the five weeks, all other parts of the degree having been stopped for this duration), where music of one culture will be studied in depth. Lectures, seminars, practical sessions and if appropriate, field work will be the mode of delivery of the project.

In year three there is a dissertation for all students, and this allows ethnomusicologists to submit a lengthy individual study on a chosen subject.

BA (Hons) Qualified Teacher Status

This degree has a module of world musics as applied to the National Curriculum. Practical sessions in West African Percussion, Indian instrumental, and Latin American styles are held - Bretton has a stock of African, Indian and Latin instruments and some experience in this work in education, over the past ten years.

**Cambridge University**

Ethnomusicology is taught in all three years of the undergraduate curriculum. The first year course, given in collaboration with specialists in other fields, is compulsory, and explores particular themes and issues common to both Western and non-Western traditions from a cross-cultural perspective. Thus in a course entitled 'Melody, Mode and Word', each of these concepts and their interrelationships were considered from the basis of Western chant, Middle Eastern, Irish, Tibetan and Twentieth Century

European repertories. The current course 'Melody as Ritual' refers to medieval Christian, Middle Eastern and Andean music cultures.

In the second year, students are presented with an ethnomusicological option as an alternative to a subject in the history of Western music. Typical titles include 'Art Music of North Africa and the Near East', 'Music in Middle Eastern Cities', 'Maqam from Tunis to Tachkent', 'Music of the Bolivian Andes', and 'Music of Northern Pakistan and the North Indian Classical Tradition'. Focusing on particular cultural/geographical areas, these courses serve simultaneously as introductions to basic methods and tools of ethnomusicology. Students are encouraged to devise local fieldwork projects, and everyone is required to do a transcription and analysis of a recording of their choice; in the Bolivian Andes course, offered for the first time last year, instrumental performance took a central role.

In the third and final year, ethnomusicology is again offered as an optional course, this time among a range of more specialised subjects in music history, analysis and cognition. Students focus on various distinct, thematically related research topics grouped under titles such as 'Performance Practice in Non-Western Music', 'Mode and Melody in Asian Music', and 'Westernisation of Traditional Music'.

Travel grants offered by the University and various individual Colleges, enable keener students to do more adventurous field projects in such diverse places as Egypt, Baluchistan, Northern Pakistan, Morocco, Nigeria, China and the Outer Hebrides. These field projects often form the basis of a third year dissertation, and in some cases, provide a springboard for future M Phil work.

## City University
BSc Honours Degree in Music

For their first year of study, students take core curriculum courses in Music from Oral Traditions - an introduction to ethnomusicology and musical anthropology - North Indian Classical Music and a Gamelan Workshop.

In the second and third academic years, students elect twelve fifteen - week modules from a programme which includes:

Music Traditions from the Far East
Indonesian Music Studies
English and European Folk Music
Jewish Music East and West
Afro-American and Popular Music Studies

Final year students are required to submit a dissertation of approximately 12500 words on a topic of their choice; each year there are seven or eight titles related to ethnomusicological study. A bursary is available for students wishing to persue fieldwork; recent expeditions have included Central India, Zaire, Java and Morocco. Related language and instrumental studies may be provided for those students specialising in ethnomusicology.

## Dartington College of Arts

Dartington's view of 'World Music' and Ethnomusicology is best characterised by the title of John Blacking's book 'A Commonsense View of All Music'. We do not promote musical hierarchies or hegemony; we accept a very wide range of instruments as a performance study. The main focus of our degree programme is twentieth century music: classical, art, world, vernacular, folk, popular and other qualifiers included. Within the degree programme there is the opportunity for students to choose to focus on world music for a proportion of their time (this is a modular programme). According to the choices they make students might be involved in some aspect of world music/ethnomusicology for up to one-third of their time in the second year, and over half the time in the third year.

## Durham University

At the undergraduate level, all first-year students are exposed to non-Western or folk musics in a course called 'Prescribed Scores'. Typically this involves learning about two or more contrasting items, such as North Indian *dhrupad* and Korean farmers' drumming. All undergraduates also have the opportunity to play in the Department's Javanese gamelan. In the second and third years, students may choose to take a full-year course in Ethnomusicology and/or various topics such as American Music (including native American music, country music, etc); Music of China, Korea and Japan; Music in Culture and Society; and others offered from time to time.

## King Alfred's College of Higher Education (Winchester)

'World Musics' can be taken as one of two or three fields in a modular BA or BSc, and also provides the Special Studies element in Music for students on the BA (QTS). The field of World Musics aims to educate students in ways of examining other musical traditions in relation to their own indigenous music tradition whatever that may be. Historical work will be based on a non Eurocentric model. Practical work in performing and composing will include work in the traditions of Jazz, Caribbean Steel Orchestra, African and Thai traditions and Classical European style. Rock musicians work alongside Grade 8 violinists, and retired people realising a life long desire to study music in greater depth learn alongside folk musicians and exchange students from many places including the US, Japan and Africa.

The three strands are performing, composing, and critical studies, all of which have a high World Musics content. The pattern of modules is as follows:

Stage 1: (Yr 1):   A Framework for World Musics
Composing
Solo Performing
Ensemble Performing

Stage 2:  (Yr 2,3)  Ethnomusicology
Kenyan Musical Traditions
Musics of the Caribbean
The Gamelan and its Music
Solo Performing
Ensemble Performing

There is also World Musics input in the Teaching Studies in Music for non-specialists or the BA (QTS) and PGCE courses.

There are visiting performers and lecturers in the fields of African, Indian, Chinese, Japanese and Gamelan music.

## Kingston University

1.   Curriculum
World Music is a compulsory part of of the BA (Hons) Music course. It also features in our B Ed and PGCE Music courses.

Ethnomusicology
Ethnomusicology is an Option within the BA (Hons) Music course.

2.   Music Activities
We have a World Music Ensemble which meets every week. Currently students have lessons from a Brazilian Drummer.

We have a Chinese dulcimer performer who is our Research Fellow from Beijing, who teaches students the Dulcimer. He is one of the finest Ducimer performers and represented China in last year's International Dulcimer Conference in Brno.

We have concerts from time to time given by musicians from Africa, China, India and Ireland.

## London College of Music (Thames Valley University)

All undergraduate and postgraduate courses offered by the London College of Music at Thames Valley University operate according to the university-wide modular scheme. At present, world musics/ethnomusicology appear in a number of different undergraduate modules, each of which represents 1/8 of a student's work in an academic year, although there is a rolling programme of new module development. 'Anthropology of Music' adopts a social anthropology perspective, asking key questions about musical behaviour, and drawing on examples principally (but not exclusively) from Africa, South and East Asia, and South America. Being aimed at BA Humanities students, we spend little time on this module analysing music structures. A range of modules on British folk and traditional musics, rock music, and black US American popular music and jazz are aimed at BMus and GLCM students, and here we prioritise music analytical approaches, while social and cultural theory provides necessary context. The music library has extensive resources (both recordings and books) to support these modules.

## London University:  Goldsmith's College
Undergraduate Courses in Ethnomusicology offered as Part of the BMus

Module: Ethnomusicology 1: World Music Survey

An introduction to the diversity of the world's music which allows students to concentrate on two areas of special interest for their written work. The world can be divided into nine music culture areas: East Asia, South-East Asia, South Asia, Middle East and North Africa, Africa South of the Sahara, Europe, North America, South America, and Oceania. The music of each region will be discussed in a series of lectures in the Autumn Term. Several LPs or CDs will be selected for each region which will be required listening.

Module: Ethnomusicology 2: Theory and Method in Ethnomusicology

An introduction to theory and method in ethnomusicology, with an emphasis on the practicalities of fieldwork. Term 1 consists of a series of lectures on the scope and aims of ethnomusicology, its history over the last 100 years, the study of musical instruments, contemporary theories in ethnomusicology, and the anthropology of music. Term 2 consists of a series of seminars on methodological and technical aspects of ethnomusicological research, linked to a small-scale research project. There will also be practical sessions on music transcription.

## London University:  School of Oriental and African Studies

In the present era of increasing international awareness, the study of the world's many and varied music traditions is assuming an ever more important role in university level education around the globe. A leading institution for the academic study of the world's music is the University of London's School of Oriental and African Studies (SOAS).

Music, like language, is a universal means of individual and cultural expression: like language, it is infinitely varied. Music is cherished by many societies of Asia and Africa as a distinctive and valued cultural heritage. The music of these societies, besides being intrinsically interesting for its own sake, has much to tell us, both about the cultures in question and about music in general.

The study of music at SOAS therefore has a dual emphasis. On the one hand we study specific musical traditions, both in terms of musical structure, repertory and performance, and in terms of the part music plays in the society concerned; and on the other hand we consider the principles and methods that may be applied to the study of any music in its cultural setting, and the problems and insights that arise when we compare musics on a worldwide basis. The term ethnomusicology is applied to this multifaceted approach to the study of music.

Music may be studied jointly with a second subject for a 'two subject BA honours degree by course units'.

The overall degree structure for Music is essentially the same whatever the second subject:

*     In the first year of the Music Syllabus, the student undergoes a basic training in ethnomusicology, comprising compulsory courses

Introduction to Asian and African Musics, Aural Training, and Instrumental or vocal performance.

*   In the second year the student selects one region of Asia or Africa for detailed study, and also follows the compulsory course Introduction to Ethnomusicology.

*   In the third year more advanced regional and/or disciplinary units may be selected.

Performance lessons are likely to be available in Javanese or Balinese gamelan and in various traditions from India, Japan, Thailand, China, Korea, Africa, and Iran.

Brief summaries of course contents:

*Introduction to Asian and and African-musics*
A survey of selected musical traditions of Asia and Africa, covering aspects of the musical structure, performance practice, and cultural roles of the musics in question.

*Aural training* (one half course unit)
Compulsory first-year course. Basic training in aural analysis and transcription of Asian and African music, using staff notation and/or other notation systems, and including discrimination of non-Western intervals and scales, polyphonic styles, rhythms and metres, etc.

*Instrumental or vocal performance* (one half course unit)
A study of the elementary techniques and repertory of an Asian or African musical instrument or vocal style, to be selected according to the interests of the student and the availability of teaching.

*Introduction to Ethnomusicology*
A broad introduction to the major aspects of ethnomusicological study: musical instruments and the human voice as sound-producers; musicians as agents of production; underlying concepts; the ethnography of musical performance; song texts; principles of transcription and analysis; music in relation to history, anthropology and linguistics.

## Music of East Asia

An introduction to understanding the music traditions of Japan, Korea and China. Basic Musical principles and aesthetic concepts will be discussed, and several genres will be introduced.

## Music in the cultures of South Asia

A survey of some of the varied traditions of music in south Asia, considered in their cultural contexts, included will be 'classical' and 'folk' traditions, religious music, film and popular music.

## Music of Japan

A survey of the major genres of Japanese music. These will include court and theatre musics, folk song and folk performing arts, and the chamber and parlour musics for instruments such as koto, shamisen and shakuhachi.

## Indian Music I

A survey of the North Indian classical music tradition in the 20th century.

## Indian Music II

Aspects of the history and theory of Indian Art Music. To include: the religious, social and cultural roles of music and musicians in ancient and mediaeval India.

## Music of the Middle East

A survey of music in the Islamic Middle East in the 20th century, covering the position of music in Islamic society, and an introduction to the various art-music traditions from North Africa to Persia.

## Music of South East Asia

A survey of the major musical cultures of continental and insular South East Asia. The course will concentrate on the various court-music traditions but will also cover the musics of the villages and regional minorities.

## Music of Africa

One or two regions will be covered in detail (especially the Manding culture area of Gambia, Mali, etc) but a broader overview will also be taken. Both traditional genres and recent popular styles will be considered.

## Music of Korea

Broadly divided into three sections: 1) folk music; 2) court music; 3) recent developments including contemporary composition.

*A Topic in Japanese Music*
Advanced study of a particular topic - for example: the instrumental music of the Noh theatre; regionalism in folk song style; mode in Japanese music, etc.

*A Topic in Indian Music*
Possible topics include: music and society; music and religion; aspects of folk music; iconography and iconology; organology; aspects of Sanskrit musicological literature; etc.

*A Topic in African Music*
Possible themes include: African polyphony; music, dance and trance; xylophone music.

*History and theory of Middle Eastern Music*
A survey, to include readings or source materials, of the development of art music in the Middle East from the 7th century; major trends in the evolution of music theory.

*An essay on a selected topic* (one half course unit)
The topic may relate either to the music of a specific region, or to an issue in ethnomusicology.

*Theory and methods of Ethnomusicology* (one half course unit)
An examination of selected theoretical issues and methodological approaches in the discipline.

*Music and Culture* (one half course unit)
A version of Introduction to Ethnomusicology for non-music students only. Broad anthropological approach to music, focusing on socio-cultural aspects rather than on musical sound 'per se'.

*Ethnomusicological fieldwork and analysis* (project) (one half course unit)
Students will be taught the skills necessary to plan and conduct a field project and to process the resulting data. This will include instruction in the use of sound recording equipment. Each student will carry out a project of his/her own devising, involving direct contact with an Asian or African musician or musicians.

## Manchester Metropolitan University: Crewe and Alsager Faculty

Some consideration is given to aspects of certain traditions, notably Indian Classical, Japanese and Indonesian in our units of study. The degrees offered here are as follows: BA (Hons) Creative Arts, BA (Hons) Humanities, BA (Hons) Combined Studies. These degrees are differentiated by the combination of Music Units with those of other subjects. Students on the different degree routes follow the same Core of Music units.

## The Queen's University of Belfast

We offer undergraduate BA degrees in Ethnomusicology at minor (4 modules), combined (4), joint (6) and major (8) honours level, following a general level one course.

Level 1 modules: World Music Cultures (survey, including the Americas, Africa, Middle East and Indian subcontinent) and World Music and Society (introduction to ethnomusicological theory). The intention of these courses is to provide a general knowledge of world musics and the means by which they may be understood.

Level 2/3 modules: There are two core courses, which provide a survey of the main currents in ethnomusicological theory, and the development of practical research skills: Theory and History in Ethnomusicology, Method and Practice in Ethnomusicology. These are supplemented by optional courses, depending on degree requirements. They are: Ethnicity, Identity and Music, Popular Music and Culture, Contemporary Ethnomusicological Writing, and the detailed regional study of music and dance in the Middle East, Mediterranean, Brazil, and Spanish Latin America. All courses are taught by lecture and tutorial, and include practical tuition as a required element on each module. Practical courses include Balinese Gamelan, Turkish Baglama (Saz), Indian Sitar, African Drumming, Brazilian Samba.

## Southampton University

This department is pursuing an ongoing policy of reformulating the curriculum so that it echoes the practice of music a bit better than the traditional one did. We have recently recruited experts in Jazz and popular music and are introducing specialist courses in those areas. While we do not have a specialist in non-western music (and do not support this at post-graduate level), we do offer an undergraduate-level introductory course entitled 'Music in a Multicultural World', co-taught by several staff with experience on non-western music; it focuses on such issues as cross-cultural relationships, modernisation, and commercialisation. It is also designed to coordinate with concerts in non-western music presented at the Turner Sims Concert Hall, which is located on campus.

## York University

Music at York is studied primarily through composition and performance, and this ethos applies to Ethnomusicology and the study of World Music. A focus is the complete Javanese Gamelan, built especially for the department in 1982 and the first to be acquired by a British teaching institution. It is used not only for regular rehearsals, open to any student, undergraduate or postgraduate, but also for frequent concerts and workshops for schools and colleges. In 1989 we also acquired a Thai PiPhat percussion ensemble. Also represented are the main instruments of Indian classical music, a set of Ghanaian Ewe drums and interrelated long zithers from China, Korea and Japan. Undergraduate courses (equivalent to elective modules) include an Introduction to World Music (for first-years), and courses open to all students, including postgraduates, on Indian Music, Javanese Gamelan Music, Thai Music, and Japanese Music. The teaching is by lectures, seminars, and practical sessions, often involving guest teachers, and students normally submit a folio including essay and transcription work.

## Postgraduate Degrees

## Bangor: University College of North Wales

Taught Courses

Diploma in Ethnomusicology
MA (Ethnomusicology)
Diploma in Welsh Music Studies
MA (Welsh Music)

One year full-time. These courses aim to provide the academic musician with the opportunity of intellectual appraisal of the traditional musician's art. Areas covered: Ethnomusicology in general, and traditional Welsh/Celtic music in particular. Three written papers and one field work project/folio, together with extended thesis on an approved subject.

Research Degrees

M Phil (Ethnomusicology or Organology)
M Phil (Welsh Music)
Ph D

## Birmingham Conservatoire

World Music Issues (route unit)

MA and PG Dip

The study of Ethnomusicology demands a knowledge of research methods, a familiarity with the pioneering work of past Ethnomusicologists and social anthropologists, as well as a critical awareness of current issues.

Aims:

- To familiarise the student with a range of research methodologies for annotated musics.
- To acquaint the student with important texts and past work.
- To enable the student to cultivate high standards of written presentation, analysis and transcription.
- To provide a platform for informal performance, the presentation of recent research work and for the debate of current issues.

Learning outcomes:

- The student will become competent in the handling of bibliographic and recorded source materials.
- The student will develop a knowledge of the work of important authors and contributors to the field.
- The student will acquire skills in written presentation, analysis and transcription.
- The student will develop a breadth of knowledge of musics outside their chosen field (studied in the Core unit) and acquire critical opinions of a variety of related issues.

The unit will encompass the following areas:

1   A brief study of the 'classic' texts: Bruno Nettl, Mantle Hood, Curt Sachs, John Blacking and others.

2   Bibliographical studies: how to find research materials.

3   Discussion of current issues eg transformation of traditional musics through the effects of mass media and mass tourism, the survival of musics of ethnic minorities in Britain, the promotion and marketing of

'World Music' through multi-national agencies and the music industry. Students will be encouraged to attend and discuss relevant local performances and events.

## Bretton Hall College

PGCE Music specialism in Primary and Secondary age ranges

Despite the brevity of this course, there are intensive world musics sessions, from both the theoretical and practical stance. (see BAQTS above). Students are directed towards material to support the necessarily small input.

MA Music Education, and one module of music on the M Ed

Both of these are two year part-time degrees, and Ethnomusicology comprises one term (10 sessions), and a weekend of practical work. This begins with the fundamental issues of Ethnomusicology, and then effects the transfer over to world music in education. Students present a seminar paper of 20 minutes at the end of term. The final dissertation may be to do with Ethnomusicology and music in schools.

MA Performance Arts

This is a two year part-time degree, for Dance, Drama and Music graduates. Ethnomusicology will appear in year one, taught in a general cultural studies way to a mixed discipline group. In year two, it is a concentrated Ethnomusicology course for the musicians.

## Cambridge University

The one year M Phil course in Ethnomusicology, like its counterpart in Musicology, is conceived as an individual training in research rather than a taught course with a standard syllabus. It comprises three research exercises: a 15,000 word thesis, a transcription and analysis project and a fieldwork report and documentation, whose contents may, but need not be, related. Recent topics have included music traditions of Mongolia, Northern Pakistan, Amsterdam, Ireland, Bolivia, Morocco, Mexico, China, the Greek community of Constantinople, and North India. These research exercises are produced in the framework of seminars for all graduate students, regardless of field, which provide a forum for staff, students and visiting scholars to present research in progress.

The M Phil degree may constitute an end in itself, or serve as a stepping stone to Ph D research; this in turn has led, in certain cases, to highly competitive post-doctoral research fellowships held at various Cambridge colleges.

## City University

### MA in Music

The MA in Ethnomusicology (one year full-time, two years part-time) is divided into three components: a thesis of 20,000 words, a folio of shorter essays, analyses and transcriptions, and either a fieldwork report or a recital on a non-Western instrument.

### Research

Research leading to the award of MPhil or PhD degrees in ethnomusicology is supervised within the department or, where appropriate, in conjunction with external specialist consultants. Recent and current research topics include 'Ornamentation in North Indian vocal music', 'Transylvanian fiddle music', 'Traditional Music of Ladakh', and 'Physiological Determinants in Blues Guitar Styles'.

## Durham University

At the post-graduate level, Durham offers MA, M Mus, and Ph D degrees in ethnomusicology. The MA is a taught degree (one year full-time or two years part-time), with the following basic course structure:

Research Methods and Resources: a standard module taught partly by the Faculty of Arts and partly by the Music Department - basic methods of library usage, information gathering, computer-assisted information retrieval, ethnomusicological bibliography, writing style sheets.

Discipline of Ethnomusicology: a study of important methods, basic issues, and scholars in the history of ethnomusicology up to the present, including such topics as transcription, orgonology, linguistic methods, and fieldwork.

Set Texts: a critical and details examination of influential ethnomusicological texts essential to a knowlwdge of the history and methods of the discipline. Authors include Bela Bartok, John Blacking, Bruno Nettl, Alan Merriam, Charles Seeger, and others.

MA students also complete a further module, either a Special Topic (investigating a particular musical culture or disciplinary topic) or a module from another MA syllabus within the department (composition, analysis, or musicology). Students must also complete a dissertation of not more than 10,000 words.

M Mus students follow the same syllabus as MA students, but write an extended thesis rather than a dissertation, and their course extends over two years (full-time).

Ph D students usually begin with the MA taught degree, then proceed for at least two further years by research, completing a substantial thesis in the field of ethnomusicology.

## King Alfred's College of Higher Education

An MA in Musical Studies is currently being prepared which develops individual skills in areas of World Musics. M Phil and Ph D work is at present mainly linked to education and child development in music, with links in China, Hungary and parts of Africa.

## Kingston University

Research

We have a University funded World Music Research Project which involves three members of staff, one research assistant and three external consultants in the areas of African Music, Chinese Music and Jamaican Music.

## London University : Goldsmith's College

M Mus Ethnomusicology

The M Mus in Ethnomusicology is intended as a foundation for those wishing to pursue doctoral studies in ethnomusicology. The degree is also suitable for those who wish to gain a secure footing in theory and method on ethnomusicology, such as museum curators, music teachers, broadcasters, and film makers. Students take five courses: History and Theory of Ethnomusicology, Special Area (which changes from year to year), Current Issues in Ethnomusicology and Research Methods 1 & 2. Apart from the varying Special Area, the course is not tied to the detailed study of any particular musical tradition or region. The emphasis in the 1st year is on theory, and in the 2nd on research methods, including problems of notation and transcription. There is a strong emphasis on the conduct of fieldwork, and on the use of video in research. The degree also caters for the student interested primarily in dance anthropology (dance ethnology) rather than ethnomusicology: in many cultures it makes no sense to look at music alone.

The M Mus can be taken either full-time in one year or part-time over two years.

## London University: School of Oriental and African Studies

The M Mus degree in Ethnomusicology

This is a Master's degree by course work. The programme is designed to provide 1) an understanding of the major issues in the discipline of ethnomusicology, 2) detailed knowledge of at least one major non-Western musical tradition and its cultural context, and 3) some training and experience in fieldwork and other research techniques. It is also intended as preparation for those students planning to undertake research. The curriculum includes:

1) A lecture course in the aims and methods of ethnomusicology, to be examined by a three-hour written paper and by two essays.

2) The musical traditions of a selected region. Possible regions of specialisation include: East Asia, South East Asia, the Middle East, and Africa.

3) A third course selected from the following:
a) An approved non-music course chosen from the SOAS MA Area Studies syllabus relating to the same area as course 2.
b) An approved course in general anthropology from the MA Social Anthropology syllabus.
c) A second music area course as under heading 2.

4) A Master's thesis (also called a 'Special Study'), not exceeding 10,000 words in length, of an aspect of the music of the chosen region OR of a topic in ethnomusicological theory or method.

In some cases the M Mus may serve as appropriate preparation for MPhil/PhD research.

The MA Area Studies degrees

The MA Area Studies programme provides an opportunity to study the music of a particular culture in depth and in relation to other aspects of that culture. Three courses must be chosen relating to the same region (Africa, the Middle East, South Asia, South East Asia, East Asia); one course may relate to music, the others to other aspects of culture. Examination comprises one written paper on each subject plus a dissertation in the major subject. In some cases this degree programme may serve as appropriate preparation for MPhil/PhD research.

The MPhil/PhD in Music

Supervision of study for the degrees of MPhil or PhD is offered to suitably qualified candidates wishing to pursue original, independent research in Asian or African Music. Students are admitted to the MPhil programme and may transfer to the PhD upon demonstration of progress and merit. Degrees involve fieldwork and a consequent supervised dissertation. Candidates without a grounding in the discipline of ethnomusicology may well be required to follow a preparatory one year MMus course (item (a) above) prior to entering the MPhil/PhD course; in any case, some course work will be required during the first year of MPhil/PhD registration. Current and recent dissertation topics include: ceremonial band-music of Nepal; political song in South Africa; *taqsim* in Nepal; *taarab* in Zanzibar; music of a Japanese 'new religion'; music of Sunda (western Java); vocal improvisation in Central Javanese shadow play music; Thai classical drumming; Thai fiddle improvisation; North Indian *khyal*; North Indian rhythm.

## The Queen's University of Belfast

We offer a taught MA (which condenses the above courses into a year of study, and includes a dissertation) as well as a research MA (2 years), and PhD (3 years) in Ethnomusicology.

## York University

Ethnomusicology and World Music may be studied at the postgraduate level, for the degrees of MA, MPhil, and DPhil. The last two are by research and thesis, while the MA involves essays, a dissertation and a recital. The areas of specialisation tend to be the same as detailed above, but others are by no means precluded.

## Additional Information

## Anglia Polytechnic University

Staff specialistation is in European folk music, particularly the Irish tradition, but lectures, workshops and recitals from visiting specialists and musicians contribute significantly to modules.

Hazel Fairbairn

## Bangor: University College of North Wales

The Archive of Traditional Welsh Music

The Archive of Traditional Welsh Music at the University of Wales, Bangor, collects, preserves and provides direct access to sound recordings collected in many areas of the Principality. Created with the financial support of the Welsh Arts Council, it serves the academic community of the University as well as individuals and institutions further afield. Although the Archive exists primarily as a research, teaching and training centre for the University's Ethnomusicology course, its collections and facilities are also utilised by members of staff and students from the Welsh, Welsh History, English, Linguistics and other departments.

The Archive (which is housed in the Music Department) is a repository of recorded musical and verbal forms which are perpetuated in the oral tradition rather than through writing or printing. Its collections are received through a number of channels - as deposits, gifts or exchanges, through the support of collecting expeditions and through purchase.

In addition to compiling or sponsoring the publication of reference books connected with the field of Welsh Traditional music, the Archive is also well equipped with tape recorders (studio and field recorders), turntables, transcribers and can thus reproduce recordings made by any device used in the collecting of folk music.

The Archive functions as a public library of recorded sound in which two major types of collections are house - commercial recording, which have been produced for public sale; and field recordings which have been collected under field conditions for research and which have not been issued commercially.

The Archive endeavours to serve educational institutions and the general public by any means at its disposal.

Wyn Thomas

## Birmingham Conservatoire

Mark Lockett
Simon Gray
John Mayer
Ranjit Singh

## Bretton Hall College

Helen Simpson

## Cambridge University

Resources

1   Non-European instruments belonging to the Music Faculty and used in teaching including a complete Javanese gamelan, gift of the Indonesian embassy; a *guchin*, a *sitar* and an *ud*. A large, private collection of Bolivian Andean instruments is on indefinite loan. Laurence Picken's collection of musical instruments, available for practice, is housed in the Museum of Archaeology and Anthropology.

2   Both the Music Faculty's Pendlebury Library and the University Library hold books and journals in ethnomusicology, including the Picken collection in the University Library. The Pendlebury library holds a substantial collection of commercial recordings in world music. All students doing field work are provided with recording equipment, tapes and a copy of their recordings on return; this policy has resulted

in individual collections of field recordings from various parts of Europe, the Middle East, Africa, Asia, and South America, whose use remains under the control of the respective collectors.

3   Music students have free use of the Faculty's Ethnomusicology Laboratory containing studio digital and analogue recording and playback equipment, portable DAT, reel-to-reel and cassette recorders, patch bay, filters for analysis, and a Mac computer running Sound Tools for digital recording and analysis. Video recording equipment, at present available in a limited capacity from the university's Audiovisual Aids unit, is also in the pipeline. An electro-acoustic recording studio, also housed in the Music School, provides additional resources, in the form of more sophisticated analytical tools, for ethnomusicology research.

Dr Ruth Davis
Dr Colin Huehns
Henry Stobart

## City University

The Department houses two Javanese gamelans and a wide variety of Indian, Japanese and Chinese instruments.

The Department possesses a wide range of computer-aided audio and audio-visual analysis systems for use in ethnomusicological study and research.

Dr Steve Stanton

## Dartington College of Arts

Dartington has a number of world music ensembles including Balinese Gamelan, Ghanaian drumming and Cuban/Brazilian percussion. There are also a range of Indian, Japanese and Caribbean instruments for students to use plus a well-stocked library. The college also offers research supervision in world music/ethnomusicology, particularly world music in education, and is intending to offer some aspects of this within a taught Master's programme in the near future.

Dr Trevor Wiggins

## Durham  University

Dr Robert Provine
Dr Jonathan Stock

## King  Alfred's  College

There is a collection of African instruments, and selections made from the Caribbean, Japan and India. In addition much use is made of the South Bank gamelan. World Music students make much use of electronic media and resources in their work, and are prepared for the practical techniques of field work.

Dr June Boyce-Tillman
Judith Deeble
Dr James Flolu (Visiting Consultant)
Malcolm Floyd
Ernest Piper

## Kingston  University

Instrumental Resources:
We have a collection of Chinese, Indian and African instruments.

Library:

We have journals, books and recordings of World Musics.

Prof. Edward Ho

## London  College  of  Music

Dr Allen Moore

## London  University:  Goldsmith's  College

Goldsmith's library, with a good collection of ethnomusicological books and essential journals such as *Ethnomusicology, Yearbook for Traditional Music, Asian Music* and *World of Music*. There is also a collection of non-Western records, and video tapes of most of the music documentaries shown on British television in the last few years. The College houses the A. L. Lloyd Library, with its collection of rare Eastern European music books.

The Computer Centre has extensive PC and Mac word processing facilities.

VHS camcorders can be borrowed from the Media Equipment Centre. A video editing suite is available in the Media Resources Centre but is much in demand and thereby hard to get much time on.

The Stanley Glasser Electronic Music Studio. Equipment includes MIDO-based sequencers, synthesizers and samplers, together with 8-track recording and stereo mastering to DAT or 1/4" analogue machines.

The Ethnomusicology Studio has basic equipment for 1/4" tape and audio cassette recording and monitoring. Multi-system video replay available.

## The Gamelan

The Department is fortunate to have on loan from the Indonesian Embassy an excellent bronze gamelan in *pelog* tuning.

Dr John Bailey

## London University: School of Oriental and African Studies

Music students have access to the large main Library of the School (holding books, journals and recordings), a Centre Audio-visual archive, the University's Senate House Library, the British Museum, National Sound Archive and other London libraries museums, and to a wide range of flourishing music traditions in the ethnically diverse metropolis. The Centre also maintains a working collection of musical instruments, principally from India, Thailand, Indonesia, Japan and Korea but with many items from elsewhere. Among special items in the SOAS collections are: field recording, films and slides of South Asian music made by Arnold Blake from the 1920s to 1956; and a number of instructional or demonstrational videotapes, mostly produced by and inherited from the Ethnomusicological Audio-Visual Archive (formerly of Cambridge University), for musical instruments including *koto, shakuhachi, changgo, pakhavaj, tabla,* and various Thai instruments.

Lucy Duran
Dr Keith Howard
Dr David Hughes
Dr Richard Widdess
Prof. Owen Wright

## Manchester Metropolitan University: Crewe and Alsager Faculty

Graham Shrubsole

## The Queen's University of Belfast

Kevin Dawe
Dr Suzel Reily
Dr Martin Stokes
Dr Hae-Kying Um

## Southampton University

Robynne Stillwell

## York University

The full-time member of the academic staff specialising in Ethnomusicology and World Music is Dr Neil Sorrell, Senior Lecturer in Music, who has published books both on Indian Music and Javanese Gamelan Music. Dr Roger March, a composer and also a Senior Lecturer in Music, teaches courses on Japanese Music. Until the summer of 1994, we were fortunate to have Yoshikaze Iwamoto, Shakuhachi player, as Fellow in Japanese Music, and in May 1995 we look forward to welcoming Ustad Amjad Ali Khan, Sarod player, as visiting Professor of Indian Music. The Department also houses the Donald Mitchell Thai Music Archive, as well as numerous publications and recordings of Indian, Javanese and other World Musics.

# Figure 11.1 Degrees containing World Musics

| | | BEd/ BA (QTS) | BA | BSc | PGDip | PGCE | MA | MMus PhD | MPHil/ |
|---|---|---|---|---|---|---|---|---|---|
| ANGLIA | (A) | | X | | | | | | |
| BANGOR | (Ba) | | X | | X | | X | | |
| BIRMINGHAM | (Bi) | | X | | | | X | | |
| BRETTON HALL | (Br) | | X | | | X | X | | |
| CAMBRIDGE | (Ca) | | X | | | | | | X |
| CITY | (Ci) | | | X | | | X | | X |
| DARTINGTON | (Da) | | X | | | | (X) | | X |
| DURHAM | (Du) | | X | | | | X | | X |
| KING ALFREDS | (KA) | X | X | | | | (X) | | X |
| KINGSTON | (Ki) | X | X | | | | | | X |
| LCM | (LCM) | | X | | | | | | |
| LONDON U: Goldsmiths | (LG) | | X | | | | | X | |
| LONDON U: SOAS | (SOAS) | | X | | | | | X | X |
| MANCHESTER MU | (MMU) | | X | | | | | | |
| QUEENS | (Q) | | X | | | | X | | X |
| SOUTHAMPTON | (So) | | X | | | | | | |
| YORK | (Y) | | X | | | | X | | X |

( ) : Proposed Course

## Figure 11.2 Areas of Research Interest

| | |
|---|---|
| Europe | A, Bi, Ci |
| East Europe | Ci, KA |
| Mediterranean | Bi, Q |
| Britain | LCM |
| England | Ci |
| Ireland | A |
| Wales | Ba |
| | |
| Africa | Bi, LCM, SOAS |
| North Africa | Ca |
| West Africa | Br, Da, KA, Q |
| East Africa | KA, Ki |
| | |
| America | Du |
| Native America | Du |
| Afro-American | Ci, LCM |
| Afro-Caribbean | Bi, Da, KA, Q |
| Latin American | Bi, Br, Da, Ki, LCM, Q |
| Andes | Ca |
| | |
| Near East | Ca |
| Turkey | Q |
| Middle East | Ca, Q, SOAS |
| Jewish | Ci |
| | |
| India & Pakistan | Bi, Br, Ca, Ci, Da, Du, MMU, Q, SOAS, Y |
| | |
| Far East | Ci, Q |
| South East Asia | LCM, LG, SOAS |
| Japan | Da, Du, KA, MMU, SOAS, Y |
| China | Du, Ki, SOAS |
| Korea | Du, SOAS |
| Indonesia | Bi, Ci, Da, Du, KA, Q, SOAS, Y |
| Thailand | SOAS, Y |
| | |
| World Musics in Education | Br, Da, KA, Q |

To conclude, there is a wide range of courses and expertise available to students in Britain who wish to pursue or initiate an interest in World Musics in some way. These can be seen in summary in Figure 11.1.

There are courses which emphasise the importance of practical experience, and which have instruments and ensembles from many places across the world. There are courses based on composing, developing the individual styles of students through exposure to a wider range of compositional practice than may have been the case previously. There are courses which include a philosophical or theoretical underpinning to the study of World Musics to give confidence to the student who will then go out into the world and experience its diversity. Such courses are often called 'Ethnomusicology', although the precise nature of this beast varies from place to place.

There are several courses which include World Musics in their teacher training, at undergraduate and PGCE levels, and into MA and research work increasingly as time goes on.

There are courses in the music of particular traditions, and Figure 11.2 shows how wide is the area covered by such courses. Some traditions are particularly well represented (Afro-Caribbean, Indian sub-continent, Japan and Indonesia), others occur much less frequently (North Africa, Turkey and so on), and there are some which do not appear at all. This may be an area where cooperation between institutions would benefit all, as particular expertise is shared, and priorities for further investigation realised.

There are institutions which base all their teaching on fundamental principles garnered from their World Music experiences, and there are others which include elements of inter-cultural work, and have free-standing modules in areas of particular interest to staff (and hopefully students).

This inclusion of a richer diversity of music may be a continuing trend as more and more students have been exposed to World Musics in school, including their appearance in both GCSE and A level examination courses.

June Boyce-Tillman argues in her chapter earlier in this book that 'academics' have been rather slower at getting to grips with the fullness of the musical world than schools. What this survey has shown is that the interest and skills exist; and that transmission of information, and transformation of students' thinking is going on. We need to continue to be open and welcoming, and avoid the impression that we are most concerned to preserve the uniqueness of our experience and the perceived exoticism of the music that has given us such joy. In short, we should continue to expand routes of access into World Musics, and prepare for the Swahili saying given at the beginning of this section:

*Penye mafundi, hapakosi wanafunzi*
Where there are experts, there will be no lack of learners

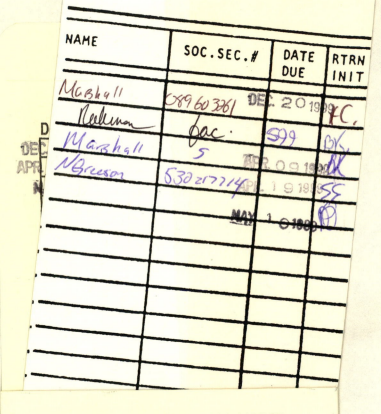

| NAME | SOC.SEC.# | DATE DUE | RTRN INIT |
|---|---|---|---|
| Marshall | 089603361 | DEC. 2 0 1999 | TC. |
| Neikman | Jac. | 599 | BK |
| Marshall | S | APR. 0 9 1999 | BK |
| N. Greeson | 530217714 | APR. 1 9 1999 | SS |
| | | MAY 1 0 1999 | P |